D1317962

LSD: PERSONALITY AND EXPERIENCE
by Harriet Linton Barr, Robert J. Langs, Robert R. Holt,
Leo Goldberger, and George S. Klein

TREATMENT OF THE BORDERLINE ADOLESCENT:
A Developmental Approach
by James F. Masterson

PSYCHOPATHOLOGY: Contributions from the Biological,
Behavioral, and Social Sciences
edited by Muriel Hammer, Kurt Salzinger, and Samuel Sutton

ABNORMAL CHILDREN AND YOUTH: Therapy and Research
by Anthony Davids

PRINCIPLES OF PSYCHOTHERAPY WITH CHILDREN
by John M. Reisman

AVERSIVE MATERNAL CONTROL: A Theory of
Schizophrenic Development
by Alfred B. Heilbrun, Jr.

INDIVIDUAL DIFFERENCES IN CHILDREN
edited by Jack C. Westman

EGO FUNCTIONS IN SCHIZOPHRENICS, NEUROTICS,
AND NORMALS: A Systematic Study of Conceptual,
Diagnostic, and Therapeutic Aspects
by Leopold Bellak, Marvin Hurvich, and Helen A. Gediman

INNOVATIVE TREATMENT METHODS IN PSYCHOPATHOLOGY
edited by Karen S. Calhoun, Henry E. Adams, and Kevin M. Mitchell

THE CHANGING SCHOOL SCENE: CHALLENGE TO
PSYCHOLOGY
by Leah Gold Fein

THE CHANGING SCHOOL SCENE:

Challenge to Psychology

LEAH GOLD FEIN

Diplomate in Clinical Psychology
American Board in Professional Psychology

President
International Council of Psychologists
1973–1975

A WILEY-INTERSCIENCE PUBLICATION

JOHN WILEY & SONS, New York · London · Sydney · Toronto

Library of Congress Cataloging in Publication Data

Fein, Leah (Gold)
 The changing school scene.

 (Wiley series on personality processes)
 "A Wiley-Interscience publication."
 1. School psychologists. 2. Personnel service
in education. I. Title.

LB3013.6.F44   371.2′02   73-19916
ISBN 0-471-25679-x

Printed in the United States of America

10 9 8 7 6 5 4 3 2 1

Foreword

Living and growing from infancy to childhood into maturity is a complicated process at best. Child study and research have revealed that what many adults have tended to believe was a simple world of childhood is for children a world filled with physical demands, hurts, and pleasures; emotional joys, grief, and tensions; fearsome as well as exciting introductions to the unknown; and pressures as new or unproven abilities are tested. Childhood has always been a period of making varying adjustments to security and insecurity experienced from parents, friends, and authorities. Many children who are unfortunate in health, in parental relationships, or in other respects need the help of specialized personnel beyond that of parent or teacher if they are to cope with situations which develop.

As technology has advanced and as population has increased the world of the school age child has become increasingly complicated, as has the world for his parents. More children need assistance beyond what they are able to receive from parents or from a teacher who knows a child well and in whom he has confidence. But problems are created in the process of providing specialized types of assistance. A family doctor is unknown to many city children. Instead, parents rely on hospital complexes, specialists, and paramedical assistance. The child rarely has long enough association with them for them to know him as a reacting person in a home and community setting. The child does not have the opportunity to learn of the human as well as the technical qualities of these specialists who seem to be doing something to him more than for him.

The child progresses through school as a member of groups that change in composition and undergo frequent change in control and direction by different teachers or other specialists.

v

Arithmetic may be taught by one teacher and reading by another, and these teachers change each year. Art and music and physical education specialists may direct the activities and learning in those fields. There may be others who administer, score, and interpret standardized tests. Still others may measure the child's height, weight, and vision. If he is absent, or taken ill at school, or is a behavior problem to the distraction of a teacher, or if his test results are very low or are normal but his classroom performance is deficient, then the attendance officer, the school nurse, the assistant principal or a counselor, psychologist, or psychiatrist may be called upon to give him brief, individual, specialized attention. His growth as a total person in school is the concern of many, and yet often of no one person. And at home increasing numbers of children face a broken parental situation or one in which the sole parent or both parents are working away from the residence enough hours when the child is not in school to leave the child on his own resources in the house or on the street for regular and often prolonged intervals. He may have no adult interested in him as a person to whom he can turn for assistance and guidance on problems which confront him during those times.

Teachers have been aware of differences in pupil behavior among those who were enrolled in their classes. They have tried, with some or little success, to use their professional knowledge and skills to capitalize on these differences and thus to make learning more challenging for each child. They have called upon others to aid them—other pupils, parents, the janitor, or special school employees such as the school attendance officer or the school nurse. In some school systems teachers have been able to call on psychologists, psychiatrists, counselors, social workers, and others for assistance with pupils having mental and social problems.

Specialized personnel have, over the years, been introduced into school organization on a piecemeal basis and as the result of varied combinations of circumstances. In some instances the help has been introduced to relieve teachers of certain duties so they may have more time to work with pupils, as in case of the introduction of custodial help so that teachers did not have to build the fire or sweep the school floor. In other cases specialists such as school doctors, school psychologists, school counselors, and school social workers were made available to work directly with individual children and their parents to provide services beyond those the teacher had the competence to provide.

Patterns of school psychological work have been modified over the years. They vary from school system to school system in part because of the way they have developed in relation to other areas of the pupil personnel services, in part because they grew with marginal funding and in part out of a scarcity in the availability of trained personnel in the school psychological field.

School administrators have sometimes assumed that one who is certified as a psychologist should be able to diagnose with a few brief contacts what prevents any child from learning at a normal rate, and that he should be able to make the necessary repairs and thus produce normal functioning. They seem to overlook the fact that among psychologists there are varied specializations. One needs to know the area of specialization within the broad term of psychologist to approximate an understanding of the kinds of service any psychologist is qualified to perform.

In many school systems specialists have been added on less than a carefully developed long-range plan, and not always in keeping with specialist training or understanding of their school responsibilities. Persons so added to an organization tend to want the organization to fit their ideas of how best they can perform their job, but they may not know fully the capabilities and interests of other co-workers. This is true because specialists in an organization frequently have little opportunity to know about and to understand the total operation to which they contribute a part. On the other hand, administrators, who are in charge of a total operation, frequently have different expectations of the services they can appropriately expect from a specialist and of the conditions needed by a specialist if he is to contribute efficiently toward a total operation.

School personnel likewise often feel frustrated in their efforts to make the specialized service that is available contribute most to pupil growth and development, and to assist most effectively parents who feel less than able to help their children grow into well adapted, competent adults. They see the importance of the specialized knowledge and skill if it could be applied early enough and long enough and if other offsetting conditions could be controlled. But they also recognize the limits in numbers of specialists available compared to the number of pupils needing special services and the limits of the specialist's time in the light of the demands on him by parents, siblings, friends, and all who come in contact with him. Thus school personnel—be they early childhood teachers, special subject field teachers, administrators, psychologists, or others —need help in developing a common perspective on their specialty in relation to other specialists as applied to the growth, learning, and development of children—their common concern.

The introduction of innovative programs in the schools often results in rearrangement of established relationships of the work of both teachers and specialists with each other and with pupils. It therefore becomes important that school innovative practices be examined by school specialists, as well as by administrators and by teachers, to determine how the role of each needs to be redefined. Those who develop school innovative practices also need the insight of the specialist in order to consider if and how proposed innovations strengthen or frustrate the reinforcements to established pupil learning and to pupil-teacher relationships.

It therefore seems appropriate that the responsibilities of specialists from the psychological field who work in varied school positions should be considered by a highly trained professional psychologist who has been intimately involved in school psychological service in the New York City school system, and has maintained leadership roles in the preparation of psychologists. So, also, it is well to have recent innovations in school practice reviewed by one who sees them in relation to the role of the psychologist and allied school personnel. School administrators and teachers, as well as school psychologists and those who prepare personnel for some aspect of school psychological service, should find in this volume challenges to their ideas and information that will help them to appreciate the work of their colleagues as each seeks to make his appropriate input to aid pupils to progress successfully from infancy through childhood and to become competent adults.

SAMUEL MILLER BROWNELL
Professor Emeritus of Educational Administration
Yale University

Series Preface

This series of books is addressed to behavioral scientists interested in the nature of human personality. Its scope should prove pertinent to personality theorists and researchers as well as to clinicians concerned with applying an understanding of personality processes to the amelioration of emotional difficulties in living. To this end, the series provides a scholarly integration of theoretical formulations, empirical data, and practical recommendations.

Six major aspects of studying and learning about human personality can be designated: personality theory, personality structure and dynamics, personality development, personality assessment, personality change, and personality adjustment. In exploring these aspects of personality, the books in the series discuss a number of distinct but related subject areas: the nature and implications of various theories of personality; personality characteristics that account for consistencies and variations in human behavior; the emergence of personality processes in children and adolescents; the use of interviewing and testing procedures to evaluate individual differences in personality; efforts to modify personality styles through psychotherapy, counseling, behavior therapy, and other methods of influence; and patterns of abnormal personality functioning that impair individual competence.

IRVING B. WEINER

Case Western Reserve University
Cleveland, Ohio

Preface

There is an urgency today to redefine the roles, goals, functions, and training of the psychologist in the schools. The earliest role of psychometrist as IQ or Binet tester, and later the clinical role of personality or intelligence tester and case study evaluator with referral for treatment, remedial education, or special class placement is viewed by many psychologists and educators today as an extravagant use of professional staff time and a futile approach to the ever increasing problems erupting in the school populations. Since 1960 or so the schools have worked feverishly to expand facilities, improve curricula and methods, and change organization patterns in response to the challenges of the population explosion and its concomitant ills, the scientific and technological advances, the flood of available knowledge, and the speed of its dissemination as well as the demands for equal education and mental health services for the underprivileged segments of our population.

The major thrust of educational experimentation and innovation today is directed toward the education of the deprived child populations, under the impact of fast accumulating evidence of widespread underachievement in basic school skills in these child populations and the recognition that these deficiencies reflect eroding impacts of "dyspedogogia," that is, poor teaching and socioeconomic and culturally deprived milieus rather than limited learning potentials. The angry, militant, and threatening demands by parents and communities for relevant and effective education of their children have "spurred" the process.

The critics of the roles and functions of the psychologist in the schools insist that present day problems and new educational technologies call for new approaches, new methods on the part of the psychologists. They claim that group and class approaches should replace individual methods in diagnosis, treatment, and reeducation; that prevention of school difficulties should be the focus rather than remediation; that the psychodynamic theories, principles, and methods should be replaced by learning theory and behavior modification methods, where the focus is on observable behavior, on symptoms; that differential diagnostic testing should focus on deficit learning, on "how learning or not learning occurs," and on facilitation and remediation of learning rather than on intelligence and affective variables.

Leading theorists in psychology recognized in the late 1950s and early 1960s that the practice of psychology is changing and must continue to change under the impact of scientific and technological advances and the chaos of change in our society:

The basis for practice has increasingly relied on learning rather than (or in addition to) personality (Bandura & Walters, 1963; Skinner, 1968; Wolpe, 1958). The goal has become coping, or personal and social competence (Loevinger, 1966; Murphy, 1962; White, 1963). The methods have become more indirect and include preventive efforts (Bower & Hollister, 1967) and the education of people in addition to or instead of treatment of people (Albee, 1966; Caplan, 1959; Guerney, 1964; Szasz, 1960). An interactive approach to understanding persons has developed (Endler & Hunt, 1966; Wallace, 1966). The school in the community is the prime target area (Brayfield, 1965; Brunner, 1965; Sarason, 1967). The funnel empties where the school psychologists are (Bardon, 1968).

School psychologists feel inundated by the overwhelming demands from school personnel to "do something" about the children who are uncontainable in the classroom and the school building, those who are chronically resistive to authority, those who "will not or cannot" learn yet are not mentally retarded, the dropouts, the drug addicted, the multiply handicapped.

Confronted with these challenges some school psychologists feel impelled to become instant "experts" in all situations. Hastily scanning the new literature for current approaches to the problems presented, they give advice and propose remedies. Other school psychologists recognize that they cannot cope with all types of problem presented or even with the massive workload imposed on them within the limits of their skills. These psychologists seek solutions through pressuring for reduced workloads and more staff. Another group of psychologists in the schools urge that the roles and functions of staff be defined in differential terms, that is, in terms of the particular skills, interests, and expertise of each. This group urging differential function insist that this approach is *the only one,* since no one psychologist can possibly "be all things to all people."

Graduate school faculty are also struggling with the challenges of change in the schools and in education at large, as well as the changing emphases within the field of psychology itself. What should be the focus of these training programs for the practice of psychology in the schools? Should there be two or more levels of training? Should the school psychologist be trained in clinical methods to provide services based on psychodynamic interpersonal theories, principles, methods, and materials for diagnosis and treatment? This model is the most prevalent today. Should he be prepared to cope with learning and adjustment problems of all school children, that is, should the focus be on developmental theories and principles of learning, on curriculum construction, content, and methods of teaching with special focus on the new educational technologies? Or should the school psychologist be trained primarily in sensory-neurological theories, principles, methods, and materials with focus on perceptual-motor deficits to serve principally the "handicapped" child? Should the emphasis be on experimental psychology, learning theory, and behavior modification methods and skills, to the end that he serve as a behavior "engineer"? Should he be trained for service to individuals or groups, for the elementary and/or intermediate and/or adolescent age groups, and/or as a consultant, researcher, designer, and/or implementer of programs? Since all these roles are essential to school programs, perhaps a differential approach to the training of psychologists for work in the schools is the answer. Differential training available at different levels of study, AA, BA, MA (one to three years of preparation), and the doctoral level, might provide the skilled personnel essential to coping effectively with the ever new challenges presented by the changing school scene.

In the chapters that follow an effort will be made to explore the innovative, experimental, and compensatory programs in the public schools with special attention to the changes in schools in deprived areas and the challenges these present to psychologists serving the schools.

Attention will also be given to the emergence of training programs for paraprofessionals outside and in some cases within the profession of psychology and the adaptations of training in university graduate programs seeking to meet the new needs of school children, staff, and communities.

This book was written for practicing psychologists, particularly those who work with children and their families in schools, clinics, and the community; for students majoring in psychology at the undergraduate level and of course at the graduate level in school, clinical, counseling, and educational psychology. It was also written for educators, teaching and special service staff who must cope with the many traditional and new target populations. It should prove a useful supplementary text in teacher training. Finally, it is intended for parents and community and government leaders who are concerned with the plethora of disturbances afflicting our school child populations and are seeking ways and means of changing school and other social organizations in the hope of eliminating the ailments and facilitating healthy development in all our children.

LEAH GOLD FEIN

New York City
September 1973

Acknowledgments

My sincere thanks go to Dr. Simon S. Silverman, former Director of the Bureau of Child Guidance of the City of New York Board of Education, and to Dr. Jessie Alozery, former Supervisor of Psychologists in the New York City Schools, for their kind support of my efforts in the Model B program. Sincere thanks and appreciation is offered to Burton Weisburger, Ida Sargoy, and Dr. Martin Farkash for their support throughout the Model B program and their contributions of data to the cross-cultural study. Sincere gratitude to Dr. Libero Arciero, Supervisor of School Psychologists in the Bronx Office of the Bureau of Child Guidance, for the extensive and intensive discussions we held about the problems affecting the roles and functions of psychologists in the schools of New York City and the types of training needed to equip this staff for effective service to the target populations in the schools of New York.

My sincere appreciation goes to Mrs. Sara Freeman, Principal of Public School 139X, and to Mrs. Elizabeth Czajowska and Mr. Jack Williky, Assistant Principals at PS 139X, for their cooperation in the conduct of the Model B program in their school. My thanks go to all the teachers, principals, aides, parents, and special service staff who cooperated with our research efforts at PS 139X, to the secretaries who facilitated our work, to the graduate students, Steve Bristran and Ellen Wolff, who assisted in the testing and statistical treatment of our data, and to Marquita Gorham and Meta Springer, school aides at PS 134 assigned to our unit.

Sincere thanks go to Ronald Kurz of the Education and Training Board of the American Psychological Association Central Office for sharing with me his early data on the training of psychologists for professional roles.

My sincere gratitude to my friends Hadassah Gold, Lois Zimmerman, Michell Milikowsky Harmon, and Kathy Detmer, who patiently typed and retyped the manuscript as required.

Finally I wish to thank Dr. Karl Zucker of Indiana State University for reading the manuscript and for his cogent suggestions and comments.

L. G. F.

Contents

THE CHANGING SCHOOL SCENE:
CHALLENGE TO PSYCHOLOGY

CHAPTER 1

Traditional Roles of Psychologists and Present Dilemmas

SCHOOL PSYCHOLOGY TO MIDCENTURY

The beginnings of school psychology may be said to date back to 1896 when Dr. Lightner Witmer, director of the James McKeen Cattell psychological laboratory at the University of Pennsylvania, presented a paper at the American Psychological Association meeting proposing "a scheme of practical work in psychology":

The training of students for a new profession—that of the psychological expert, who should find his career in connection with the school system, through examination and treatment of mentally and morally retarded children and in connection with the practice of medicine. (Brotemarkle, 1931, p. 346)

1

Witmer's proposal appears to have initiated the development of applied psychology as a clinical descipline in both the schools and the hospitals. During the next ten years, Witmer trained students, predominantly teachers, in clinical psychology and learning remediation methods. The training program at his laboratory appears to represent the first "practicum" or "internship" program in clinical and school psychology. The year 1896 also saw the beginning of the testing movement in the United States with the APA publication of a five-page series of tests that "could be given in one hour." The testing movement grew rapidly over the next decade as evidenced in the publication in 1904 of E. L. Thorndike's *Mental and Social Measurements.*

The development of special classes for children who were not profiting from the educational programs offered in the public schools contributed to the development of school psychological services, since selection of such children is based in part on psychological examination. As early as 1871 New Haven, Connecticut, established a special class for disruptive children "who were running wild on the streets and becoming a public nuisance." The first public school Department of Child Study was established in 1899 in Chicago, Illinois, "to study and serve mental and physical conditions of school children." This led to the establishment of ungraded classes for the benefit of children with such handicaps. In 1909 special classes for juvenile delinquents were established in Chicago as a result of the work of Dr. William Healy and Dr. Augusta Bronner.

The development of the Binet tests, 1905, 1908, and 1911, and their translations, revisions, and adaptations to the American culture by Dr. H. H. Goddard at the Vineland Training School in New Jersey gave further impetus to the development of the psychological study and treatment of the school child. The Terman 1916 Stanford Revision of the Binet-Simon Intelligence Scale became the most widely used form of the test in the schools of the nation during the following 25 years. It is noteworthy that Dr. Arnold Gesell served as a school psychologist: "In 1915, the Connecticut State Board of Education appointed a School Psychologist to make mental examinations of backward and defective children in rural, village and urban schools, and to devise methods for their better care in the public schools. Connecticut was the first state in the Union to create a position of this kind" (Cutts, 1955).

The introduction of group tests by Dr. Arthur Otis, who devised the Army Alpha Examination in response to the urgent need for large-scale evaluation of men's abilities during World War I, gave impetus to the development of standardized group tests of intelligence for use in the public schools. The use of these tests expanded the functions of the school psychologists. Educational achievement tests had been devised by psychologists as early as 1908 and were developing at a rapid pace during these same years, but their use was primarily the function of educators. This group movement served to point out the wide range of abilities and achievements in children and alerted psychologists and educators to the need to attend to and provide for individual differences in learning. These insights further expanded the concerns and functions of school psychology.

By 1938 there were 650 child guidance clinics in 35 states, either connected directly with the schools or with hospitals serving their communities and schools. These services continued to expand through the next decade with the expectation that they were meeting the needs of disturbed and/or educationally handicapped children. However, during the 1940s and the early 1950s, with the unprecedented increase in public school enrollment, educational administrators, public health officials, and mental health specialists became alarmed at the rise of juvenile delinquency and the increasing incidence of mental illness. Attention turned to the schools as the critical preventive agency, since juvenile delinquency is obviously a problem affecting the school child and mental illness often has its beginnings in childhood experience.

Confronted with these clinical challenges, school psychologists turned to their clinical colleagues for new approaches to school problems. During these same years, the 1940s and early 1950s, the psychodynamic interpersonal theories, principles, and methods of diagnosis and treatment were the methods of choice, as professional psychologists were rapidly entering the private practice of psychoanalysis and other forms of dynamic psychotherapies. Accordingly school psychologists *en masse* sought to change the thrust of their efforts from IQ or Binet testing to projective testing, psychodynamic and interpersonal interpretations, and psychotherapeutic methods of treatment. These changing practices by school psychologists, combined with the rapidly expanding use of psychological services in the schools of the nation, plus the shortage of well-trained and qualifed school psychologists, aroused grave concern among the members of the Division of School Psychology (Div. 16) of the APA. Services rendered by poorly trained people might well endanger the children served and cast disrepute on the whole profession (Cutts, 1955).

Concerned about the poor qualifications of psychologists in the schools and the lack of graduate training programs for school psychology, T. Ernest Newland of the University of Illinois initiated preparations in 1952, in cooperation with the members of Division 16 of the APA, for a conference on the definition of the goals, roles, functions, training, and qualifications of school psychologists. With the support of the APA and funding by the National Institutes of Health of the Department of Health, Education and Welfare, the Thayer Conference was held in August 1955 at the Hotel Thayer, West Point, New York. The plans for the conference were based on the experience of the Boulder Conference held by clinical psychologists in 1949 (Raimy, 1950).

Briefly, the conference offered the following definitions and recommendations for the training and functions of psychological personnel in the schools:

1. A school psychologist is a psychologist trained in education with special skills in assessment, learning, and interpersonal relations.
2. He assesses with tests of intelligence, achievement, aptitude, and personality to gauge needs and evaluate change. He studies exceptional children and prescribes treatments and programs for their education.
3. Two levels of training are necessary: the doctoral level to be called school psychologist and the subdoctoral level commonly called psychological examiner.
4. Doctoral programs should be 4 years with 1 year internship in a child setting. Subdoctoral training should be 2 years with 6 months practicum training in a school situation under supervision of a school psychologist.
5. Doctoral people will serve on the policy making level, plan curricula, effect behavior change, do research, supervise, effect attitude change of school staff, parents, and community, do individual psychotherapy. They will be expert in personality assessment methods including projectives.
6. Subdoctoral people will assess abilities, aptitudes, and intelligence; they will recognize maladjustment but refer such cases to fully trained psychologists or community clinics. They will not use projectives and above all [the subdoctoral workers] must know their own limitations and avoid attempting functions which exceed their competence (Cutts, 1955).

It should be noted that the participants of the Thayer Conference were deliberately cognizant of the fact that their recommendations for the roles and functions of school psychologists had little meaning without acceptance by school administrators and teachers, since the school psychologist serves the needs of the school as perceived by the principals and teachers of any given school.

Preconference surveys of opinion from superintendents, principals, and teachers disclosed many dissatisfactions with the services of school psychologists at midcentury. The most frequent criticism was that the school psychologist "tends to be a law unto himself," as reflected in his tendency to come and go without notifying the school principal. Other criticisms included the following: "tends to give orders to principals"; has "poor human relations skills"; "doesn't understand the practical problems of the classroom"; exhibits "unfortunate personal characteristics"; is "inflexible"; "indulges in spectacular dress, manner, and conduct"; "fails to communicate"; "makes inadequate recommendations"; "has inadequate training"; "fails to recognize his own limitations"; and "has poor community skills." The conference participants took a dim view of these "failings" of the school psychologists and cautioned them to correct their faults and improve essential skills. On the other hand, in defense of the school psychologists, the conference members recommended that "Correct organization cooperatively designed by teachers, principals, superintendents and school psychologists" is essential and the school must provide the psychologist with adequate facilities for his work: "a chair behind a screen in the hall is not a desirable meeting place" (Cutts, 1955).

CURRENT DILEMMAS AMONG SCHOOL PSYCHOLOGISTS

Experience in the schools today reveals that the attitudes of many school people are still critical of the school psychologist and as a consequence the roles and functions of the school psychologist vary with the attitudes and expectations of the school personnel in any given school situation. Bardon aptly describes attitudes of school personnel toward the school psychologist from personal experience:

School personnel accept my status as a psychologist; they are not quite sure, however, why I am working in the schools and why I want to affiliate with them. My colleagues in social work and guidance, if they like me, think I am doing essentially what they are doing, and they forgive me my little idiosyncrasies such as the use of puzzles, figure drawings, and vocabulary lists. Those social workers and guidance counselors who do not like me seem to perceive me as a poorly trained and badly misplaced clinical psychologist (Bardon, 1968).

In spite of the many changes on the educational scene, a substantial number of school psychologists still function as clinicians, using the clinical model in the traditional manner. Bardon notes that this model was quite universal up to 1964 at the time of the conference on New Directions in School Psychology at Bethesda, Maryland. The conference participants recognized that change was urgent if school psychology was to survive as a profession. Clinical psychology had been changing for a decade in response to the exploding scientific and technological advances, and the consensus was that if clinical psychology changes, school psychology also must change.

School psychologists today are aware of the pressures for change in their roles and functions and are searching for effective direction. There are different views among them. Some insist that the clinical model is still the *sine qua non* in school service and they seek to continue with this model, feeling comfortable in these skills and competent to make a contribution through these methods. Other psychologists have turned to diagnostic tests of basic school skills and to tests of perceptual motor skills such as the Durrell Reading Analysis Test, the Slingerland Tests for Identifying Children with Specific Language Disability, the Illinois Test of Psycholinguistic Abilities, the Frostig Program for the Development of Visual Perception. Many kinds of tests are available, as listed in *Buros Mental Measurements Yearbook* (published every few years), and new forms of such tests are proliferating through the efforts of university researchers and research staff at independent educational research agencies.

Some psychologists prefer to dispense with testing, considering these procedures too time consuming and even useless in terms of contributing to an understanding of how to prevent or remediate learnings or change behaviors and attitudes on the basis of their test findings. These psychologists seek to meet the massive school problems through various forms of group therapy such as reality therapy, commitment, actional, experimental, nondirective, directive, occupational, and rational. Other school psychologists seek to relieve the pressure of the massive underachievement in the school populations by training paraprofessionals, parents, community volunteers, and child peers as tutors and classroom and therapeutic aides. Finally, there are those who consider the latest innovation on the psychological and educational scene the method of choice; these psychologists use behavior modification and the derivative programed curricula, machine teaching, computer aids, prescriptive teaching, and the like.

Application of behavior modification methods to school programs appears to have been stimulated in part by the sudden popularity of these methods in the therapeutic dyad, that is, among professional practitioners in the open society. During the past ten years, Yates (1970) notes that behavior modification methods have gained significant status under the impact of a "veritable explosion of work in this area." These methods have been used successfully not only with phobias, tics, stuttering, and addiction but also more recently with autistic children, mental retardates, and those with severe learning deficiencies in reading and arithmetic (Bijou, 1965; Birnbrauer et al., 1965; Haring & Phillips, 1962).

Other trends receiving scattered attention in the nation's

schools include "social engineering" to facilitate integration, group decision procedures to change emotional cli-
mates in communities, simulation and game theory to study
coping behavior in the classroom versus the earlier focus on
adjustment per se, and milieu modifications based on accumulating evidence that behavior of an individual changes in
response to changes in the setting, that is, in terms of the
degree and type of structure and ambiguity in the setting
(Bardon, 1968; Cummings & Cummings, 1963; Gray,
1970; Fein, 1967; Gold, 1940; Bruner et. al., 1966).

These new trends threaten many psychologists in the
schools, challenging them to seek training to equip them for
participation in these new educational designs. These trends
also challenge training schools to adapt their training programs to equip graduating school psychologists with the
new skills to cope with the burgeoning problems and the
new technologies.

A word of caution is necessary at this point. No matter
how well trained the psychologists are or become in new
methods, their functions and services will be determined in
great measure by the attitudes and preferences of school
personnel, the degree of cooperation given the psychologist,
the trust in his expertise, and the facilities provided him to
carry on. This means that principals, teachers, social workers, guidance counselors, special service staff, and parents
will need to be educated to the values of the new approaches to learning and behavior change if the psychologist is to be free to implement such programs. Changing attitudes of school people will be a slow process, for "great
bodies move slowly." There is the further danger that the
new programs will be introduced into some school situations without adequate understanding of the theories and
principles underlying them so that implementation may
well be arbitrary. In such cases, programs are bound to fail.
The implementers, frustrated by failure, may reject the
methods rather than seek the causes of failure in inadequate
planning, design, organization, staffing, facilities, skills, and

methods. Psychodynamic interpersonal methods may be
losing status in the schools due to their application by unqualified people who use these methods with limited skill
and little or no understanding of the underlying theories
and principles. In recent years not only poorly trained psychologists but also social workers and guidance counselors,
ill trained in psychodynamic principles and methods of diagnosis and treatment, have administered projective and intelligence tests and made interpretations about child personality and behavior, and even parent pathology
underlying child pathology, on the basis of their "clinical"
observations and "their test findings."

These widespread practices reflect ignorance of the ethical and professional standards for psychological testing as
defined in the *APA Standards for Development and Use of
Educational and Psychological Tests* (3rd draft, 1973,
APA). It is noteworthy that hearings on testing standards
were recently held under the auspices of the APA Office of
Scientific Affairs. One of the critical principles underlying
the standards of test use is that the "test user, in selecting,
administering, scoring, or interpreting a test, should know
what he is doing and the probable consequences of his activity. . . . The user must know what procedures are necessary to maximize the effectiveness of the testing program
and to minimize unfairness in the use of test results. He
must evaluate the many factors which may have influenced
test performance in the light of his purposes." Where "certain factors would unfairly influence performance, his procedures for using the test and interpreting the results should
be designed to minimize such influences." (p. 3). These
standards require that diagnostic psychological testing be
conducted by or under the direct supervision of *fully qualified psychologists* optimally skilled in test selection, administration, scoring, and interpretation and uses of test results.

Similarly, during the past few years the limits on who may
do therapy in the schools have been ignored in the name of

urgency so that guidance counselors, teachers, student teachers, educational aides, and volunteers are trying their hands at these treatments. It would be enlightening to explore the relationship between these many poorly conceived testing and therapeutic efforts by unqualified people in the schools, and also in many of the increasing numbers of clinics, and the failure of these "psychodynamic" practices to turn the tide of learning deficiencies and behavior problems in school children. There can be little doubt that "poor services by unqualified people" today are just as dangerous as they were at midcentury when the Thayer Conference participants noted that "poor services by unqualified people calling themselves psychologists not only brings the whole profession into disrepute, but more serious, endangers children" (Cutts, 1955).

Old methods and new methods of coping with problems of school children can be effective if they are used by skilled professionals whose approaches are based on sound developmental, learning, behavioral, or psychodynamic theories and principles and if these services are respected by the school people and supported with adequate facilities and ancillary staff. To be sure, psychologists in the schools must keep up with the new scientific and technological advances as they apply to school learning and behavior. In fact, many school psychologists are developing skills in coping with the many educational challenges today but their efforts are futile unless school people view them with "positive regard" and "positive expectations." Experience reveals extreme variations among school people in attitudes toward the school psychologist, conceptions of his role and skills, the application of his skills, and the implementation of his recommendations. There are some school situations when the psychologist cannot work at all due to the negative, critical, rejecting attitudes of school people, inadequate facilities, excessive demands, conflicting directives, and manipulatory tactics—"games" played by school people. A few examples of current school situations confronting school psychologists are offered to document these observations.

To Test or Not to Test

In a junior high school in a deprived inner city school, the school psychologist stopped testing and diagnostic studies to concentrate his energies on classroom observations, evaluations, and teacher consultation. The school principal in charge of guidance requested diagnostic clinical testing of several students with long histories of school disturbance, to facilitate educational planning for these students. The psychologist offered to write reports on these children on the basis of his observations and interviews. When the principal discovered that his reports contributed no more to the planning than the material already on hand from teachers, guidance counselors, and social workers, he again asked the psychologist to do diagnostic psychological testings. Since the psychologist resisted these requests, the principal turned for help to a psychological consultant serving the school on a special project.

The consultant soon discovered that the school psychologist was caught between *two different administrative views* about the type of psychological method appropriate to the problems of this school population. The school psychologist had to make a choice, whether to follow directives given by the district guidance supervisor working out of the superintendent's office (who incidentally had no direct authority over the school psychologist) or to respond to the requests of the school principal. The psychologist had a third choice, his responsibility of making a decision in terms of his own professional judgment relative to effective means of serving this school at this time. The school psychologist in question chose to follow the directives of the district guidance supervisor "to play it safe" since he saw this man as the power figure in this setting. The difficulties confronting this psychologist derived apparently from the conflicting demands by two school administrators, but his problem was compounded by his own need to "play to power" at the expense of his professional responsibility.

Diagnoses on Sight

A special project serving children with serious behavior problems was initiated in an inner city district, in five schools in seven classes with a total population of 120 children, from grade 2 to grade 8. An experienced cinical psychologist was assigned to do diagnostic testing, evaluations, and psychotherapy, consult with teachers, principals, and parents, and serve as consultant to the team (a guidance counselor and a coordinator). Within a week after the psychologist joined the project he was told to stop all testing and consultations; to select, by observation, the most disturbed children up to half the number of children involved in the project and involve these 60 or so children in individual and group therapy on a weekly basis. The less disturbed children were to be carried in "group therapy" by the guidance counselor, a *veteran of two years teaching, who had passed the guidance examination that year.*

When the psychologist explained that the approach was untenable, could not be defended theoretically, and if it could, was not possible to implement on a weekly basis by one person no matter how expert, he was ignored. As the psychologist continued to carry out the program he deemed appropriate, the coordinator sought means of removing the psychologist from the project and succeeded. It is noteworthy that the psychologist in this situation, in contrast to the preceding psychologist, refused to "play to power" at the expense of his ethical and professional judgment. These two problem situations might have been resolved with dignity for the school psychologists involved had the administrative and supervisory staff of the psychology department of the system come to the aid of the staff on the firing line. They did nothing, suggesting that they too were "playing to power."

Limited Space and Staff

In contrast to the foregoing situations is a junior high school in a very deprived area of an inner city where the principal and staff depend on the psychologist for help with school and child problems, calling for a wide variety of skills. In this situation the psychologist serves as diagnostician, therapist, motivation expert, referral agent, classroom milieu modifier, and critical contributor to the decisions relative to student placement and promotion. Although the attitudes of the school people here are positive and encouraging, the facilities are limited and the pressures for help great. What should the psychologist do under these circumstances, assuming he has the skills required to meet the demands? What should he do if he knows that he does not have the necessary skills to cope with the challenges?

The Principal as Obstacle

In still another junior high school in a similar inner city area the school principal informs the newly appointed psychologist that there is one authority in this school, the principal. He further informs the psychologist that not having had a psychologist on hand very often in the past, he has been obliged, himself, to give children and their parents essential mental health services. He shows the psychologist objects in his office to attest to his claim of competence in this area of function, objects sent to him as gifts by families in appreciation of his services. The psychologist is impressed. Then the principal informs him that he is to serve as a resource expert to the school and is to communicate to the principal about every contact he has with students and staff. The psychologist is impressed with the intense involvement of this principal in his school, an involvement that might well stifle the work of the staff.

As work begins the psychologist's fears are realized. This principal wants him to serve as a "yes man," a "tool" to implement the principal's decisions. The main goal of this principal, "a martinet," is to maintain a well ordered school. He will not tolerate disturbances in classrooms, halls, grounds. His immediate reaction to disturbance is to threaten suspension. However, since suspensions may have legal ramifications and are frowned upon by the superintendent of schools and parent groups alike, the principal seeks to avoid these limitations by "demanding" that the school psychologist "get" a medical suspension for the given student. When the psychologist explains the time consuming procedures to obtain a medical suspension from the school psychiatrist, the principal dismisses the psychologist as "useless," claiming that he needs a psychiatrist rather than a psychologist on the staff, for a psychiatrist can sign a medical supension when directed. The guidance and teaching staff here are very guarded, for their work is also closely watched by the principal, so they seek help from the psychologist furtively. What should the psychologist do in this situation?

Guidance Counselor as Obstacle

In an elementary school in a deprived metropolitan setting the guidance counselor has top powers for some obscure reason. Even though the principal and the assistant principal view the psychologist as a highly skilled professional and expert in teacher training as well as in clinical skills, their efforts to use the psychologist in these challenging ways are sabotaged by the guidance counselor. She sees

herself as the clinical expert, responsible for child evaluations, teacher training, individual and group therapy, and
as a referral agent. She decides which children should be
medically suspended and she tells the psychologist to "get"
the medical suspension from the school psychiatrist. It is
apparent that the psychologist in this situation must be will-
ing to serve the power needs of this guidance counselor if
he is to remain in this setting. What should he do?

Positive Attitudes Are Not Enough

In an experimental elementary inner city school the psychologist is expected to develop and implement a diagnostic
program to facilitate individual prescriptive teaching. In
addition, the psychologist is called upon to intervene in
crises in the classrooms, screen new admissions, provide in-
service training for teachers in methods of coping with dis-
tressed and problem children in the classroom and adapting
teaching methods to the learning styles of the children. Further, the psychologist is expected to test children suspected
of mental retardation at the request of the guidance counselors. In this situation the staff generally expresses positive
attitudes toward the psychologist and has positive expectations, so that the psychologist is highly motivated to productive efficiency. However, the demands are beyond the
energies and time of any one psychologist no matter how
skilled. The psychologist here needs additional psychological staff, secretarial and clerical help, and appropriate work
spaces, none of which are available. What should the psychologist do in this situation?

The Principal as Facilitator

In privileged communities the challenges are not as critical
in terms of space and facilities, which are generally ade-

quate. However, the attitudes of the school people in these communities are as varied as in deprived settings and determine in good measure how the psychologist functions. In a school in an upper middle class suburban community the school principal views the psychologist as clinical, educational, and research expert. He is concerned primarily with the problem of limited achievement among his many gifted children. He presents this problem to the psychologist asking for help in motivating these children toward utilization of this high potentials. Here the psychologist is given a free hand to plan in-service training for teachers, serve as liaison to parent and community groups to enhance the effectiveness of school-community relations, and to plan programs to meet the needs of the school as defined above.

The Psychologist "Should" Know His Place

In contrast, a principal in another upper middle class area uses the psychologist simply for IQ testing while in a third suburban system the school psychologist is expected to take orders from the school administrator of mental health services, in this case the school social worker, who views the psychologist as a "tester" obliged to provide IQ scores and subject matter scores to facilitate the clinical work of the social workers in the department. In still another privileged community each of the three psychologists are burdened with the responsibilities of serving five schools each week, an assignment that is unrealistic under any circumstances calling for *services* to children. In this setting the psychologists are further frustrated in their efforts to introduce new approaches such as training teachers to cope with many of the problems of the children, classroom management techniques, positive reinforcement approaches to learning. The general view of school people in this community dictates that the psychologist is a tester and that their efforts to introduce these other methods encroach upon the domains of the guidance counselors, principals, social workers, and subject matter and methods supervisors affiliated with the superintendent's office. What can the psychologists do in such a school community to change the attitudes of the school people?

Doing Your Own Thing

It is noteworthy that there are schools in which the principals are not involved in the role and functions of the psychologist in his school. Here the psychologist is left to explore the needs of the school in conference with the guidance counselor, social worker, assistant principal, and special service staff. In this type of situation what the psychologist selects to do will be determined in great measure by his own interests and skills as well as by the needs defined by the school staff, their ability to assign priorities to the needs, to arrive at consensus about the projects to be initiated, and to cooperate in facilitating the work of the psychologist. The popular phrase used by psychologists to describe this particular type of assignment is "doing your own thing." In these situations the roles and functions of the psychologist are as varied as are the interests and skills of each psychologist, given positive regard and professional respect by the school people.

The situations presented illustrate that the roles and functions of the school psychologist vary with the demands made on him by the power authorities in each situation. The demands vary from that of simple IQ tester, to "tool" of the power figure, to expert contributor to solutions of a wide variety of challenging school problems. Although these sample situations reveal great differences in the expectations from psychologists in the schools, all reveal that the psychologist is in the schools to serve the needs of the schools as determined by the school administrators and staff. They also reveal that the "felt" needs of school personnel for psychological services are so diverse as to call for different levels of training of psychological personnel in the schools. If these school needs, as defined by school personnel, can be demonstrated as valid, legitimate needs, to facilitate education of children, then the training of psychological personnel for the schools must encompass differentiated programs, from technician through policy maker, program designer, evaluator, and consultant. These roles will be examined further as we move on to the changing school scene.

REFERENCES

Bardon, J. I. School Psychology and School Psychologists. A new approach to an old problem. *American Psychologist,* 1968, *23,* 187–194.

Bardon, J. I. & Bennett, V. Preparation for Professional Psychology: An Example from a School Psychology Program. *American Psychologist,* 1967, *22,* 652–656.

Bijou, S. W. Experimental Studies in Child Behavior. Normal and Deviant. In L. Krasner & L. P. Ullman (eds.), *Case Studies in Behavior Modification.* New York: Holt, Rinehart & Winston, 1965, pp. 66–81.

Birnbrauer, J. S., Wolf, M. M., Kidder, J. O. & Tague, C. E. Classroom Behavior of Retarded Pupils with Token Reinforcement. *Journal of Experimental Child Psychology,* 1965, *2,* 219–235.

Brotemarkle, R. A. (ed.) *Clinical Psychology: Studies in Honor of Lightner Witmer.* Philadelphia:University of Pennsylvania Press, 1931.

Brownell, S. M. (ed.) *Issues in Urban Education.* New Haven: Yale University Institution for Social and Policy Studies, 1971.

Bruner, J. S., Oliver, R. R. & Greenfield, P. M. *Studies in Cognitive Growth.* New York, John Wiley and Sons, 1966.

Cohen, A. S. Dyspedagogia as a Cause of Reading Retardation: Definition and Treatment. In B. Batemen (ed.), *Reading*

Disabilities. Eugene: University of Oregon Press, 1970. (mimeograph copy of chapter)

Cummings, J. & Cummings, E. *Ego and Milieu.* New York: Atherton Press, 1963.

Cutts, N. (ed.) School Psychologists at Mid-Century. Washington, D.C.: American Psychological Association, 1955.

Durrell, D. *Analysis of Reading Difficulties.* New York: Harcourt, Brace, and World, 1955.

Fein, L. G. Non-Academic Personality Variables and Success at Nursing School. *International Mental Health Research Newsletter.* New York: Post Graduate Center for Mental Health, 1967, p. 9.

Frostig, M. & Horme, D. *The Frostig Program for Development of Visual Perception.* Chicago: Follettt, 1964.

Gold, L. Functionalism in Education. New Haven: Yale University Graduate School of Education, 1940. (unpublished manuscript)

Gray, S. Intervention with Mothers and Young Children. In H. C. Haywood (ed.), *Social and Cultural Aspects of Mental Retardation.* New York: Appleton-Century-Crofts, 1970.

Haring, N. G. & Phillips, E. L. *Educating Emotionally Disturbed Children.* New York: McGraw-Hill, 1962.

Kirk, S., McCarthy, J. & Kirk, W. *Illinois Test of Psycholinguistic Abilities.* Urbana: University of Illinois, 1968.

Korten, F. F., Cook, S. W. & Lacey, J. I. (eds.) *Psychology and the Problems of Society.* Washington, D. C.: American Psychological Association, 1970.

Myklebust, J. R. *The Pupil Rating Scale.* New York: Grune and Stratton, 1971.

Raimy, V. *Boulder Conference on Clinical Psychology.* Washington, D. C.: American Psychological Association, 1950.

Slingerland, B. *Screening Tests for Identifying Children with Specific Language Disability.* Cambridge: Educators Publishing Service, 1969.

Standards for Development and Use of Educational and Psychological Tests. (3rd draft) Washington, D. C.: American Psychological Association Office of Scientific Affairs, 1973.

Susskind, D. J. Franks, C. M. & Lonoff, R. Desensitization Program with Third and Fourth Grade Teachers: A New Application and a Controlled Study. *Newsletter of the Association for the Advancement of Behavior Therapy,* 1967, *2/3.*

Yates, A. J. *Behavior Therapy.* London: John Wiley and Sons, 1970.

CHAPTER 2

The Changing School Scene

To determine what new roles and functions are required of psychologists serving the changing schools and communities, it is essential to examine the various innovations, experimental and compensatory, introduced into the nation's schools over the past decade and ongoing today. The focus is on the target populations and conditions and the rationales underlying the programs. Those aspects of the new developments that call for psychological skills and knowledge are discussed even though no reference was made to the roles of psychologists in these situations in the designs and implementations.

For more than a decade school systems in the United States have been developing compensatory educational programs in inner city schools and deprived rural areas. These are designed for the following purposes:

1. To remediate and reverse the widespread learning deficiencies and progressive learning retardation in basic school skills and content mastery in children of deprived cultures.
2. To stem the tide of school dropouts and motivate prospective dropouts toward achievement through special programs geared to their abilities and interests.
3. To modify organizational elements in the schools that appear to promote and maintain behavior problems in school children.

In addition, various innovative educational elements have been and are being explored in schools across the country in communities at all socioeconomic levels, in efforts to facilitate teaching and learning under the impact of the new knowledges, technologies, and materials flooding the marketplace. In essence, the thrust of the innovations is to prepare children to cope effectively with life challenges in the world today. There is general consensus that to achieve these goals the focus of teaching must change from content mastery to a functional command of basic school skills and the development of cognitive skills, functioning flexibly and discriminately; that is, the focus must be on learning to think critically, to reason, judge, analyze, categorize, compare, evaluate, synthesize, and integrate ideas, and to think and perform creatively. The new goals also seek development of differentiated perceptual motor skills, of independent self-directive behaviors, of socially appropriate attitudes and behaviors, of positive self-concepts, of widening interests in new contents and measurable outcomes; in other words, the new goals seek to teach children to act meaningfully and skillfully rather than "to be educated."

These new emphases in education are not new when examined in terms of goals set by teachers and administrators in our nation's schools in the past. Even today teachers believe they are teaching children to think, yet most observers of the classroom scene find that rather than teaching children to think, practice tends to emphasize recall and recognition of bits of information, calling for rote memory rather than for thinking and problem solving. Suskind (1969) examined the extent to which schools meet the highly valued objective of fostering curiosity (questioning and problem solving) in young children. Based on 30 minute classroom observation units he found that teachers asked on the average about 50 questions during the 30 minute observation unit against an average of 7 questions by the classroom children. Analyses of teacher questions revealed further that simple questions of fact predominated significantly over thought-provoking questions by the teachers.

Over the years, as our schools became institutionalized and insulated from current societal needs, they increasingly failed to prepare children for coping effectively with changing conditions in our society. The present innovative approaches are motivated by awareness of the urgent need to bring the school culture into an organic relationship with today's culture in our open society. The school experience thus will equip today's children with skills essential to occupational flexibility and mobility and to the maintenance of American democracy, which ensures equality of justice for all.

CAN LEARNING BE FACILITATED?

The new emphasis in our schools on cognitive, perceptual, motor, and ego skills and behavioral outcomes is in sharp contrast to the school concerns of the past 50 years when subject matter mastery, as measured by standardized achievement tests, was the measure of school success and IQ scores were sacrosanct evidence of intellectual power and ability to learn. Over the years, subject matter achievement age-grade norms and mean IQ scores of children from culturally rich upper socioeconomic homes and neighborhoods were found to be consistently and significantly higher than corresponding norms for children from low socioeconomic and deprived cultures. These statistics were viewed by many guardians of society and the educational gatekeepers as unequivocal evidence of the hereditary nature of learning potential, that is, of the rate and power to learn. This evidence, accepted as absolute truth, led teachers to expect school success from upper cultural level children and minimal achievement from culturally deprived children. Since children respond to teacher expectations of them (Rosenthal & Jacobson, 1969), teacher prophecies of school achievement by their pupils from different cultural backgrounds were fulfilled frequently enough to reinforce teacher belief in the genetic influences on learning potential and ability.

The view of the ascendance of genetics over environment is current today not only among many teachers and school administrators but also among educational and psychological leaders at renowned universities. Thus Jensen (1969) reignited the age old nature-nurture controversy when he attempted to answer the question *How much can we boost the IQ and scholastic achievement?* Eysenck (1971) reinforced this controversy when he sought to support Jensen in his book *The IQ Argument.*

If we accept the view of these authors that genetics plays a most critical role in the massive learning retardation among our deprived child populations, then our continued involvement with efforts to design effective compensatory educational programs seem futile. On the other hand, if we can provide research evidence that nurture is the critical variable in the massive learning retardation manifest in deprived child populations, then our efforts to facilitate learning in these children must be intensified.

Support for the Genetic View

Jensen notes after a thorough review of published studies of cross-cultural, cross-national, and cross-racial IQ score differences that genetic factors account for 80% of the differences and environmental factors account for 20% of the differences. Of the environmental factors affecting intellectual ability, he considers prenatal factors, particularly deficit nutritional influences during the gestation period, most critical. Jensen limits these influences further by noting that only very gross nutritional deficiency during the prenatal period seriously affects intellectual development and that these impairments are reversible only during the first few years of life. Jensen discounts the impact of mild nutritional deficiency on intellectual potential during the prenatal period. Since we do not yet know the nutritional ingredients essential to full development of intellectual potential, we are in no position to determine what is gross and what is mild nutritional deficiency as related to nurture and development of the intellectual structure and function. In view of the limits of our knowledge in this area, it seems essential that we view any evidence of malnutrition in children as potentially detrimental to cognitive development.

Jensen accounts for the failure of Head Start programs on the premise that the intellectual powers of the children exposed to those programs are not modifiable, being fixed by genetic determinants. He further states that these programs were bound to fail for they are based on two untenable theories, the "average children concept" and the allied "social deprivation hypothesis" (p. 4). The average children concept assumes that all children will reveal equal potential for learning if exposed from birth to the same environmental stimulations and experiences. This concept is essentially the blank slate (*tabula rasa*) theory of Locke. The social deprivation hypothesis postulates that ethnic minorities and the economic poor, who do poorly at school, do so because they begin school lacking critical experiences essential to school learning. The proponents of this thesis state that these deprived children lack perceptual, attentional, verbal skill experience, self-confidence, self-directional practice, teacher attitudes conducive to classroom learning, and parental help and encouragement needed to promote school achievement.

Challenging the voluminous evidence cited by Hunt (1961) attesting to the modifiability of IQ scores and school achievement, Jensen presents data "proving" the fixed nature of intelligence. He refers to genetic studies revealing deviant chromosomal counts as unequivocal evidence of the genetic nature of intelligence. He cites Turner's syndrome, which is genetically demonstrable by lack of one chromosome (subject has 45 rather than 46 chromosomes); this syndrome appears to impair the subject's fertility, accounts for certain physical characteristics, and seriously impairs space-form perceptions and ability to cope with mathematical concepts. In this context Jensen might have included studies of impaired chromosomal structures as represented by Downe's syndrome, Mongolism (Trisomy 21), which causes varying degrees of mental retardation along with distinct physical anomalies.

There is no argument that these genetic studies contribute to our understanding of specific intellectual *disabilities* in a selected number of children, but these studies do not explain the widespread learning lags among masses of children from deprived population samples in the United States and other nations of the world. There is little if any support today for the concept that the mind is a blank slate at birth. In fact supporters of the nurture or environmental theory of mental development acknowledge that genes determine the *limits* of intellectual potential just as they determine the color of the eyes. However, whereas the color of the eyes is directly discernible, to date we have no way of measuring the contributions of genes to the limits of intellectual potential in the general populations of the world. Any claims about different intellectual limits between various ethnic, cultural, national, economic, or racial population samples are based on inferences from test data that presumably tap functional intellectual limits. In other words, such claims are merely educated guesses based on culturally determined standards. In spite of the difficulties inherent in tapping objectively the real limits of intelligence by the tests at present available to us, Jensen claims that "Intelligence . . .

meets the usual scientific criteria for being regarded as an aspect of objective reality and just as much as do atoms, genes and electromagnetic fields" (p. 19). He states that "it is a biological reality and not just a figment of social convention" (p. 19).

Citing the work of Shuey (1966) in detail, Jensen notes that Negro IQ score distributions fall consistently 1 standard deviation below that of the white population in the United States, thus the norm for Negro samples is 15 IQ points below the national intelligence test norm, at 85 versus the national norm at 100. Jensen notes further that "as a group, Negroes perform somewhat more poorly on those subjects which tap abstract abilities . . . and they perform relatively better on verbal than on nonverbal intelligence tests" (p. 81). Jensen notes also that Negro children do as well as white children on tasks calling for associative learning abilities such as memory span and serial and paired associate rote learnings. On the other hand Eysenck notes that cross-racial studies reveal that *Negro children surpass white American children* during the first three years of life on development of sensorimotor skills, which are of course *nonverbal*. However, Eysenck adds that white children catch up to the Negro children in these nonverbal skills after age 3 and in fact surpass the Negro children as they get older.

These data do not permit conclusions about the relative impacts of heredity and environment on intellectual potentials. If anything these reported items appear to blur the issue. These data fail to provide convincing evidence of the relative contributions of nature and nurture to learning. Instead they suggest the intrusion of intervening variables that need to be identified with precision, whose impacts must be measured so that methods may be devised to counteract those variables that are destructive to continuing development.

The apparent contradictions in the various studies on comparative intelligence based on IQ scores suggest that the use of intelligence tests per se in efforts to gain an understanding of the learning potentials of masses of children is a simplistic approach to a complex problem. The contradictory findings reveal the inadequacy of the concepts employed to define complex cognitive processes. Serious research into intellectual potentials and abilities calls for refined operational definitions of the intellectual processes to be studied, identification of the intervening variable that have a profound impact on these developing processes, and precise instruments that measure the impacts of the intervening variables as well as the skills under question.

Jensen notes that there is a need for studies to explore the spectrum of abilities and potentials of children, presumably with innovative refined instruments, yet he also recommends a differential educational curriculum for disadvantaged children, one that caters to their "demonstrated" strengths and circumvents their "demonstrated" lacks. Does this mean that disadvantaged children should be educated via curricula that stress "rote learning" and circumvent problem solving and abstract ideas?

Eysenck defends Jensen's thesis and adds evidence from the work of Lemos (1969), who tested two groups of Australian aboriginal children, one group part-aboriginal and the other group full-aboriginal. Results revealed that the part-aboriginals performed consistently better on "conservation" in Piagetian-type tasks than did full-aboriginals. Lemos speculated that these differences were probably due to *genetic drift, extreme environmental conditions, and natural selection* affecting the ancestors of both groups of children. Eysenck notes further that many studies of intelligence on native English and Irish children reveal consistently superior IQ scores for the English than for the Irish samples. He acknowledges that the crimes against Negroes over centuries and against the Irish (by the English) may well have contributed to these intellectual deficiencies and he urges that maximum use be made of the abilities these unfortunate children possess. He also hopes that educators will nurture the 20% intellectual potential that is modifiable in these children, granting that 80% is not modifiable, being genetically limited. It is in the best interests of children that educators not take this 20% modifiability too seriously, since this figure has been arrived at statistically, not by direct measurement of the intellect itself. One might concede that all things being equal, children with optimal prenatal and postnatal nurturance should be motivated to increase their intellectual productivity by at least 20% beyond their characteristic fine performances. On the other hand, children deprived prenatally and/or through infancy, early childhood, and up to adolescence have been thwarted in the natural development of their intellect, so that their education presents a double challenge. First it is essential to release or revive their natural maturational potentials, which may well have been aborted by deprivations, and second it is essential to provide them with the critical experiences that facilitate continued development up to native potentials. In other words, the potential for modification among these deprived children may well be closer to 80% than 20%.

Support for the Nurture View

In contrast to the research findings on comparative studies of child intelligence that Jensen and Eysenck present to support the idea of a fixed nature of intelligence are the results obtained by Vane (1973) and Collier (1972) in support of the modifiability of intelligence under impact of social and cultural influences. Vane's findings derived from a comparative study of English, Irish, and American children aged 4 to 7 tested with the Vane Kindergarten Test (VKT) and the Boehm Test of Concept Formation (BTCF). The Boehm test is designed to assess knowledge of basic concepts such as "around," "between," and "almost"; the Vane test is designed to assess intelligence through the use of three subtests: vocabulary, perceptual motor, and draw-a-man test. Both tests are designed for kindergarten age children and have been standardized on children from all socioeconomic backgrounds. The purpose of this study was to test the hypothesis that differences in intelligence and achievement test results of school children are associated with social class rather than with race. The present study compared achievement and intelligence test results of kindergarten age children from the white-collar class and children from the blue-collar class in England and Ireland with the performance of children from these classes in the United States. Vane hypothesized that there would be larger differences between the classes within each of these English-speaking countries than between the same classes of the different countries. The English children were predominantly from London and the Irish children were all from Dublin. Since three of the five English schools did not lend themselves to the group administration called for by the Boehm test, it was administered to only 111 children, whereas 300 children were tested with the Vane test.

The results obtained indicated that the differences between classes on the VKT total scores and on almost all subtest scores were highly significant in favor of the children from the white-collar class. No significant differences were found between the sexes with the exception of the scores on the draw-a-man subtest, which favored Irish girls over Irish boys. The differences between classes in both England and Ireland were found to be similar to such differences in the United States, 11.3 for England, 10.6 for Ireland, and 13.8 for the United States. In contrast the differences between the countries for same class children were significantly smaller than for between classes, thus there was a 5.7 point difference between white-collar children in England and the United States and an 8.2 point difference between the blue-collar children of these two countries. These results suggest that existing differences in intellectual performance, as measured by the VKT, are related to class rather than race, since the children in both England and Ireland were white and native born. Results on the BTCF indicate that English white-collar children score significantly higher on these concepts than do the blue-collar children. In Ireland the results showed no difference between classes on the BTCF, but it is noteworthy that the blue-collar children in Ireland were 8 months older, on the average, than the white-collar sample.

The results of this study suggest that there are significant differences between intelligence and achievement test scores in different socioeconomic classes in England and Ireland, much as in the United States. These results support the hypothesis that test result differences between socioeconomic classes within countries are greater than test result differences within the same socioeconomic classes in different countries. Vane calls attention to the fact that children in the blue-collar classes in all three countries show a similar pattern of subtest scores, with the vocabulary subtest lower than the other two subtests. This finding supports the view of many educators that children from deprived backgrounds lack adequate verbal skills essential to maximal benefit from schooling offered. Vane also notes that the vocabulary scores for the Irish samples of both socioeconomic classes were lower than these scores for the English and American samples. She suggests that this finding may be due to the fact that Irish children must use both Gaelic and English in school, whereas the English and American children are required to do all their work in English. The results of the Vane study cast doubt on Eysenck's inferences that the Irish as a nation have a lower native intelligence than do the English and on his effort to account for this phenomenon. It is far more likely that the studies reported by Eysenck did not control for the impact of social class on performance of the Irish and English samples studied.

Collier's data cast doubt on the speculations of Lemos about intellectual differences between two samples of one culture, the aboriginals. Collier's study focused on the question of the development of the ability to conserve in 350 Turkish children as it relates to social status and differential conditions of socialization. The population studied was drawn from four segments of the Turkish child population: (1) private urban; (2) private village; (3) public urban; and (4) public village. The children were all in the 7 to 8 year old range. A concept development test introduced by Freyberg of New Zealand was used to measure conservation attainment. Eighteen dimensions of concept development were assessed including such areas as conservation of continuous quality, conservation of mass, ordination and conservation of weight. The Goodenough-Harris IQ test was also administered to all children. Significant differences in mean test scores were found between children who attend private and public schools, between those who attend urban and village schools, and between 7 year olds and 8 year olds. Village boys scored significantly higher across the board than did village girls. The Goodenough-Harris IQ scores were significantly correlated with concept development scores at the .05 level. Collier concludes that her results support the thesis that intelligence, as measured by the tests used in this study, is vulnerable to social class, socialization processes, and cultural factors. Compared to the speculations of Lemos, one must conclude that Lemos ignored the law of parsimony: no more causes or forces should be assumed to account for an observed phenomenon than are necessary.

Additional critical evidence *undermining* the concept of a fixed intelligence is emerging from the work of Kagan at Harvard University. Kagan (1972) recently released findings from his long range investigations of species-specific influences on intellectual growth from infancy through puberty which present a major challenge to proponents of the fixed nature of intelligence. Kagan's findings indicate that cognitive retardation in infancy does not permit prediction of future function in all environments; that young children who are poor achievers in school, whether the children come from developing countries, deprived family backgrounds, or from highly cultivated backgrounds, do not necessarily lack intelligence. He notes that children who start slowly in mathematics and reading may later gain vital confidence needed to become proficient in these areas of learning. In short, he finds a serious *discontinuity* in the development of particular cognitive competencies from infancy through preadolescence. The samples he studied were in the United States, Guatemala, and India. Kagan notes that the data collected by his research team seriously question the continuity hypothesis of cognitive development and the hypothesis that early childhood *"cultural* deprivation" leads to a lifetime of inferior intellectual functioning. Kagan's results underscore the complexities of human intellectual development and the futility of seeking to *predict limits of intellectual potential* from test performances during infancy and childhood up to preadolescence.

Results of current well controlled studies (Heber, 1972; Hunt et al., 1973) should put a stop to the circular argument of the relative merits of nature versus nurture, an argument that unfortunately distracts critical attention, time, energies, and funds from the task of developing programs to counteract and finally eliminate the correlates of poverty and prejudice that erode learning in children exposed to these insidious influences.

STEREOTYPED ATTITUDES TOWARD IQ SCORES IN TRADITIONAL SCHOOL SETTINGS

In traditional school settings where school success is measured by age-grade achievement norms and where IQ scores are viewed as true measures of learning potential, the role of the school psychologist is accordingly stereotyped. In such school settings, psychological personnel administer "IQ tests" and compare obtained scores to standard achievement scores or teacher classroom grades in one or more content areas; they then determine which children are "overachievers" (whatever that may mean) and which children are underachievers. It is noteworthy that often when a child from a deprived background is identified as an "overachiever" he is encouraged to lower his sites, although an underachieving child from a deprived background is viewed with "pity" by the school staff "because his parents are not interested," or because "they are not really involved in the child's school progress" and "the school can't do it all." Rarely is any effort made to involve the parents of these children, to spur them on to use their learning potentials, and seldom is any effort made to investigate disparate specific abilities and disabilities in these children, an approach that has been effective in educating exceptional children, including brain damaged, retarded, and cerebral palsied children. On the other hand, rarely if ever is a child from middle or upper middle class background identified as an "overachiever," and when such a child is identified as an underachiever his parents are called in and plans are set afoot for more thorough psychological study to develop individually prescribed interventions to facilitate this child's school learnings.

Such stereotyped practices by psychological personnel in the traditional school programs serve to support and reinforce school staff expectations of children under their tutelage, expectations that discourage children of deprived background from striving for higher achievement.

In defense of the school psychologist it must be pointed out that even if the psychologist should try to change his interventions, explore specific abilities and disabilities of children, and modify teacher expectations of privileged and deprived children, his efforts are doomed, since he must work within the *regularities* (Sarason, 1971) of the school system "where the more things change the more they remain the same . . . ." However, the present forced acknowledgment that cultural deprivation impairs learning and motivation for learning, that school curricula are not relevant to the demands of life, that educational goals need to be operationally defined in terms relevant to preparation for effective coping behavior—these awarenesses are provoking changes in school organizations, curricula, methods of teaching and evaluations, and it is hoped in teacher expectations of all children, so that all children may be motivated to achieve under positive teacher expectations. Under these changing conditions the roles and functions of the school psychologist may change accordingly, to meet the new needs of teachers and children in these new settings.

NEW DIAGNOSTIC APPROACHES TO LEARNING DIFFICULTIES

Since functional mastery of basic school skills is critical to continuing learnings, widespread attention is being given to developing new teaching and evaluation methods of these basic school skills, "reading, 'riting, 'rithmetic." One new approach is based on task or skill analyses of the significant discrete sequential learning steps in each skill, an approach that emerged from efforts to devise computer aids to teaching reading and from behavior modification approaches to learning remediation and was further influenced by the diagnostic and remedial methods used in Special Learning Disabilities (SLD) programs. The task analysis approach to teaching and learning provides continuous feedback to progress since movement through hierarchical sequences depends on mastery of each preceding step. This approach individualizes teaching and learning even as it permits the teacher to work with each child within the whole class setting. This approach to teaching can alert teachers to intraindividual as well as interindividual rates and modes or styles of learning different skills and to the *irregularities of learning both within any one child and between children.*

Psychologists in such settings must change their approach to the uses of standard intelligence tests, viewing them as diagnostic instruments tapping cognitive, perceptual, verbal, and motor skills rather than as an absolute measure of learning potential as implied in a global IQ score. Through task and skill analyses approaches to testing, teaching, and learning, teachers can more readily detect learning difficulties in selected children and make referrals to the psychologist in precise problem terms rather than in traditional global terms such as learning problem, reading problem, behavior problem, day dreamer. In school settings where the new approaches to teaching are introduced, the psychologist, the psychological examiners, the interns, and the trainees face the challenge of developing operational understandings of learning sequences in basic school skills and of the underlying cognitive, perceptual, and motor processes. Such understanding is essential to the selection, administration, analyses, scoring, and interpretations of test performances. In these settings the traditional global use of the IQ score and age-grade achievement norms on standardized tests have little meaning. Psychologists in the schools can also look to behavior modification methods and principles for guidelines to interventions in the classroom with behavior problem children.

LEARNING IS MORE THAN COGNITION

Evidence has been accumulating over several years indicating that behavior modification principles and methods are effective in modifying behaviors such as social and self-management skills, symbolic learning, sensitivity for others' needs, and verbal learnings in retarded, autistic, and emotionally disturbed children (Bandura, 1969; Lovaas, 1966; Lovaas et al., 1965; Lovaas et al., 1967). Lovaas and his co-authors (1967) indicate that self care skills, play patterns, appropriate sex role behavior, intellectual skills and interpersonal modes of behavior can be established in autistic children more rapidly than lingustic patterns by modeling the appropriate activities and rewarding the childrens' emulations. Bandura (1969) notes that evidence is also accumulating that a wide variety of neutral and socially approved behavior can be substantially increased in all learners as a function of witnessing the action of real life or symbolic models in action. Although these behavior modification methods have been precisely defined and described and demonstrated as effective in experimental settings, little progress has been made over the years in applying these various methods of modeling, shaping, contingency systems, reinforcement schedules, and so on, in widespread and consistent ways to changing behavior of groups of school children in classrooms.

In short, widespread application of these behavior modification procedures in a consistent way to classroom teaching and learning needs to be encouraged, particularly with respect to facilitation of maturation and continuing development of healthy personality dynamics, positive self-images, independent self-directional skills within appropriate age limits, socially and emotionally effective behaviors, both approaches and responses, sensitivity for the needs of others and ultimately for the generalized other, ethical and moral values and attitudes that become embedded in the developmental matrix of the personality. Attention needs to be given also to the use of action methods like role playing and psychodrama, simulated reality practice for evaluation and modification of attitudes and behaviors, methods that lend themselves to classroom teaching.

PITFALLS OF OVERSIMPLIFYING LEARNING PRINCIPLES

Recognition of the responsibility of the school for development of the personality dimensions just noted are implied in the dictum of John Dewey, "teach the whole child," a challenge that was iterated and reiterated through the past five decades in all teacher preparation programs. Though well intentioned, this dictum received little attention beyond lip service, just as the intention to teach children to think in the traditional school program was constantly verbalized but never implemented. To be sure, some efforts were made by progressive educators to implement approaches to facilitate development of cognitive processes and personality dynamics, but the results have been discouraging to date. The failure of progressive education perhaps may be accounted for in the same terms that present innovations may fall short of their goals, that is, failure to invest the necessary time, effort, funds, and expertise in the definition of constructs to be taught and analyses of the behaviors to be modified as well as failure to test new practices with sound controlled experimentation. Rather than experimentally testing new approaches based on critical constructs from Dewey's philosophy of education, progressive educators, guided by a simplistic interpretation of Dewey's principle that "children learn by doing," removed structure from the classroom and courses of study, eliminated sequential learning steps, and substituted permissive unstructured classrooms and activities, encouraging children to do what they "like to do, what interests them." For some reason difficult to comprehend progressive educators failed to recognize that children's interests and talents are expanded from exposure to ever-widening experiences and that learning and interests are aborted and regressed if selection of activities is left solely to the child's preferences. In short, progressive programs, like many of the new programs today, were implemented in haste without benefit of appropriate research and based on simplistic interpretations of learning theory. This progressive view of learning is as destructive as the view that rigid conformity and content mastery prepare for life. Neither progressive education seeking to teach "the whole child" nor traditional education seeking to teach "content mastery" has provided convincing evidence that it is an approach that facilitates development of healthy personality dimensions.

THE CHALLENGE

The challenge to the new education remains. Can the schools effectively teach the millions of children, passing through every year, problem-solving styles and strategies in the various culture content areas and the social and emotional skills essential to appropriate and effective interpersonal coping in critical life contexts. Such questions were explored by the participants at the Invitational Conference on Testing Problems conducted by the Educational Testing Services of Princeton, New Jersey, in New York City in 1969.

Relative to content selection and organization toward the new process goals of education, passing consideration was given to the task analysis and essential content mastery approach. It was noted that although the approach attends to the sequential ordering of content, it fails to attend to the more critical branching aspects of content organization essential to facilitation of cognitive manipulations of facts in a variety of contexts so that contents may become meaningful, flexible, functional, and transferable even as cognitive skills are mastered and generalized. At this conference there was majority consensus that teaching and testing for content mastery is a sterile approach to education, that psychologists must develop new ways focusing on processes or strategies of problem solving, on developing means of fostering self-discovery, and on encouraging development of decision-making skills. The question to be answered is how does each child learn rather than what does he learn. Note was made of the need for evaluating the nonrational aspects of achievment, detecting the unintended and harmful outcomes of teaching/learning, the unexpected side effects as well as the process aspects or modes of behavior as opposed to products of behavior.

The urgency of developing evaluation procedures that are appropriately validated was emphasized as was the fact that validation depends not on the test but on one's purpose in using the test. Tests per se are not valid, but their uses and interpretations for any stated situation need to be validated. It was noted that to date evaluations have been designed to measure success against some fixed standard so that test results are given comparative interpretations and have little absolute significance per se. Such uses of test data suit content mastery goals but are meaningless in evaluations of cognitive processes, self-directional skills, self-respect attitudes, and the like. If our goals are focused on development of each child in his mode rather than on competitive development, then evaluations must permit absolute statements concerning any given trait or process in any given child in a defined situation rather than in terms of relative status.

NEED FOR RIGOROUS RESEARCH IN
THE CHANGING SCHOOL SCENE

In spite of the many problems that still confront educational and psychological researchers seeking to develop new approaches to teaching and evaluating learning processes in the classroom, some ground has been broken in these areas by research designers at the preschool and primary school levels. Such programs appear to have significant short term effectiveness but they are too new to permit evaluation or prediction of their long term impacts. It is noteworthy that in some of these innovative programs, the designers define, in detail, the evaluative approaches to be used and the personnel to carry out the evaluations, whereas in other programs the designers leave evaluation methods to the discretion of school administrators and staff in each setting.

Needless to say, evaluation techniques used in such programs need to be rigorously standardized for reliability and their uses need to be precisely defined to permit determination of the validity of the use to which the test results are put. Since such research skills generally are not part of the equipment of school administrators, teaching staff, special service staff, or psychological examiners (usually employed in schools at MA level), educators and psychologists with expertise in educational and clinical research need to be involved to ensure meaningful research implementation and evaluation. Without such expert direction the new programs are doomed to failure.

In the next chapter we describe the various educational innovations that are changing the school scene with a view to determining what new roles and functions these changes impose on the psychologists in the schools.

REFERENCES

Anastasi, A. *Differential Psychology.* New York: Macmillan, 1957.

Bandura, A. *Principles of Behavior Modification.* New York: Holt, Rinehart and Winston, 1969.

Boehm, A. E. *Boehm Test of Basic Concepts.* New York: Psychological Corp., 1969.

Collier, J. A Study of Cognitive Development in Turkish Children: Conservation Attainment as a Special Issue. In L. G. Fein (ed.), *International Understanding.* New York: Ms Publishing Co., 1974. (ICP publication)

Educational Testing Service. *1969 Invitational Conference: Toward a Theory of Achievement.* Princeton, N.J., 1969.

Eysenck, H. J. *The IQ Argument.* New York: The Library Press, 1971.

Gold, L. Functionalism in Education. New Haven: Yale University, Graduate Department of Education, 1940. (Unpublished manuscript)

Gordon, H. Mental and Scholastic Tests among Retarded Children. London: Board of Education Pamphlet 44, 1923.

Hebb, D. O. A Return to Jensen and His Social Science Critics. *American Psychologist,* 1970, *25,* 568.

Hebb, D. O. Whose Confusion? *American Psychologist,* 1971, *8,* 736.

Heber, R. The Milwaukee Project. *Time Magazine,* March 8, 1972.

Hunt, J. McV. *Intelligence and Experience.* New York: Ronald Press, 1961.

Hunt, J. McV., Paraskevopoulos, J., Schickedenz, D., & Urgiris, I. C. On the Range of Reaction for Age of Achieving Object Permanence. Preliminary report presented at Annual Symposium of ICP, Hawaii, 1972. Full report to be published in L. G. Gold (ed.), *International Understanding.* New York: Ms Publishing Co., 1974. (typed copy, 1973)

Jensen, A. R. How Much Can We Boost IQ and Scholastic Achievement? *Harvard Educational Review,* 1969, *39,* 1–123.

Kagan, J. *Change and Continuity in Infancy.* New York: John Wiley and Sons, 1972.

Lemos, M. N. de. The Development of Conservation in Aboriginal Children. *International Journal of Psychology,* *1969,* 4.

Lovaas, O. I. A Program for the Establishment of Speech in Psychotic Children. In J. K. Wing, *Early Childhood Autism.* London: Pergamon, 1966, pp. 115–144.

Lovaas, O. I., Freitag, G., Gold, V. J., & Kassoria, I. C. Experimental Studies in Childhood Schizophrenia. Analysis of Self Destructive Behavior. *Journal of Experimental Child Psychology,* 1965, *2,* 67–84.

Lovaas, O. I., Freitas, L., Nelson, K., & Whalen, C. The Establishment of Imitation and Its Use for the Development of Complex Behavior in Schizophrenic Children. *Behavior Research and Therapy,* 1967, *5,* 171–181.

McClelland, D. Testing for Competence Rather Than for Intelligence. *American Psychologist,* 1973, *28,* 1–14.

Rosenthal, R. & Jacobson, L. Changing Children's IQ by Changing Teachers' Expectations. In M. Gottsegen and G. Gottsegen (eds.), *Professional School Psychology*, Vol. 3. New York: Grune and Stratton, 1969, pp. 172–197.

Sarason, S. *The Culture of the School and the Problem of Change*. Boston: Allyn and Bacon, 1971.

Shuey, A. M. *The Testing of Negro Intelligence*, 2nd ed. New York: Social Science Press, 1966.

Simpson, B. R. The Wandering IQ. *School and Society*, 1939, *50*, 20–23.

Suskind, E. C. Questioning and Curiosity in the Elementary School Classroom. Unpublished doctoral dissertation, New Haven: Yale University, 1969.

Vane, J. Intelligence and Achievement Test Results of Kindergarten Age Children in England, Ireland and the United States. *Journal of Clinical Psychology*, 1973, *29*, 191–193.

Vane, J. The Vane Kindergarten Test. *Journal of Clinical Psychology*, 1968, *24*, 121–154.

CHAPTER 3

Compensatory and Experimental Educational Elements in the Schools

In the preceding chapters we delineated the various forces that dictated imperatives for change in the nation's educational system. These forces combined with the rapidly accumulating evidence of learning retardation in masses of deprived child populations challenged the traditional public school administrations and organizations, the teaching principles, methods, and goals, the learning theories espoused, and the roles, functions, and services of mental health staff in the schools. In response to the imperative for change in our schools, to cope with the burgeoning problems among our child populations, educators across the nation devel-

45

oped and implemented compensatory and experimental programs. Although these innovations delineated the new contents, methods, and evaluation techniques to be used by the teaching and administrative staff, few of the designs recognized the disruptive impacts of these innovations on the traditional roles, functions, and services of the mental health professionals in the schools. The dilemmas of the psychologists in the schools under the impact of these innovations have been detailed in an earlier chapter. In an effort to define the new roles and services of psychologists in the changing school scene, it seems essential to examine some of the more popular compensatory and experimental elements and programs with a view to identifying those areas calling for the skills of psychologists at different levels of training and expertise.

Among the frequently used compensatory educational elements in the schools today are reduced age at school admission, enriched language programs, improved teacher resources and supports, teacher aides, reduced pupil / teacher ratio, special resource centers, and home and community involvement. Experimental educational elements include individualized prescribed instruction, heterogeneous versus homogeneous groupings, same age peer, high school, college, and paraprofessional tutors, team teaching, and class clustering.

LOWERED AGE FOR SCHOOL ADMISSION

Preschool programs that lower the age at which formal public school instruction is provided to deprived child populations give these children experiences and learning opportunities that have long been available to privileged child populations through private school facilities. Financed by Head Start federal funds, private foundations, and state and local grants, preschool experience is now available to deprived children in many parts of the country. These children enter school at age 3 and continue in this type of program through the primary school grades. It is noteworthy that the one common feature of all these experimental programs is the admission of children at age 3, but beyond that similarity each program is dinstinct in the formulations of the learning theories and the principles underlying the organization of the classroom facilities, the focus of the teaching, the methods of teaching, and the evaluations of progress. Differences are highlighted in the descriptions that follow.

The *Follow Thru Program* (the *Ypsilanti Perry Preschool Project*), one of the federally supported programs involving the lowered age for school admission, was established in 1962 under the direction of Dr. D. P. Weikart of Eastern Michigan University. This program is cognitively oriented, guided by Piagetian theory of cognitive development. This cognitive program is based on the premise that intellectual growth is the result of the child's ability to create representations of himself and his environment. These representations may be called concepts, thoughts, images, or symbols, and they refer to objects, problems, and situations of everyday life. When a child can create representations or symbols for concrete objects and can relate these symbols, he is free to reason, plan, and predict, for he is no longer bound by concrete limits. With these representational skills the child can think in terms of consequences rather than immediate concrete qualities and so has "power" to control his own thinking.

The program provides the teacher with a highly structured cognitively oriented course of activities designed to develop concepts, language, and behaviors that facilitate learnings. The learning objectives are stated in behavioral terms, operationally defined; that is, the type of behavior expected from the child as a result of the learning activity is described, and measurement of progress is based on behavioral outcome in coping with assigned tasks. Presentation of tasks is always from simple to complex, concrete to abstract. For example, on the motoric level the child first uses his own body to experience concepts before moving on to abstract meanings. Thus the child learns the meaning of the concept "roll" by rolling on the floor; in like manner he learns the meanings of prepositions up and down, in and out, over and under, by first experiencing these positions with his own body, then with objects, then with pictorial representations of the objects, then with symbolic representations (printed and written language). Through these experiences the meanings are expected to generalize and the child is expected to be able to cope with abstract meanings. On the verbal level, that is, in developing an extensive, meaningful vocabulary, teaching proceeds from the child's direct experience, sensations, and perceptions and moves on to externals and abstractions.

Weikart notes that the concepts that seem to have the greatest relevance to the child at preschool and primary levels are those related to spatial relations, time relations, size and seriation, classification, and conservation. (Educational materials useful for such teaching and learning are available from Developmental Learning Materials, Chicago, Illinois.) Approaches to evaluating the development of these cognitive processes are illustrated graphically by Piaget (1952) in his text on development of cognitive processes.

Although this program is primarily directed to the teacher, teaching aides, and children, the school psychologist plays a significant role in evaluation procedures. Educational and clinical psychologists were involved in the planning, design, and organization of the program, the identification of the teaching and learning principles, and the formulation of evaluation procedures. School psychologists were involved in the initial testing with the selected intelligence test (1937 revision of the Stanford-Binet) and with periodic retesting to measure progress of children over a three year experimental period. The use of the Binet form LM to measure progress in this project seems meaningful, first because this test samples operationally the cognitive, verbal, and perceptual motor skills being taught in the program, and also because this test is organized around mental ages, which are more functional concepts for teachers' use than are IQ scores. Weikart notes that continuing development of cognitive skills in these children calls for opportunities to practice these skills in reality or in simulated reality problem situations in the classroom, home, and neighborhood, as they move on up the educational ladder. Analysis of reality practice situations, designing simulated reality problems, and developing criteria for measuring performance in these situations require high level behavioral research design and evaluation skills. Reality performance and simulated reality testing are commonly used by industrial psychologists but rarely by psychologists serving school children and clinic populations. This is a critical challenge to psychologists in educational, clinical, developmental, and social fields of specialization.

The *Klaus-Gray preschool program* (DARCEE), developed by Rupert Klaus and Susan Gray of the Demonstration and Research Center for Early Education at George Peabody College in Nashville, Tennessee, was begun in 1961 after several pilot studies had been completed during the previous two years. These authors sought to develop a systematic approach to improving the educability of young children. (Such projects are commonplace today but they were rare at the start of the 1960s.) This study, funded by NIMH, was built around a strategy of putting together an intervention package based on relevant research from the fields of cognitive and motivational development and from social class studies. The major focus of this early-training project was to explore the means of offsetting the progressive retardation among deprived child populations and to study the "spillover" effects on other children in the families and the community.

The overall rationale for the intervention program was organized around attitudes and aptitudes relating to achievement. Under attitudes, the authors were specifically interested in achievement motivation for school type activities, persistence, delay of gratification for distant goals, and interest in reading and graphic materials used in school. Under achievement aptitudes, the authors were concerned with perceptual and cognitive development and with language development. The study involved four groups of children, two experimental and two controls. The first experimental group (T1) attended a 10 week preschool for three summers and had three years of weekly meetings with a trained home visitor during the three year period. The second experimental group (T2) had similar experience except that they began school a year later, so they had two rather than three years experience. The two control groups (T3, T4) had no preschool or home visitation experiences; they simply were tested before the program began and each time retestings were conducted for the experimental groups. One control group resided within the research community in proximity to the experimental children; the other control was located at some distance from this community but was matched to this community in composition of population and socioeconomic factors. By establishing two control groups, one proximal and one distal, it was possible to measure the spillover effects of the experimental programs on the children and families in proximity to the experimental populations. It is noteworthy that several compensatory educational elements were introduced into the structure of the classes, including reduced pupil-teacher ratio, with 20 children to a class under the direction of a head teacher (experienced first grade black teacher) assisted by three or four teacher aides.

Testing administered before the program was initiated and repeatedly administered at the end of each summer included the Stanford revision of the Binet form LM, the Peabody Picture Vocabulary Test, and the Metropolitan Achievement Test (first administered at the end of the first year of the program).

The instructional programs in the experimental classes

seek to develop skills necessary to perceive and discriminate environmental stimuli, to order this information in a conceptual framework, and to express the results of this structuring process (Camp, 1970). It is expected that the child will learn (build cognitive maps) ordering and structuring through exposure to ordered experiences, and he will in turn be able to impose order and structure on his disordered environment (home and community). These skills will permit him to process information and experience more economically and efficiently. Such experiences are especially critical for children coming from homes and communities that are disordered, chaotic in terms of time, space, activities, and relationships.

The specific goals of these instructional programs are to remediate lags and facilitate continued development of sensory skills, abstracting and mediating skills, and response skills. The sensory skills (critical to input of information), including the visual, auditory, tactile, kinesthetic, taste, and olfactory, permit the child to learn to attend, discriminate, integrate, and sequence such concepts as color, size, shape, number, volume, time, space, texture, temperature. The development of each of the sensory skills is programed over time through developmental sequences of behavioral expectations which require increasingly finer and more precise responses to ever more complex stimuli, moving from simple, concrete, one to one relations to multiple relationships among concrete objects, on through to abstract comparisons and configurations such as designs, letters, words, numbers. Abstracting and mediating skills, which include conceptual associations, classifications, and critical thinking, involve processes that permit assimilation of stimuli into logical and orderly conceptual frameworks allowing retrieval of information and facilitating transfer of learnings. Response skills (output skills) permit expression of learned experience verbally and motorically. The purpose of the curriculum in this area is to develop verbal and small muscle coordination skills essential to self-expression and

effective communication of thought processes. *It is significant that very carefully programed reinforcement schedules
are presented sequentially to realize continuous improvements in articulation and sentence structure.* The programing for developing motor coordination skills again moves
from gross motor controls such as in modeling with clay to
fine controls required in tracing, following dots, directions
in space, coloring small areas, printing, and ultimately writing.

Content of the curriculum is organized around a central
theme to encourage meaningful learning for the child. This
core or unit approach facilitates ordering the units from the
simple to the complex, from the known, proximal, to the
unknown, distal. Thus the units begin with the child's self
and move to the family and home, on to the neighborhood,
to the community, and to the city. These programed schedules with reinforcements consistently applied were selected
as the teaching method of choice on the premise that children from deprived homes and communities learn more
effectively from direct instruction rather than from incidental experiences, since these children have not developed
cognitive frames of reference for selection of material for
learning, as have children from privileged homes and communities.

The effectiveness of the program, as determined by test
results at the end of each year from 1962 to 1968, revealed
an initial sharp rise in intelligence test scores, which then
leveled off and began to show a decline. The control group
showed a slight but consistent decline throughout except for
a spurt at the end of the first year. However, differences between control and experimental groups on the Binet were
significant at the end of the third year after intervention
ceased. The results of the Peabody Picture Vocabulary Test
were similar, but the differences were not significant at the
end of the third year. On the Metropolitan Achievement
Test no significant differences were demonstrated in 1968,
although the experimental groups did show gains at the end

of the first and second years testing. In short, the results suggest that the intervention program is effective through the first grade but by the end of the fourth grade this program of intervention fails to sustain the initial gains.

An interesting insight was obtained by comparing the achievement scores of a group of children who had changed schools (moved to middle class schools) and a group that remained in the school in the low socioeconomic area. The test scores of the children who changed schools reflected a three year gain in school achievement over a three year period, whereas the children who remained in the deprived area school made less than a two year gain over a three year period, from grade 1 through grade 4. Additional findings based on test results of younger siblings of experimental and control subjects revealed that the intervention programs with mother involvement through home visitors had a salutary effect on the younger siblings in the home (vertical diffusion) and also on the neighboring children and mothers (horizontal diffusion).

The Early-Training Project at DARCEE is one of the best examples of early intervention efforts in the United States. It was begun four years before Project Head Start and Title I and III elementary and secondary education acts which have since stimulated widespread efforts in these directions. Furthermore, the Early-Training Project design is superior to many of the hastily implemented efforts, since the DARCEE program was experimentally tested through pilot studies and was conducted with controlled design and testings in settings where administration was fully committed to experimentation and so did not speak premature results, which many school administrators often demand.

This form of experimentally controlled intervention appears to raise the Binet IQ scores continuously during and for two years after interventions and stimulate horizontal and vertical diffusion so that effects go beyond the target children. The authors recognize, however, that lasting reversal of progressive performance retardation calls for continuing intervention throughout the school lives of these children along with enrichment of their homes and neighborhoods.

The development, implementation, and evaluation of this type of program calls for expertise in developmental, educational, and clinical psychology with sound research skills supplemented by psychological skills that can be provided by school psychologists in the school situation. The description of the program as presented by the authors suggests that it was guided throughout by a variety of learning theories, principles, and practices, each applied where meaningful. Thus learning and behavior theory, principles, and procedures, through graded sequencing and positive reinforcement schedules, facilitated learning consistency and generalizations of responses. Gestalt perceptual theory guided teaching from the concrete to the abstract, whole to part, simple to complex, from the known to the new. Cognitive and social learning theories and principles also appear to have guided the design and implementation of this program, as reflected in the goals to develop cognitive skills, patterns, maps, and modifications of home and community, social and emotional vectors.

Considering the broad dimensions of this program, one wonders why no effort was made to evaluate social development through the use of scales like the Vineland Social Maturity Scale (Doll, 1965); and why self-image and dependency attitudes, which are readily evaluated by the Fein 3DPT Dependency and Self Image Scales (1960, 1968), were not included in the evaluation procedures. It seems reasonable to expect that three years of exposure to a richly structured educational program would have had very positive impact on these dimensions of personality development, attitudes, and behaviors that are often more critical to effective coping with life challenges than are increasing school achievement scores.

The *Ashton-Warner preschool program* (1963) reflects a psychodynamic rationale founded on the premise that creativity is released as the child learns to understand his important emotions and learns how to use his emotions constructively. The teacher's role in this program is essentially "therapeutic": deliberately passive, listening, watching, waiting, although she does draw out each child as need indicates. The program includes a "key vocabulary," "creative writing," and "creative dancing" as well as the "golden section," which includes nature and number and discussions that help children understand and cope with their critical problems around fear and sex. The key vocabulary is different for each child, being developed from the child's expressed interests. The children learn to read and write the words by perceptual motor practice, that is, they watch the teacher write the word on a large durable card, listen to her pronunciation of the word, repeat the word, trace the word with their fingers; then they practice reading, repeating, and tracing their words as they practice with a class peer. The creative writing follows the "key vocabulary" and here the children *write whatever they wish, the teacher never criticizing the productions, since "the child's work is an outgrowth of his internal emotions."* (A limited view, from learning theory stance.)

The *Bereiter-Engleman program* is in sharp contrast to the Ashton-Warner cited previously, guided by classical and operant conditioning learning theories, principles, and methods. This program is based on the premise that a child's learning rate can be accelerated by intensive drill, precise logical sequential presentations of materials to be learned, modeling and shaping of precise pronunciations. *Classroom time is not spent on social-emotional problems, which these authors believe can be more effectively treated elsewhere.*

The *Integrated Day in the English Infant School Program* (Sealy, 1966) appears to reflect the influences of John Dewey's educational principle that a child learns by doing, by exercise, and by effect. This program also operates on the premise that a child learns by freedom to select what is relevant and meaningful to him within given choice limits, as well as through sequential progression and management of consequences, which are behavior modification principles. The integrated school has no scheduled classes or time periods for specific activities; rather each child selects his own activities and devotes as much time as he wishes to them. The classroom is structured by subdivisions into specially equipped working areas for science and math, reading and language arts, visual arts, general activities, programed learning areas, and so on. Reading and writing are both taught on an individual basis, the children receiving letter and word cards, primers, story books, and even reference books. Structure is provided by given directions to follow, names to learn, events to describe. The children and teachers keep records of progress.

The *Learning to Learn Program* (Sprigel, 1968) developed by Hubert Sprigel of the Learning to Learn school in Florida, is a comprehensive approach to the education of children, parents, and teachers. The program is based on the following three concepts:

1. Education is continuous from early childhood upward through organized sequential curricula.
2. Children need to learn how to learn. Learning must follow the orderly sequence of cognitive growth and development.
3. Drive for mastery is innate and needs to be guided appropriately.

The program development was guided by nine principles derived from the research literature in psychology, education, and child development, together with classroom observations. Briefly the nine principles may be defined as follows:

1. Learning calls for active participation in process.
2. Internal satisfactions and feelings of adequacy stimulate growth toward independence, responsibility, and performance.

3. Feedback to child of contributions made by him builds self-confidence and self-worth.
4. Problem solving stimulates interest and facilitates learning when the discrepancy between what he knows and what he needs to learn to solve problems is small enough to insure success.
5. Immediate use of learnings facilitate their integration into a permanent repertoire of intelligent behavior.
6. Learning is facilitated by extensive exposure to multiple sensory and motor activities and opportunities to talk about these experiences.
7. Timing, continuity, and structure of learning experiences are critical to learning.
8. Effective communication is developed from meaningful feedback that guides thinking and reasoning.
9. Lasting effects of school experience call for parental involvement in and commitment to the objectives of the program.

This program is built on Piaget's theoretical principles of learning that mental development proceeds along an orderly sequence of motor-perceptual symbolic phases with periods of transition. According to Piaget's formulations, spoken language comes only after the development of mental images, which in turn develop out of repeated encounters with objects the children move and manipulate. This second stage of mental imagery is replaced by the third stage of symbol formation, which enables the child to talk about things in their absence.

Two teachers and two rooms are essential to conduct this program, a large room to accommodate 24 children engaged in a variety of activities and a small room to accommodate a teacher and 4 children, where the children have opportunities to apply the knowledge learned in problem solving, decision making, games, and activities. In this setting the child does most of the talking, the teacher serving to supply missing information, correct misinformation, and help synthesize all parts to feed back to the large group later in an organized fashion. Essentially the purpose of the second phase is to provide an opportunity for each child to experience repeated reinforcement of his learnings by talking about them, using them in problems, hearing his peers and teacher use them repeatedly. Evaluation of progress is built into the sequential curriculum with mastery of performance the critical index toward more challenging tasks rather than mastery of content.

The Head Start Program (Passow, 1963) developed by Deutsch and his staff at the Institute of Developmental Studies seeks to develop multiple modalities for learning, including language, visual and auditory discriminations, motivation, and positive self-concepts. The Deutsch team has designed special materials and autoinstructional methods including the Letter Form Board, the Language Lotto, and the Language Master. They have adapted Montessori equipment for use in stimulation of auditory and semantic differentiation. They use mirrors and photographs to assist in the development of the child's sense of identity. Concentration is on those tasks a child cannot do, identifying those deficiencies by definitive screening of basic school learnings. Continuous adaptations of materials and teacher training is provided by curriculum specialists working at the classroom level.

Measures of basic school skill progress are built into the sequentially programed curricula of the Head Start Program. Positive self-concept development is explored by teachers through children's graphic representations of their self-images; functional development of appropriate social behavior and relationships and self-directive skills in the classroom setting are evaluated by observed behaviors in the classroom and school grounds. Psychological assessment of progress in functional development of cognitive skills, social and emotional maturation, self-image, and dependency and interpersonal attitudes are left to the discretion of the school psychologists or psychological examiners and other special service personnel in each situation. The tests used most frequently in these programs include an intelligence test, generally the Binet or the WISC, the (Draw a Person Test) (DAP), the Bender, and possibly one of the picture story projectives. Results reported to date indicate that these programs facilitate learnings through the preschool years while the programs are ongoing but the gains recede as the children move on into the elementary grades.

It seems unfortunate that Head Start Programs have been implemented in widespread communities without definitive guidelines indicating the target behaviors to be changed and the instruments that demonstrably tap the critical variables of the target behaviors.

Zigler (1972), the designer of the Head Start Program, acknowledges that many mistakes were made in the design and implementation of these programs, but he notes that significant benefits derived from them. The two major benefits are the health benefits to children attending the programs and the benefits to the parents of children in the programs. In the health area Zigler notes that 40% or 400,000 children entering the program over a period of five years had some identifiable physical defect and of these children 75% had their physical defects treated. Furthermore, the parents who participated got a new sense of dignity and worth and a feeling of having some control over their own lives and the destiny of their children. The negative aspects of the program are acknowledged by Zigler to be the narrow evaluative procedures and the use of the IQ as a measure of growth. The actual purpose of the programs was not to increase the IQ but to *improve social competencies of the children, to modify their motivations and their negative self-image attitudes and expectations toward accomplishment and self-confidence.*

The policy and practice of limiting the Head Start programs to children of deprived milieus was another error notes Zigler. He is convinced now that such programs must have heterogeneous socioeconomic-cultural mixes for the children to gain an understanding of society at large, instead of their current parochial vision of society. Zigler recommends a program he calls Home Start, which sends individuals into the homes at the request of parents to help the parents with problems with which they themselves cannot cope.

Whether heterogeneous groupings are more effective for child development of competence and learning than homogeneous groupings is at present a moot question. The relative merits of these two groupings are discussed later in this chapter. The Home Start program sounds promising, if it is patterned after similar programs that have been used in Israel for some years with families from Oriental cultures. However, the Israel program does not wait for parents to ask for help; rather the planners educate the parents of these deprived families to accept the "home teachers" assigned.

LANGUAGE PROGRAMS

Special language programs have been designed to facilitate verbal usage, enrichment, and understanding in children, particularly in children from foreign speaking homes and from homes using dialects or idiomatic vernacular English, characteristic of populations living in circumscribed geographic districts of the nation. The language programs also focus on children from homes of limited cultural experience where communications are limited to daily mundane activities involving a verbal repertoire of about 500 stereotyped words.

The *Tucson Early Education Model* (Hughes et al., 1965) was developed in 1965 at the Arizona Research and Development Center-Early Childhood Education Laboratory and is now operating in 68 classrooms, grades 1 to 3, in metropolitan Tucson. The child population is predominantly Mexican American from economically deprived homes. The program, theoretically based on behavior modification theory, is built on the premise that specific skills and attitudes are essential to function effectively in a technical and changing society. It is designed to remediate the deficits in these basic skills, characteristic of children from deprived cultures. The skills that are assumed to be essential to an efficient intellectual base for success at school and in the open society include labeling and identifying, ordering, time orientation, recall, planning, and understanding of cause and effect relationships. This program seeks to develop the special language skills necessary to the elaboration of these basic intellectual processes. The milieu is structured to facilitate child experience in a wide variety of behaviors including exploration, manipulation, and other forms of interaction with objects and materials. Interest centers are structured around common tasks such as science, cooking, number and measurement, art, reading, writing. These interest centers are defined, focused, and changed through arrangement of tables, chairs, play equipment, graphic and other materials. A teacher and her aid are the permanent adults in the classroom while a program assistant visits the class weekly to communicate new techniques and ideas to the teachers through demonstrations within ongoing class activities. *The classroom adults deliberately model, elaborate, extend, and reinforce language. All classroom adults are trained in the techniques of social reinforcement—praise, attention, and the like—and reinforcement effects are built into the materials and activity sequences.* Experience is extended into the child's neighborhood and wider community and classroom adults seek to generalize learnings through field trips, walks, visits to the child's home, and the like. The authors of this program caution that implementation of such innovative practices requires changes in roles of school personnel and organizational structures, so that a school system that seeks to implement such a program must be able to tolerate the strains and stresses that such change generates.

The foregoing description suggests that the school psychologist working in such a setting would need to develop a functional mastery of behavior modification principles and methods to meet the needs of teachers and children that emerge in such an educational setting.

The *Perception-Language-Concept Development Program* (Goldberg and Boehm, 1968) developed at Teacher's College, Columbia University, is essentially designed to facilitate learning to read. The program seeks to develop these perceptual skills, language, and conceptual processes that appear to be prerequisite to success in reading. Perceptual activities stress awareness of body in space, visual and auditory discrimination, directionality, likenesses, and differences. To develop language, children are encouraged to ask questions or to describe their immediate environment, always paying attention to sentence structure, grammatical usage, and logical thinking. Each child has his own workbook, from the SRA Thurston Learning to Think series. The Ginn "Language A" program, Continental Press materials, selected portions of SRA economics program, and John Day photograph albums from the Urban Cities series are used. Science units, mathematical concept cards, and manipulative materials are also supplied.

IMPROVED TEACHER RESOURCES AND SUPPORTS

In efforts to reduce the pupil-teacher ratio (the element considered most critical to effective teaching and learning), several innovative educational elements have been combined to provide additional support for teachers. Teacher aids have been trained and assigned to classrooms to relieve the teacher of arduous mechanical tasks like record keeping, managing materials, managing the groups during study periods, and even tutoring individual pupils or small groups of pupils. A great variety of instructional materials have been classified, stored, and inventoried in special instructional material resource centers and laboratories manned by specialists, serving the needs of the teachers, classes, and individual children. Principals and assistant principals have presumably been relieved of mundane administrative chores to provide educational leadership, teacher training, and supervision. Teachers are supposed to have more free time for cooperating with the special service staff, guidance counselors, psychologists, and social workers in the study of problem children and in developing classroom approaches in efforts to reduce these problems in the classroom rather than through an outside agency.

Increased involvement of parents and community in the school programs and processes also increases the number of adults available in the school and thus serves to provide additional resources and support to teachers. Furthermore, involvement of parents and community leaders in the planning of the school programs is expected to lead to the development in these people of positive attitudes toward the school, which in turn may be expected to build positive attitudes toward school in the children. Positive attitudes engender trust in the school and teachers, and trust frees children for learning, so that the involvement of parents and community leaders in the school program becomes one of the most significant innovations. In fact, involvement of home and community appears to be a universal goal in school systems in the United States, as reflected in trends toward decentralization, election of local school boards, school parent training programs, increased participation in school improvement by parent and community associations. Many schools have added a staff member whose sole responsibility is stimulating increased involvement of parents and community in the educational programs.

What children gain when schools are flooded with a large variety of adults, such as parents, community leaders, trained paraprofessionals or in some cases potential paraprofessionals (learning *in situ*), is unknown. To date little evidence has been reported of the salutory effects on school children of adult flooding in schools. Since these practices are continuing and spreading rapidly, it is urgent that the formats of adult interventions in the schools and the models the adults present be analyzed and evaluated in terms of their impacts on the children exposed. Development of evaluation designs of such programs is a challenge to psychology.

It is noteworthy that as parents and community leaders become sophisticated in the educational process they demand justifications for procedures and materials used. Their critical view of the educational process extends to the evaluative process, so that they question the purposes, formats, and contents of tests administered and the interpretations and uses of test results. Parents and community leaders not only question the values of tests administered by teachers and the school system but they also question tests administered by school psychologists. Although parent enlightenment about public school education is essential for betterment of the school program, the side effects of their involvement in testing can become a source of threat to school psychologists, particularly to those who function in traditional routinized ways without clearcut rationales for their activities in each testing situation. Even more threatening to a school psychologist is the situation where the parent, and sometimes the school administrator, challenges in conference the interpretations of test results offered by the psychologist. Since accountability is a key word in school programs involving widespread parent participation, it seems wise to appoint mature, highly experienced psychologists with a rich repertoire of skills to schools with heavy parent involvement. Naive, inexperienced school psychologists, particularly if they are below the doctoral level, will be hard pressed to cope effectively in such settings.

Parent protests against the invasion of privacy through psychological testing of children are well documented (Gross, 1962). Another aspect of the problem of invasion of privacy that psychologists must be alert to is the need for confidentiality of records in the schools; psychological reports cannot be accessible to any other personnel except with parent permission for children under 16 and with student permission for those 16 years of age and over. At present writing, communications of school children to pupil personnel workers, particularly psychologists, guidance counselors, and school social workers, are not considered privileged communications, so that they are available to school principals, teachers, and clerks at will; they may be subpoenaed by the courts, sent to draft boards, picked up by parole officers without permission of the student, his parents, or the health worker involved. However, psychological associations and boards of education are attempting to effect legislation classifying these school records as privileged communications (Legislative Affairs Bulletin, May 1970, NYSPA).

TUTORING: PEER, PARAPROFESSIONAL, AND OLDER STUDENTS

Among the various approaches to reducing the pupil-teacher ratio and thus provide increased individual attention to children in the schools, paraprofessionals, upper grade and high school and college students, and same age peers with advanced skills are used as tutors. Such tutoring programs have been widely used in schools throughout the United States, in most cases as emergency measures, to cope with the widespread learning deficiencies among deprived child populations where teacher shortages are extreme. This "innovation" is hardly new, for it has been used for decades in the one-room schoolhouse and is still common in families with several siblings, where the older children in a family tutor, supervise, and model for their younger siblings. It is also common to see children in neighborhood life teaching each other games and skills and serving as models for each other, although not always as desirable models. In brief, children are socialized not only by their parents and parent surrogates and by generalized ideal models like movie, TV, and stage heroes and heroines, but also by interactions with their peers, siblings, and neighbors. In these relationships they learn and practice values, attitudes, roles, and role relationships and gain knowledges even as they attend school for formal education. Since they learn from their peers—same age, older, and at times even younger—in the natural process of socialization in most cultures, it makes good sense to use such relationships deliberately to facilitate learning school skills and directing the modeling into constructive channels.

The *Homework Helper Program* was begun by Mobilization for Youth in 1963 with 110 eleventh and twelfth graders employed to tutor fifth graders. Tutors were trained and supervised in established centers by parent attendants and master teachers. The South Vermont Tutorial Program was organized by the Western Student Movement of College Students and recent college graduates of Oakland, California. Orientation and training sessions were led by the Los Angeles City School personnel and University of California at Los Angeles faculty members. The tutors, high school students, worked with elementary school children two and three afternoons each week and concentrated on basic school subjects. The Ohio Civil Rights Commission sponsored a program in which high school students from both inner city and suburban schools were trained by reading specialists to tutor inner city elementary school children.

The effectiveness of such programs was explored by a team of psychologists at the University of Michigan Institute for Social Research during the early 1960s (Lippitt & Lehman, 1965). In these pilot projects sixth graders were involved as academic assistants in the fourth, third, second, and first grades. They helped children in these primary grades with reading, writing, arithmetic, spelling, and physical education. *The children serving as tutors were trained in skills of relating to younger children as well as in skills for teaching subject matter material.* The results indicated that the younger children helped, as evidenced by their improved school skills, but even more significant was the finding that the majority of the older pupils were eager to be involved in this type of helping program. This was particularly true of low achieving students of low socioeconomic status. Through these experiences, their relationships to the authority figures, teachers, were improved and their motivation to learn increased substantially. Such programs provide the tutors with opportunities to take initiative and responsibility to try out their own newly developing skills, integrate their own learnings in these skills, discover the satisfactions of achieving and of helping others achieve, develop more effective skills in relating to others, and facilitate self-understanding and understanding of others.

In these Michigan programs psychologists served as trainers of tutors in interpersonal skills, a creative maneuver that can be adapted readily to other tutorial programs with confidence in the benefits accruing to all the children, tutors, and learners.

HETEROGENEOUS VERSUS HOMOGENEOUS GROUPINGS

The relative merits of homogeneous versus heterogeneous ability groupings have not yet been determined experimentally, although the debate has been raging for more than half a century (Passow, 1963). However, empirical evidence suggests that both groupings have advantages and disadvantages. Homogeneous groupings are justified on the basis that such clusters reduce demands on teachers, especially where teacher competencies are variable. Heterogeneous groupings on the basis of abilities and/or cultural, ethnic, and economic backgrounds are justified by experience demonstrating that learning is facilitated by such mixings in minority group children and slow learners, whereas learnings are retarded in such children in homogeneous settings. Another advantage of heterogeneous groupings is that bright children consolidate their own gains while tutoring the slow learners, who of course benefit from the tutoring. However, until controlled studies designed, implemented, and evaluated by expert educational, clinical, and developmental research psychologists demonstrate the "true" values of each grouping, decisions will rest with the teaching and administrative preferences in any given situation.

INDIVIDUALIZED INSTRUCTION

Individualized instruction programs are based primarily on learning and behavior modification principles and methods and are often facilitated by use of computer aids in teaching individual as well as masses of children. Such programs seek to make learning student directed and to develop student autonomy and initiative. Two such programs that have caught the interest and imagination of school administrators and are being implemented in school systems in various parts of the country are PLAN (Program for Learning in Accordance with Needs) in cooperation with AIR (American Institute for Research) and LRDC (Learning Research and Development Center)-IPI (Individually Prescribed Instruction) programs.

The *Plan Program* was developed by the American Institute for Research in cooperation with the Westinghouse Learning Corporation, teachers from participating schools, and university-based consultants. The program first prepared for grades 1, 5, and 9 is now ready for grades 1 to 12. The key components of Plan are teacher diagnosis of individual child learning levels and needs, development of tailor-made teaching-learning units, use of computer for processing, storage, and retrieval of curriculum and pupil information, continuous evaluation of individual child's progress and effectiveness of curriculum materials. Placement and survey tests are given at appropriate times to check retention and status on short and long term objectives. These programs are now installed in several districts of California, the Quincy Public School District in Massachusetts, Hicksville Public School District of New York State, Bethel Park, Penn Trafford, and Pittsburgh Public School districts.

The *IPI Program* was developed by the Learning Research and Development Center of the University of Pittsburgh (Bolwin and Lindvahl, 1965). Begun in 1963 in one elementary school (K-grade 6) in suburban Pittsburgh, it now operates in more than 120 schools.

IPI "consists of planning and conducting with each student a program of studies that is tailored to his learning needs and to his characteristics as a learner." The basic aspects of this program include a curriculum based on sequenced and detailed behaviorally defined teaching objectives, each child progressing at his own rate in terms of performance on sequentially graded tasks and each pupil performing most of his work without teacher help. The teacher's time is spent in diagnosing the pupil's needs, preparing individual learning prescriptions, helping children with instructional problems, and evaluating pupil records while the ancillary tasks such as maintaining records, scoring objective tests, and maintaining materials supply are done by paraprofessional teacher aides.

Diagnosis of each child's learnings is made on the basis of rate of learning; placement tests measure mastery of each unit, indicate strengths and weaknesses of the pupil, and indicate areas that need further exploration for more precise diagnosis. Pretesting and posttesting are standard procedures to provide indices to mastery of units. A pupil must display at least 85% mastery of one unit before he is moved ahead to the next unit of work in the given area. This program calls for a special floor plan within the school, to provide for a learning Materials Center and study halls opening into the classrooms so that pupils may obtain the materials they need with ease as they progress from unit to unit.

Children who do not move ahead at a normal or expectable rate are referred to the school psychologist or psychological examiner for IQ testing, on suspicion that these children lack adequate learning potential at age grade. This simplistic approach to slow learners in these sequenced programs suggests an indifference to the differential learning rates and styles of the children involved, a view that intellectual potential and abilities are fixed and fully measurable by IQ tests and an indifference to the responsibility of turning over such children to qualified psychological consultants who are in a position to make differential diagnostic studies of these children to ascertain the blocks to their learnings.

TEAM TEACHING AND CLUSTERED CLASSES

Team teaching and clustered classes (Gordon, 1968) are strategies intended to provide reduced pupil-teacher ratios as well as collective planning, peer supervision, and multiple teacher exposure to elementary school children. The program involves assignment of four or five teachers to three or four classes with individual teachers primarily responsible for specific content areas across classes. A master or leader teacher is either appointed or elected from within the teacher team to move from class to class for supplementary teaching. Generally there is collective responsibility for all children served by this team, specific and total group planning is coordinated in the group, and consultation and supervision are available within the group.

Efforts at evaluation of these programs report tendencies toward acceleration of pupil achievement, good pupil and teacher morale, positive teacher and administrative acceptance. However, in the experience of this writer many primary grade children fall out of these programs due to their inability to cope with the multiplicity of teacher exposure, daily periodic movements from room to room, and the intellectual stance required of them during the "mass" lecture periods. Children who fall out of such programs generally are referred to the psychologist for study and plans for suitable programs to meet their earning needs. Personal experience in such a program revealed that the majority of children referred for study were emotionally and socially immature, needing a *constant relationship with one teacher to serve as parent surrogate, all day residence in one room to call their "home," and daily consistent peer relations to provide them opportunities to establish close, warm peer relations which could carry over into out of school activities.*

The team teaching, clustered classes programs appear to frustrate the basic social and emotional needs of such children. In these settings the school psychologist studies the child through teacher behavioral reports, parent reports, direct classroom and other school activity observations, through psychodiagnostic testings including cognitive, perceptual, motor, and projective methods as well as in reality play situations and play therapy settings. Insights so derived permit preparation of prescriptions of classroom organizations and teacher interventions essential to the continuing development of each child, emotionally, socially, and academically. In this setting the responsibility of the psychologist extends to continuing supervision of the child's progress in the classroom and general school life. This is carried on through periodic classroom observations and teacher conferences and supplemented by a selected form of therapy outside the classroom, either individual or group, as the situation indicates. In short, the psychologist in this setting is a consultant to school staff, a psychodiagnostician, behavior evaluator, program prescription writer, behavior modifier, and/or psychotherapist, all challenging roles calling for a rich educational/clinical background.

This sampling of compensatory and experimental educational elements in the schools reveals many challenges to psychologists in the schools and communities, challenges that call for thorough understanding of learning theories and processes and the ability to implement them, understanding of the sociological and milieu impacts on learning and development, command of broad diagnostic and prescriptive skills, and appropriate interventions. Additional insights into the challenges facing psychologists in the changing school and social scenes may be gleaned from examination of the innovative Great Cities Programs presented next.

REFERENCES

Ashton-Warner, S. *Teacher*. New York: Bantam Books, 1963.

Bereiter, C. & Engelman, S. Teaching disadvantaged children in the preschool. Englewood Cliffs, N.J.: Prentice Hall, 1966.

Bolwin, S. & Lindvahl, C. *IPI: An Approach to the Problem of Individual Differences*. Learning Research and Development Center, Pittsburgh: University of Pittsburgh, 1965.

Camp, J. A Skill Development Curriculum. Nashville: George Peabody College for Teachers, April, 1970. (mimeo).

Coffman, W. E., Manning, W. H., Harris, C. W., Chronbach, L. J. & Guttman, L. Toward a Theory of Achievement Measurement. 1969 Invitational Conference. Princeton, N. J. Educational Testing Service, 1969.

Coombs, P. H. *Educational Strategies for the 1970's. Lectures in Education*. New Haven: Yale University Institution for Social and Policy Studies, 1970.

Deutsch, M. The Disadvantaged Child and the Learning Process in Depressed Areas. In H. Passow (ed.), *Education in Depressed Areas*. New York: Teachers College Press, Columbia University, 1963.

Deutsch, M. *The Disadvantaged Child*. New York: Basic Books, 1967.

Doll, E. *Measurement of Social Competence*. Princeton, N.J.: Educational Test Bureau, 1953.

Doll, E. *The Vineland Social Maturity Scale. Circle Pines,* Minn. : American Guidance Service, 1965.

Duker, J. National Trends in School Psychology. Paper read before Div. 16 of the APA., Washington, D.C., 1969.

Fein, L. G. *The Three Dimensional Personality Test: Reliability, Validity and Clinical Implications.* New York: International Universities Press, 1960.

Fein, L. G. Roosevelt Hospital Screening Program for Special Class Placement of Emotionally Disturbed Children. New York: Roosevelt Hospital, 1968. (mimeo)

Gallistel, E. Psychoeducational Assessment and Remediation. Paper read before Div. 16 of the APA, Washington, D.C. 1969.

Goldberg, M., Passow, A. H. & Justman, J. *The Effects of Ability Grouping.* New York: Teachers College Press, Columbia University, 1966.

Goldberg, M. & Boehm, A. *The Perception-Language-Concept Development Program.* New York: Teachers College Press, Columbia University, 1968.

Gordon, E. *Final Report to the Superintendent of Schools.* New York: Board of Education, 1968.

Gray, S. Intervention with Mothers and Young Children. In H. C. Haywood (ed.), *Social Cultural Aspects of Mental Retardation.* New York: Appleton-Century-Crofts, 1970.

Gray, S. & Klaus, R. *DARCEE. Child Development.* Nashville, Tenn.: George Peabody College of Teachers, 1970.

Gray, S. & Wickers, D. *DARCEE.* Nashville, Tenn.: Demonstration and Research Center for Early Education, George Peabody College for Teachers, 1968.

Gross, M. *The Brain Watchers.* New York: New American Library, 1962.

Hall, M. Psychology and Education. A Partnership. Paper read before Div. 16 of the APA, Washington, D.C., 1969.

Heber, R. Heading Off Retardation. *Behavior Today,* 1971, *33,* 816.

Holbrook, S. Differentiation of Functions in Delivery of Psychological Services. Paper read before Div. 16 of the APA, Washington, D.C., 1969.

Hughes, M. M., Henderson, R. & Taylor, J. *The Tucson Early Education Model.* Arizona Research and Development Center, Tucson: University of Arizona, 1965.

Ilg, F. & Ames, L. B. *School Readiness.* New York: Harper and Row, 1965.

James, H. T. Supporting Big City Schools. Frank Ellsworth Spaulding Lecture, 1970. New Haven: Yale University, Institution for Social and Policy Studies, 1970.

Kadrie, A. The School Psychologist in a Community Mental Health Center. Paper read before Div. 16 of the APA, Washington, D.C.: 1969.

Lippitt, R. & Lehman, J. E. Cross-Age Relationships: An Educational Resource. *Children,* 1965, *12,* 113–117.

Montessori, M. *Dr. Montesorri's Own Handbook.* Cambridge: R. Bently, 1964.

NYSPA. *Legislative Affairs Bulletin, 1970.*

Passow, A. H. (ed.) *Education in Depressed Areas.* New York: Teachers College Press, Columbia University, 1963.

Piaget, J. *The Origins of Intelligence in Children.* New York: International Universities Press, 1952.

Project Plan. *Individual Instruction with the Computer.* Palo Alto, Calif.: American Institute for Research, 1965.

Rivlin, A. M. Experimentation in Urban Education. Frank Ellsworth Spaulding Lecture, 1971. New Haven: Yale University, Institution for Social and Policy Studies, 1971.

Sarason, S. *The Culture of the School and the Problem of Change.* Boston: Allyn and Bacon, 1971.

Sealey, P. Looking Back at Leicestershire. Watertown, Mass. ESI Quarterly Report, 1966.

Sprigel, H. A. The Learning to Learn Program. Jacksonville, Fla.: Learning to Learn School, Inc. (mimeo.) (Also see abstract in Gordon, 1968.)

Suppes, P. Technology in Education. Lecture on Education, New Haven: Yale University Institution for Social and Policy Studies, 1971.

U.S. Department of Health, Education and Welfare. *Toward a Social Report.* Washington, D.C.: U.S. Government Printing Office, 1970.

Weikart, D. P. & Ericson, M. Cognitively Oriented Follow-Thru Project. Ypsilanti: Eastern Michigan University, 1969. (mimeo)

Yeomans, E. *Education for Initiative and Responsibility*. Boston: National Association for Independent Schools, 1967.

Zigler, E. Children's Needs in the 70's: A Federal Perspective. *Journal of Clinical Child Psychology*, 1972, *1*, 3–6.

CHAPTER 4

The Great Cities Programs

Brief descriptions of the Great Cities programs as conducted in Detroit and New York are offered here to provide further insights into the new title roles, functions, and services required of psychologists operating in the changing school scene.

As early as 1957 the superintendents and board of education members of the 14 largest city school systems of the nation met in Atlantic City, New Jersey, to explore the problems of education in large urban areas. They focused their attention on three critical problems: the world of work, the widespread unemployment of youth, and the corresponding limits of work opportunities for deprived youth; the funding of effective education in large cities; and the problems of educating the ever increasing numbers of children from limited backgrounds. Intensive and extensive study of the problem of educational deprivation revealed a series of factors that contribute to educational deprivation. These factors include lack of preschool and kindergarten experience, poor attendance, high rate of failure, and the variety of home and community deprivations. To guide their planning for change, to alleviate the eroding impact of socioeconomic and cultural deprivations, family instability, broken homes, decaying neighborhoods, crowded and antiquated school buildings, and urban blight and depression compounded by economic, social, and political crises, regionally, nationally, and even internationally, the Great Cities Team developed the Central Hypothesis that the problems of children with limited backgrounds can perhaps be resolved by:

1. Programs of education adapted to the needs of these children.
2. Organizational modifications within the schools.
3. Improved instructional materials and equipment.
4. Parent and community involvement in the schools.

THE DETROIT EXPERIMENTS (Marburger, 1963)

In September 1959 the Detroit project was initiated to test the central hypothesis. It was under the leadership of Professor Samuel Brownell of Yale University and under the direction of Dr. Carl Byerly of the Detroit Public School System. This pilot project involved three schools and was financed for the first year by the Board of Education of Detroit, Michigan. In July 1960 and 1961 the Ford Foundation provided funds to support this and other Great Cities School projects for a period of five years. With this financial help the Detroit project was expanded to include seven schools, from kindergarten through grade 12. The purpose of the Detroit project was to work toward "More Effective Schools," a design that has since become known as the

"MES model." The Detroit Experiment also included parent and community projects, using the school buildings throughout the day and evening, a design that has been adopted experimentally by many other school systems under the title "All Day Neighborhood Schools."

The objectives of the Detroit experimental MES programs were to increase the academic, social, living, job, and work skill competencies of the "whole child" for effective urban living. The Detroit model is multidimensional, including in-service teacher training, additional special school personnel, consulting specialists, special expense funds for materials that may not be ordered through regular board of education channels and for enriching out of school trips. In addition the program focused on revision of curriculum content, materials, and methods of teaching basic school skills. After-school and evening programs for children, parents, and the community at large were instituted in an effort to bring all community forces to bear on the challenge of adapting the education to the needs of the children.

In-service training courses for teachers designed to change teacher attitudes was given priority in the implementation of the Detroit program, since teacher attitudes play a critical role in child learning and many teachers have negative expectations of children from deprived backgrounds. Negative expectations by teachers have disastrous effects on the learnings of children they teach. This self-fulfilling prophecy has been experimentally demonstrated in the classroom by Rosenthal et al. (1968). The first attempts to provide in-service training of teachers through exposure to lectures by experts in education, psychology, and sociology failed to make any significant changes in teacher attitudes. As might be anticipated, teachers with positive attitudes were impressed with the lectures whereas those with negative attitudes rejected and resisted the expert teachings, continuing to expect negative performance from culturally deprived children, in subtle and at times in direct ways.

To involve these teachers meaningfully in the need for change of attitudes, the in-service programs were reorganized on the basis of the unique school needs and problems defined by the staff in each school, since schools differ from each other in most critical areas. Each school staff examined its own unique community, youth problems, strengths and weaknesses, organization and facilities. Accordingly the in-service training programs took several forms, depending on the felt needs of the staff, so that some school staff took courses at local universities for credit, others attended as auditors, others instituted Saturday and summer courses. To encourage attendance, released school time was given, course fees were paid, and salary payments were made for after-school time invested in study. As a result of these in-service courses, changes began to take place; these include nongraded primary classes, block time and core classes, and team teaching. However, much resistance was expressed against changes in teaching approaches, such as approaches to the teaching of reading. To encourage modification in the reading curriculum, an effort was made to revise the content of the reading primers, since it is recognized that children learn more readily when they begin with the known, the familiar, and move toward the new. Thus it was expected that Negro children would be more likely to learn to read if the content of the primers was more nearly like their own living experiences, depicting the living activities of the Negro child and his family.

Accordingly the Detroit committee-on-writing set about to prepare and illustrate primers adapted to the experiences and levels of achievement of the Negro children in the experimental schools. The first efforts by the project writers alerted them to the hazards of writing nonconventional revolutionary primers: they discovered that their "remedy" for teaching could be more destructive psychologically than the ailment, the conventional primer, with its focus on the middle class style of life of the white child. For example, the artist depicted "some typical housekeeping situations such as brooms leaning in the corner, a kitchen sink with exposed pipes beneath it." These pictures were viewed simply as poor housekeeping among some Negroes, thereby serving to imply derogation of the Negro, since this booklet depicted the Negro family. Other material in this primer that served to derogate the Negro family was the complete omission of the father figure and the name assigned to the little boy, "Sammy." With these lessons in primer writing for this special child population, the committee finally produced for experimental use the first three preprimers of this series in September 1962.

The MES programs sought to reinforce the efforts of the teachers by providing additional personnel who worked with children who had difficulties in reading, arithmetic, and/or speech and with their families, to establish stronger ties to the school and better understanding between home and school. The staff added to facilitate the work of the teachers included a "visiting teacher" to do case work with children and families, a remedial coach, and a school-community agent to facilitate school-community cooperation. In addition, after-school and evening programs were provided as were full summer programs, and each school received extra funds for special enrichment out-of-school activities. It is noteworthy that the Detroit committee introduced these special services and funds even though the members of the committee were aware of the limited value of extra monetary and staff provisions when the school atmosphere operates against teachers' freedom to be experimental and innovative in the classroom.

The atmosphere of the school is determined by the attitudes and administrative styles of the school principal, which may be restrictive or nonrestrictive, authoritarian or democratic, legalistic or expeditious. The most destructive attitudes of teachers' enthusiasm and imaginative efforts to teach are the authoritarian and the legalistic. "The authoritarian sees his school as an armed camp which admits a school population in the morning, regiments them until early afternoon and then sends them home, five days a week. More insidious and difficult is the legalist, who processes each decision with perfect logic but imperfect premises, who operates exclusively through a tight chain of command, who so dampens enthusiasm and subverts innovation that any external assistance provides only short term palliative results" (Marburger, 1963). Additional hazards to effective teaching derive from overinvolvement of some parents who operate to stifle the work of teachers. To limit such influences the families in the Detroit project were limited in the number of school days they could participate in the school programs.

Evaluations of the programs were built into the project from the start with two types of control school, Type A, those schools in the same geographic area as the experimental schools, and Type B, schools in upper middle socioeconomic areas where the achievement and ability scores of the pupils reflected consistently higher levels of attainment. The evaluation design included such categories as pupil achievement, attitude change, behavior change, effectiveness of materials and techniques, school-community relations, and school health. Answers were sought for such questions as What is most effective to change attitudes: workshops with experts lecturing or those that involve staff in planning or curricular changes? Which is more effective to child learnings, modification of teacher perceptions or a more intense school health program?

It is noteworthy that the Great Cities School Improvement Program took advantage of the data made available by the various city-wide testing programs, the Iowa Tests of Basic Skills, the SCAT-Step, and the various group intelligence testings administered at certain grades of the systems. In addition, other group achievement and intelligence tests were administered to the children in the experimental and control schools, including the California Achievement Tests and the Lorge Thorndike Tests of Intelligence, Verbal and Nonverbal. The plan calls for a five year follow-up study of these children. Furthermore, school and sociological base-line data were collected regarding attendance, failure, lack of kindergarten experience, delinquency, youth and adult crime, population density, and transiency in each school's service area. Questionnaires were developed to tap pupil and teacher attitudes.

Project staff noted short term improvements in IQ and achievement scores and parent and community participation and cooperation with the school. However, long term impact of the MES programs on positive IQ and achievement score changes, parent and child aspirations, self-image attitudes, and increasing development of independence versus pronounced dependency attitudes characteristic of these child and parent populations must wait for detailed evaluations to be made over an extended period of time. Here again one wonders why the evaluation design did not include measures of self-image and dependency needs and attitudes, which are critical factors in learning and aspirations. These dimensions of personality are readily tapped by the DAP test and 3DPT Fein Testing of Limits Self Image and Dependency Scales and by controlled observations of behavior in school, neighborhood, and home. These variables are modifiable by appropriate milieu, teaching, and role structures and can be measured before, during, and at the end of the experimental programs (Fein, 1967, 1968).

NEW YORK CITY PROGRAMS (Gordon, 1968)

The MES programs in New York City were initiated in 1963 and are now ongoing in 14 schools in deprived areas, from prekindergarten to grade 12. The main elements of the New York programs are reduced class size (12.3 per class), team teaching and class clustering, additional teaching specialists, and heterogeneous groupings. Composition is primarily Negro and Puerto Rican. Per capita costs ap-

pear to increase yearly, reaching $932 in 1965 in contrast
to the stable costs of regular classes at $485 per capita an-
nually.

In 1967 these programs were evaluated under Title I
funds in terms of the value of expanding such programs
and in terms of determining their effectiveness in raising the
reading level achievements of children in these programs.
The evaluation procedures included rating scales, questionnaires, and objective tests to obtain data on children's attitudes toward class and school, achievement level, and
changes in arithmetic and reading scores, teachers' and administrators' attitudes toward various aspects of the program, and their perceptions of pupil performance. The research teams noted that although interest, climate, and
enthusiasm favor the MES schools studied, achievement in
reading and arithmetic do not differentiate the MES
schools from their controls. However, when the criterion of
improvement was changed from grade level means to "reduction in reading retardation," the MES groups showed
greater reduction in retardation than did the control groups
in 17 out of 20 comparisons: The conclusions drawn from
this reanalysis is that two and three year attendance in
the MES school is associated with a reduction in reading
retardation.

Although these findings are encouraging, their reliability
and validity are questionable in view of the weaknesses of
the evaluation programs. First, the research efforts in the
New York schools were seriously hampered by the fact that
the Board of Education does not allow research teams to
begin their evaluations before a program is implemented.
This hurdle prevents the team from introducing and collecting preprogram measures of dependent variables and building research controls into the fabric of the program design
to permit ongoing collection of meaningful critical data
during the life of the program. Furthermore, the urgency to
implement programs without benefit of research controls
forestalls adequate definition of precise goals to be attained,

essential to development of valid and reliable evaluative questionnaires and observation schedules, so that data collected with such hastily constructed instruments and inferences drawn from these data are suspect. These same pressures lead to neglect of detailed descriptions of expert skills of special personnel needed, the precise contributions expected from special staff, and types of new material to be used, so that the implementations are fragmented, made piecemeal on the basis of expediency.

When administrators of these emergency innovations are confronted with the vagaries of the design and implementations, they seek to justify their activities in terms of practicality. Many administrators openly express disdain for the researcher, accusing him of being involved with "nitty gritty" nonsense and frills. Given such arbitrary program implementations and evaluations, little useful knowledge can be gained to provide guidelines to further educational improvement. Unless programs are designed and defined with precision and with built-in research controls, efforts to test their benefits to the target children are futile. Examination of the programs introduced into the schools of New York City suggest that the primary purpose of these programs has been to make use of the funds provided for expansion of educational innovations and compensatory programs in the deprived areas, and to appease the citizens of these communities in their urgent demands for improved schooling for their children.

Personal experience in deprived school settings in New York City convinces this writer that many school people resist introduction of research controls, the need for working hypotheses, and development of scientifically based rationales underlying all activities, materials, and evaluation procedures out of fear of the unknown, that is, fear of research theory and methodology as well as fear of exposing their felt inadequacies.

Perhaps there is one critical justification for carrying on, in spite of poor research design and arbitrary implementations. The communities involved have long suffered neglect at the hands of national, state, and municipal government and educational administrations and suddenly they and their schools are in the limelight, receiving national and even worldwide attention along with funds, expert staff, and special services. Under impact of this multidimensional enrichment, the Hawthorne effect is realized; suddenly, all the children seem to be profiting, growing, advancing along with the adults in the schools and the whole community and suddenly everyone has hope and trust in their futures and the future of their children. Under the influence of these enrichments, bringing parents and community leaders into the schools and into close contact with a mixture of fellow beings from varied sociocultural areas and levels, there can be little doubt that the endogenous community members become sophisticated about many educational matters and soon have courage to ask definitive questions about the gains to the development and learnings of their children. At this point they may discover that *more does not necessarily equal better* and the *too much can be unhealthy*. At this point they may be ready to cooperate with the researchers, calling for postponement of implementations until adequate research studies provide effective guidelines to ensure "optimal" education for their children. These parents and community leaders may then become as potent a force for controlled research of innovations as they were in pressuring for hasty implementations.

The *All Day Neighborhood Schools* (ADNS) programs (Gordon, 1968) for the culturally deprived children, introduced into the New York City schools in 1963, are now ongoing in 14 schools of the city. These programs are limited to elementary schools from grade 1 to 6 and provide an extra teacher for each class and an administrator of each program. The ADNS teachers work with the classes or smaller groups of children from each class from 11 AM to

3 PM on basic school subjects, and from 3 PM to 5 PM they meet the children in clubs for social, artistic, and recreational development.

Evaluations of these programs by a team of researchers from New York University, studying third and fifth graders from six schools, three experimental and three control, two predominantly Negro, two predominantly Puerto Rican, and two mixed Negro and white, revealed serious obstacles to obtaining valid results. The obstacles to reliable and valid results included limited number of sample schools, poor matching of school populations on significant control variables, and the introduction into the control schools and one experimental school *of after-school study programs* which sought to reinforce the ADNS goals. This last factor, the introduction of after school programs into the control schools, would spoil the research even if the sampling was of adequate size, since it completely blurred the distinctive contributions that might have been made by the experimental elements. Unfortunately, in spite of the inadequacies of the research controls, the research team proceeded to observe, administer teacher rating scales and the Ohio Social Acceptance Scale to tap children's attitudes toward work, peers, and teachers, and to administer written themes to judge verbal gains.

From records of vandalism, teacher's ratings of aggressive behavior, and the OSCAR classroom conduct scale of pupil destruction, results were reported on development of social responsibility. Additional time, effort, and materials were wasted on administration of the Ohio Mental Ability Test, Metropolitan Reading Test, Peabody Picture Test, and California Test of Personality to measure differences between "experimental" and "control" programs on scholastic aptitude, reading achievement, aspiration, curiosity and responsiveness, personal and social adjustment, and classroom conduct. As might have been anticipated, results were blurred and contradictory. One wonders why the research team proceeded with the expenditure of funds, time, and energy in the face of such poor design. Here again it seems that the "action" was implemented in response to community pressures to use up the funds allocated for the program.

The *Experimental Primary Program* (Gordon, 1968), ongoing in five schools of New York City, includes prekindergarten to grade 6 with special emphasis on prekindergarten and kindergarten. These programs provide for additional teachers, teacher aides, guidance counselors, and social workers. The school day extends to 5 PM. The *Reduced Pupil-Teacher Ratio Programs* are ongoing in 262 schools of New York City, with 15:1 and 20:1 ratios in first and second grades, respectively. Observations and reports by university consultants indicate that there is little staff enthusiasm for and commitment to the Experimental Primary, due to shortage of adequately trained staff and vagueness of purposes and guidelines. The Reduced Pupil-Teacher Ratio Programs also suffer from newness, inadequately trained staff, and the difficulties deriving from the efforts of two teachers to work cooperatively in one classroom—much like two housekeepers running one house or two cooks making one broth.

PROGRAMS WITH MULTIPLE EXPERIMENTAL ELEMENTS

As of June 1968, New York City readied itself for the implementation of four new experimental programs involving a variety of program elements judged by the design committee to be important for education of high quality (Gordon, 1968). Different elements were grouped to form four experimental models, since the use of single educational elements appears to have limited promise of effectiveness. "Evaluation research," states the report, "will seek to evaluate single as well as combined elements in these new programs." Basic conditions of these four experimental models *must* include reduced pupil-teacher ratios, adequate staff in terms of number and competence, extended school day and year, integrated child populations, adequate classroom space and facilities, modified organizational structure to allow full participation by indigenous community members in the affairs and decisions of the programs, and adequate educational leadership. Furthermore, a detailed plan for comparative study and evaluation of the models was expected to be developed well in advance of implementation, spelling out the specific goals of each model. Training programs were to be provided for all types of staff including paraprofessionals and parents; adequate space and facilities were to be provided for the activities of the special staff added to service the school.

The four experimental models, identified as Models A, B, C, and D, were implemented in four schools in each borough of New York City during 1970–1971. Experience with these programs to date indicates that the directives written into the programs for the introduction of research controls and methods for continuing comparative study and evaluations are hardly sufficient to ensure effective implementation of such measures. In most instances the efforts at implementation are running into obstacles in the following areas: staffing and training; coordination difficulties, intraprofessional and interprofessional conflicts and competitions relative to roles, role relations (status control), and responsibilities; conflicts and competitions in identification and definition of critical learning variables; purposes of testing and selection of testing procedures; type of data to be collected and methods of analyzing data collected; selection and development of materials relevant to program goals. Efforts to resolve the conflicts and confusions are generally made by the school principal in collaboration with the supervisors of special service staff. These interveners are inclined to assume that all problems derive from "personality conflicts" among the various professionals and caution the staff with a pat on the head to try to work together. These interveners avoid tackling the problems in terms of the program goals and differential expertise of the staff needed for each critical task. As might be anticipated, interventions based on assumptions of personality conflicts blur the issues, compound the confusions, and frustrate the staff so that conflicts do develop between staff on matters tangential to the issues at hand, thus fulfilling the expectations of the administrative interveners. Limited long range benefits may be expected from these new programs if the obstacles cited are not resolved in terms of the real issues —clarity of design, definitions, purposes, staff skills, and expertise—free of the obstacles of hierarchical control, tenure and seniority in employment, criteria that now carry overwhelming weight in these implementations in New York City schools.

These four New York City experimental programs (A, B, C, D) are similar in several educational elements but are different in organizational patterns and primary focus. Thus Model A is organized on the concept of the extended school day; Model C is directed primarily toward non-English speaking children, users of English-based dialects, and children whose spoken and written language repertoire is limited to the minimal stereotyped words (in our society, about 500 words). Model D is unique in its focus on the accountability of the school to parents combined with improved parent education and home, school, and community liaison. Finally, Model B is unique in the respect that it is geared to facilitate learning through detailed diagnostic procedures, individualized prescriptive assignments, and programed curricula.

Model B is selected for detailed description here because this model calls for much more extensive use of psychological staff than do the other models and further because this writer participated in efforts to design diagnostic procedures and efforts to implement this design in an inner city school.

The Model B Design

Model B (Gordon, 1968) calls for the establishment of a learning diagnosis facility to provide continuing qualitative assessment and educational prescriptions for each child and a resource development facility that would design individualized programs for each child as recommended by the diagnostic facility. The diagnostic facility was expected to be staffed by five school psychologists, two curriculum development experts, one educational psychologist, one social worker, one paraprofessional to act as community liaison, two secretaries, and two clerks. The Resource Development and Supply center was to be staffed by a coordinator who is a specialist in curriculum and instruction, two language arts specialists, two reading specialists, one social studies specialist, one math and one science specialist. In addition it was required to have one resource specialist to administer the Resource Supply Center, one librarian, two paraprofessional library aides, two paraprofessional audiovisual technicians, one coordinator of audiovisual instruction, and one specialist in the use of mechanical teaching media to maintain the teaching machines and supervise their uses.

The functions of the diagnostic unit are described as follows (Gordon, 1968):

> The staff of this unit should provide a qualitative appraisal of each youngster in the school, develop a file on each child including the description and analysis of his social, intellectual and personal characteristics. Sources of such information may be: achievement tests, standardized intelligence tests (item analysis to reflect patterns of intellectual functioning), medical history, material descriptive of child's temperament and social interaction, of his responses in new and laboratory learning situations, of those factors in his home and community that directly relate to his learning needs and style. Diagnosis should be reviewed and updated every four months. Further the staff of the diagnosis facility should consist of a team having those skills and competencies necessary to evaluate:

1. The functional abilities and disabilities of the child and the conditions which facilitate or inhibit their expression.
2. The conditions under which functioning is adequate as well as those in which functioning is impaired.
3. The preferential and stylistic trends in the adaptive behavior of the child.
4. The level and quality of intellectual functioning.
5. The level and quality of academic functioning.
6. The health and nutritional status of the child.
7. The social and environmental factors relevant to the child's academic and social development.

On the basis of these extensive studies the diagnostic staff was expected to prepare individualized prescriptive recommendations quarterly, to be translated by the Resource Development Facility staff into individualized prescriptions which were then to be implemented by the teachers and the pupils.

It is noteworthy that the design as defined by the research committee does not detail the behavioral traits or methods to be employed to collect data on specifics of social and personal characteristics, temperament, social interaction, type of laboratory learning situations, home and community factors that directly relate to each child's learning needs and styles. Apparently the task of defining the critical variables to be evaluated in the Model B program was intended to be the responsibility of the *Diagnostic Facility Team*, which was further charged with reviewing and updating diagnoses every four months. This directive suggests that the evaluation methods should be fully objectified and routinized so that quarterly reevaluations are readily conducted, recorded, and interpreted. On the other hand the directive to provide qualitative appraisals of functional abilities and disabilities, facilitating and inhibiting conditions of learning, preferential and stylistic trends in adaptive behavior, and quality of intellectual and academic functioning, appears to call for clinical, judgmental, case study approaches that do not lend themselves readily to quarterly reviews and updating.

Since the traditional case study approach hardly lends itself to extensive educational experimentation, one must conclude that the research designers expected the diagnostic experts to select or develop reliable and valid group evaluation instruments that would permit quarterly testings and reviews and provide "qualitative appraisals" of the critical dimensions noted above. To do this the diagnostic experts would be required to (1) identify the discrete critical abilities, disabilities, learning needs, styles, temperamental traits, home and community factors, social and personal characteristics; (2) define these in operational terms; (3) research and select standardized instruments or construct such instruments to measure each of the critical variables in objective terms. This would permit routinized testings with readily recorded scores that could at once be meaningfully interpreted. The diagnostic staff would also need to run pilot studies to obtain local norms on each critical variable to control the impacts from different sociocultural milieus, homes, and communities.

These then were the challenges confronting the staff charged with implementing the Model B program in four New York City schools. Under the direction of the school principals, IPI programs in reading, arithmetic, and language mastery were conducted by university teams expert in these programed applications. The diagnostic battery for evaluating psychological dimensions of personality was the responsibility of the senior psychologist and staff assigned to the diagnostic facility, with approval of the directors and supervisors of the Bureau of Child Guidance of the New York City Board of Education.

To develop such a program, the present writer was invited to join the Bureau of Child Guidance with the proposal that she apply to the Model B program devices she had used in a New York City public school in 1967 while serving as Research Associate to the Department of Child Psychiatry at the Roosevelt Hospital. The diagnostic schedule and its application to the Model B program are presented in the next chapter. This program is described to demonstrate the challenges confronting a clinical/educational/research psychologist charged with designing evaluation procedures of multiple complex personality and behavioral dimensions, vaguely defined by program designers.

REFERENCES

Fein, L. G. *The Three Dimensional Personality Test: Reliability, Validity and Clinical Implications.* New York: International Universities Press, 1960.

Fein, L. G. Non-Academic Personality Variables and Success at Nursing School. *International Mental Health Research Newsletter,* 1967, 9/4, 2–9.

Fein, L. G. Roosevelt Hospital Screening Program for Special Class Placement of Emotionally Disturbed Children. New York: Roosevelt Hospital, 1968. (mimeo)

Gordon, E. *Final Report to the Superintendent of NYC Schools.* New York: Board of Education, 1968.

Marburger, C. Considerations for Educational Planning. In A. H. Passow (ed.), *Education in Depressed Areas.* New York: Teachers College Press, Columbia University, 1963.

Rosenthal, R. & Jacobson, L. *Pygmalion in the Classroom.* New York: Holt, Rinehart and Winston, 1968.

CHAPTER 5

Implementing Research Directives to the Model B Program

In Chapter 4 it was noted that experimenters working in the Great Cities programs are confronted by many obstacles to effective implementations and evaluations of the innovative educational elements designed to remediate learning lags and facilitate optimal learnings. Among the more critical obstacles to effective implementation and evaluation of the programs are teacher expectancies of limited learning potential in deprived children; teacher and administrative resistances to changes in teaching methods, contents, and school and classroom organizations; difficulties in collecting preexperimental data on critical learning, attitudinal, and behavioral dimensions in the children, teaching staff, administrative staff, and parents; difficulties in controlling the experimental inputs in the various schools involved in the studies so that evaluative results were blurred; failure to identify and define with precision the critical learning, attitudinal, and behavioral variables to be modified in the subjects under study, which again provided blurred evaluative results and thus provided little guidance to continuing changes in the school programs. Perhaps the most defeating aspect of the Great Cities Experimental programs was the effort to modify and measure a multiplicity of variables in learning, attitude, and behavior changes in a large variety of samples, all at one time, a herculean task that can rarely if ever be accomplished in an ongoing multifaceted human action system.

Accordingly, to avoid some of these pitfalls, the writer sought to develop a research design that was precisely circumscribed in goal and population samples, that sought to modify precisely defined dimensions of learning and attitudes that are critical to optimal school achievement.

OBSTACLES TO LEARNING IN DEPRIVED CHILD POPULATIONS

Culturally deprived child populations reveal pronounced learning deficiencies in basic school skills when measured against standard middle class norms (Masland et al., 1958; Gordon, 1968; Passow, 1963). These widespread lags appear to be functions of the eroding impact of deprived milieus to which these children have been exposed from birth.

Since the ultimate goal of this experimental program was to facilitate school learnings in deprived child populations in the Model B school, it seemed essential to use psychological instruments that would tap levels of *developmental skills* and *adaptive behavior trends* that impair or facilitate learning of basic school skills: reading, writing, arithmetic.

Mastery of basic school skills depends in good measure on sequential maturation of basic developmental skills such as perceptual acuity, differentiation, visual motor coordination, and expressive verbalizations, and upon self-image and dependency attitudes (Straus & Lehtinen, 1947; Straus & Kephart, 1955; Fein, 1968; Ilg & Ames, 1964). Furthermore, these basic developmental skills and self-image and dependency attitudes, even at age appropriate levels, are vulnerable to the eroding impact of deprived and/or chaotic milieus as revealed in the studies on sensory deprivation and psychological differentiation (Solomon et al., 1961; Schlatz, 1965; Bexton et al., 1954; Simpson, 1939; Witkin et al., 1962). These data suggest that deprived child populations will reveal, on examination, significant lags in basic developmental skills, impaired self-image attitudes, and profound dependency attitudes, all of which may be expected to serve as obstacles to learning basic school skills. Accordingly, the diagnostic test battery selected for use in this study, guided by these considerations, included tests to tap levels of developmental skills and patterns of self-image and dependency attitudes.

TEST BATTERY AND VARIABLES TAPPED

The test battery included the Vane Kindergarten Test (KT) (Vane, 1968), which screens visual perceptual acuity and differentiation, visual motor coordination, and expressive verbalizations. This test was standardized on a large American child population aged 4 to 10 years. It is easily administered to groups of 10 to 12 children within an hour testing time. The manual provides mental age scores for each chronological age level to 10, scores that facilitate prescriptive writing and are more meaningful for teacher use than are IQ scores. The Vane includes three tasks: copying geometric forms, defining a list of graded words, and drawing a picture of a man. The drawing test lends itself to measurement against the Koppitz (1968) Emotional Index (KEI) Scale, which gauges level of emotional adjustment and maladjustment. This measure seemed worthwhile since emotional distress and maladjustment contribute to developmental and learning lags, impair self-image attitudes, and increase dependency needs.

The usefulness of the Vane KT with deprived child samples aged 5 to 10 was demonstrated in a pilot study conducted by this writer in 1968 (Fein, 1968) in an inner city school of New York City. Pilot study results revealed that the Vane and Koppitz national norms were significantly higher than grade norms obtained by our deprived child samples on perceptual motor coordination, expressive language, and emotional adjustment. Accordingly, grade norms were developed for each grade included in the Model B program on each of the variables tapped with the Vane, and the performance of the children was measured against their own grade norms. The KEI scores were also measured against each child's grade norms rather than against national norms provided by Koppitz. This procedure permitted us to set realistic goals for the prescriptive assignments for each child.

In addition to the Vane group test, the 3DPT Fein Testing of Limits Dependency and Self Image Scales (Fein, 1960, 1968) (see Chapter 6 and Appendix B), were administered individually to a small sample of fourth grade children. These scales measure self-image and dependency attitudes under ambiguous and role structured conditions. Also included was the Vineland Social Maturity Scale (Doll, 1965) in anticipation of collecting data from parents on child social development, and the New York Child Development Scale to obtain teacher observations on child social development behaviors. Unfortunately, the Vineland was not used due to the withdrawal from the program of the social worker who was to collect the Vineland data from parents. The data collected by the teachers with the New York Child Development Scale (Board of Education, 1950) was nonetheless useful, since in the process of using these scales the teachers were alerted to the importance of controlled observations and the need to define and record behaviors operationally to permit valid evaluations. These data also alerted teachers to the importance of classroom milieu climate and structure and stimulated study and exploration of these variables in the training seminars held with the teachers.

The original diagnostic design also included six tasks from the Wechsler Intelligence Scale for Children (1949) to obtain additional measures of perceptual, motor, and verbal skills. The tasks included:

1. Comprehension—to tap judgmental skill.
2. Digit span—to measure attention to aural stimuli and immediate recall.
3. Similarities—to tap ability to abstract.
4. Picture completion—to tap attention to visual details of mundane objects of the milieu.
5. Picture arrangement—to tap alertness to cues in sequential behavior.
6. Block design—to tap visual motor organization skill and synthesis.

Although these tasks were administered to 47 children in the fourth grade, limits of staff and time did not permit analysis of these test results relative to the other test data analyzed.

IMPLEMENTING THE DIAGNOSTIC/PRESCRIPTIVE PROGRAM

Due to limits of staff and time, the full testing program could not be administered as planned. Instead of five school psychologists and one educational psychologist called for in the research design for the diagnostic facility, only one psychologist, the present writer, was assigned. Fortunately, with the help of two paraprofessional aides whom the writer trained to assist in group administration and scoring of the Vane, and with the belated help of two graduate students whom the psychologist trained in administration of the Fein Dependency and Self Image Scales and who treated the data statistically, the program was implemented.

In this program 565 children from prekindergarten through grade 4 were tested with the Vane. These data were scored for perceptual discrimination, acuity, perceptual motor coordination, expressive language, and perceptual differentiation as measured against the Vane Developmental Tables and for emotional adjustment as measured against the Koppitz Emotional Index Scale. In addition, 47 children from grade 4 were tested individually with the WISC and with the Fein Dependency and Self Image Scales (Fein, 1968).

Time limits were imposed by lack of psychological staff and by the fact that the school year was drawing to a close. Furthermore, no plans could be made for the next year's continuation because the program was to be discontinued, by directive of the district supervising psychologist, an MA psychologist with seniority. He replaced the program with simple administration of the WISC by a staff of five school psychologists. No rationale was offered for this change except that "school psychologists are required to administer intelligence tests," and "IQ scores are required by law."

Fortunately, before the close of school for the year, the research data were put at the disposal of the school staff to guide implementation of the prescriptions written for each child. Each teacher and grade principal received class and individual reports of each child's performance on the Vane, KEI, and Fein Dependency and Self Image scales with prescriptive assignments based on child needs as revealed in these tests results. Teachers and principals found these reports useful guides to promotions at the end of the year. Further, the data collected provided an opportunity to compare the significance of differences between grade means on each variable and also to compare these data with similar data collected in middle and upper income schools, with the help of three school psychologists who volunteered to help in the project on their own time. Analyses of these data in terms of the significance of the mean age grade and mean age lag cross-cultural (socioeconomic) differences are reported in Chapter 6.

CLASSROOM USES OF TEST RESULTS

The classroom records detailed each child's MA and SD scores from their grade means on the VKT variables and KEI point scores and SD's from the KEI mean grade point scores. (Mean grade scores and standard deviations were listed on all reports given teachers and principals, for ready reference.) These data provided the teacher with comparison data on each skill measured within each child and between the children in her class. These class reports were used as guides to groupings for prescriptive teaching, as follows (Appendix A.1.):

Upper level: +2 or more SD's from the grade mean
Middle level: ± 1 SD from grade mean
Low level: − 2 or more SD's from grade mean

Four principles guided prescriptive teaching assignments:

1. Learning proceeds developmentally from the known to the unknown, from concrete (body→other objects→abstract concepts) to abstract.
2. Precision of output depends on precision of input, thus ambiguous output would presumably derive from ambiguous input and precise learnings (output) from precise teaching and practice (input).
3. Development of skill efficiency calls for a good model accompanied by consistent "shaping" (encouragement) of each closer approximation to the model, until efficiency is attained.
4. Sufficient practice is needed to overlearn each skill so that it becomes automated and functionally available as needed.

Examination of the test protocols of the children tested revealed the following deficiencies in skills and concepts:

1. Poor sense of directionality; no conception of right and left.
2. Confusion in space: up-down, in-out, on-under, close-near-far, next to-beside, and so on.
3. Little experience with geometric forms and limited conception of the meanings of geometric concepts.
4. Blurred perception of details of geometric forms.
5. Blurred conception of word meanings, for example, *"calendar is numbers," "quiet is stand in line," "straight is don't talk in line."*

It is noteworthy that our findings are similar to findings reported by Weikart (1969) in the Michigan "Follow-Thru Project."

Materials to teach directionality were prepared by the Resource Materials team with the help of the psychologist. A variety of rat mazes were prepared on desk sized cardboards with arrows indicating the routes, to be marked in pencil by the child, within the narrow road borders. The sides of the cardboards were marked "right" and "left" corresponding to the child's "right" and "left" sides. Children were alerted to their right and left hands and sides at the start and to the fact that the cardboard signs corresponded to their sides, right and left. Furthermore, they were encouraged to say softly "Right" and "Left" as they drew the "rat" routes on the mazes. In addition, black block letter signs designating Right, Left, Enter, Exit were posted around the building at strategic points for routing the classes. Teachers reviewed these signs in class daily until every child could identify and follow them correctly.

To teach precise word meanings teachers met weekly with the grade principals and the psychologist to develop a lexicon of the words commonly used by teachers in school in their "directives" and "exhortations," since words used in these contexts appeared to be commonly misunderstood by the children. In addition, other words were added as the teachers introduced them for definition. Precise meanings suited to the understanding of the children of each grade were formulated and recorded. Teachers were alerted to the imperative of defining meanings of words used and to provide special practice periods for these learnings.

To refine perceptual differentiation of the human body and self-image, teachers were encouraged to provide mirrors for the children to view themselves during a specific period of the school day, and then to draw pictures of themselves, with guidance about body details. In addition, human puzzles were provided from developmental learning materials.

To orient the children in space and acquaint them with geometric forms, developmental learning materials provided for practice included three sizes of geometric stencils, geometric shape puzzles, and spatial relations picture cards. The teachers were advised to have the children practice spatial relations sequentially, beginning with their own body movements in space, then on to object movements, and then to identification of spatial relations in the pictures. Other developmental learning materials used included lacing cards for the prekindergarten and kindergarten children who had very limited eye-finger coordination skills, counting picture cards, association picture cards, sequential picture cards, alphabet picture cards, and prewriting designs. These developmental materials are graded on each skill tapped, thus they are readily adapted by the teacher to each child's skill needs.

In addition to the classroom records discussed earlier, teachers received individual charts for each child indicating his MA and SD scores from the grade mean on the VKT variables and KEI point scores and SD from the mean grade points. Space is provided on these record blanks for four recordings of test scores from repeated testings through the year as required by the Model B design directives. These records were placed in each child's permanent record folder and used at the end of the year to help determine promotions (Appendix A.2).

To provide prescriptions for development of self-direction (independence) and self-acceptance, teacher guidance sheets were prepared by the psychologist on which Suggested Classroom Treatment and/or Special Considerations were checked off, on the basis of each child's dependency and self-image needs and attitudes in response to ambiguity or structure as revealed by the 3DPT Fein TL Dependency and Self Image Scales (Appendix A.3).

Grade principals received reports detailing the grade means and SDs on each skill measured as well as class means and SD from the grade mean for each section within each grade. These reports revealed at a glance the strengths and weaknesses of each section within each grade on each skill measured, facilitating the principal's interventions in each class in her grade (Appendix A.4).

The school year was coming to a close, so no follow-up could be done in the regular classrooms since the teachers were busy with all the details of the end of the school year. However, with the help of two first grade teachers released for this project, the diagnostic team (psychologist, two paraprofessionals, and two graduate students) met for one hour a day for five days with 25 children (from kindergarten to grade 2) scoring at or below -2 SD of their grade means on perceptual motor skills. In these sessions the children practiced on geometric stencils to develop perceptual motor coordination and perceptual differentiation skills and on spatial relations exercises as defined previously. These children were retested with the VKT the last day of school to see what learning had occurred in so short a time. It was gratifying to discover that every child made significant gains, raising scores $+2$ SD and in some cases $+3$ SD from the first set of scores on the geometric copying test of the VKT. Although this experiment cannot be designated a research study, it does provide a caution to school psychologists and other special service staff to the dangers of labeling children of deprived cultures "brain damaged" or "mental retardates" when such children reveal extreme deviations from their grade means and especially from national norms on perceptual motor coordination and perceptual differentiation skills. Our study suggests that developmental skills, though dependent on maturation, still need to be nurtured by regular daily practice in an appropriate manner so that input matches expected output, if skill efficiency is to be developed to a high level.

This study is described to demonstrate one type of diagnostic approach to meet the challenges presented to psychologists by designers of compensatory "experimental" educational programs. The report also highlights the obstacles to effective program implementation and professional functioning, obstacles imposed by vagueness of research constructs to be explored, insufficient professional staff (one psychologist where six were called for), limited secretarial assistance, poor space allotment for individual conferences and testing (a supply closet), and noise pollution (the diagnostic staff worked in the same area with other research staff conducting various programed curricula courses). Further obstacles were presented by the social service and guidance staffs who sought to use the psychologist in the traditional role of IQ tester, demanding IQ scores daily for children they had "identified" as "brain injured" or "mental retardates," whom they expected to move to special classes when the IQ scores were obtained. Apparently these staff members were unable to change their habitual modes of operation and their attitudes toward deprived children with learning deficits even in the midst of a school-wide research project seeking ways of facilitating learning in these children. The final obstacle in the course was imposed by the arbitrary decision of the district school supervisor (an MA psychologist with tenure) to discontinue this program and substitute the traditional "IQ" testing program of all children in the school. He assigned a team of *five* school psychologists to carry out his "design."

It is noteworthy that this writer met the school psychologist assigned as chief of that five person team in the summer of 1972. This chief psychologist reported that the teachers and principals of the Model B school were very unhappy with the IQ testing program, finding no use for these scores in the efforts to remediate learning in the children. She confided that the teaching and administrative staff requested the psychologists on this team to work with the records left by this writer, to assist the teachers to translate the prescriptions into actual classroom practice. She confided that her psychology staff found the records most useful in working with the teaching staff and cooperated with the school staff, though furtively, for fear of angering their district supervisor.

Before bringing this chapter to a close it is worth noting the many ways in which the school staff made use of the time and talents of the psychologist over and beyond the duties of the Diagnostic-Prescriptive Research-Through-Service Program. The psychologist held seminars with the teachers and principals on classroom management of children, milieu modification to meet the learning needs of particular children, methods of coping with behavior problem children in the classroom, crisis prevention, and intervention. The seminars were problem focused, the teachers and principals bringing the problems to the seminars for exploration. In addition, the psychologist was called on daily to cope with "child emergencies" at the request of teachers, principals, and even parents.

IMPLICATIONS

The experiences presented in this chapter are not unique many colleagues reporting similar frustrations in trying to serve the changing school scene (personal communications). The variety of challenges, obstacles, and demands made upon the psychologist in this setting reflects the varied conceptions among school people of the roles and functions of the psychologist in the schools and the fixed nature of many of these attitudes and resistances to change in practice. The foregoing description also suggests that school administrators are often indifferent to the conditions essential to effective psychological practice in the schools. The obstacles to effective psychological practice described here are not different from those noted by Cutts at midcentury (1955). This fact suggests that psychologists in the schools have done little to change the attitudes of school people toward psychological practices over the past two decades.

This book attempts to alert the readers, psychologists and educators, to the critical contributions psychologists can make to the teaching and learning goals of the schools, under appropriate working conditions and meaningful requests by school personnel. It is hoped that these insights will lead to more effective collaboration between the school teaching and administrative staffs and the psychologists serving the school needs and that psychologists in the schools will be motivated to use the design described here and test the benefits of this type of program over the long haul.

REFERENCES

Bexton, W. H., Heron, W. & Scott, T. H. Effects of Decreased Variation in the Sensory Environment. *Canadian Journal of Psychology, 1954,* 70.

Board of Education. *New York City Developmental Scales.* New York City: Board of Education, 1950.

Cutts, N. (ed.) School Psychologists at Mid-Century. Washington, D.C. American Psychological Association, 1955.

de Hirsch, K., Jansky, J. J. & Langford, W. *Predicting Reading Failure.* New York: Harper and Row, 1966.

de Moreau, M. & Koppitz, E. Relationships between Goodenough Draw-a-Man-test IQ scores and Koppitz HFD

Scores. *Interamerican Journal of Psychology,* 1968, *2,* 35–40.

Developmental Learning Materials. Chicago, Ill.

Doll, E. *Vineland Social Maturity Scale.* Circle Pines, Minn.: American Guidance Service, Inc., 1965.

Dunn, L. M. *The Peabody Picture Vocabulary Test.* Nashville, Tenn.: George Peabody College for Teachers, 1959.

Fein, L. G. The Three Dimensional Personality Test: Reliability, Validity and Clinical Implications. New York: International Universities Press, 1960.

Fein, L. G. Non-Academic Personality Variables and Success at Nursing School. *International Research Newsletter.* 1967, *9,* 2–9.

Fein, L. G. Roosevelt Hospital Screening Program for Special Class Placement of Emotionally Disturbed Children. New York: Roosevelt Hospital, 1968. (mimeo).

Gold, L. Contributions of teachers to dental health knowledge and behavior of students. *Journal of Experimental Education,* 1945. (Dissertation Abstract, Yale University)

Gold, L. Changing Student Food Habits through the School Program. *Journal of School Health,* 1945; National Council, Washington, D.C., 1945 (mimeo).

Gordon, E. *Final Report to the Superintendant of NYC Schools.* New York: Board of Education, 1968.

Ilg, F. & Ames, L. B. *School Readiness.* New York: Harper and Row, 1964.

Koppitz, E. D.A.P. Emotional Indices Scale. *International American Journal of Psychology,* 1968, *2,* 42–43.

Koppitz, E. & de Moreau, M. A Comparison of Emotional Indicators on Human Figure Drawings of Children from Mexico and the U.S.A. Interamerican Journal of Psychology, 1968, *2,* 41–38.

Machover, K. *Personality Projection in Drawing of Human Figure.* Springfield, Ill.: Charles C Thomas, 1949.

Masland, R. L., Sarason, S. & Gladwin, T. *Mental Subnormality.* New York: Basic Books, 1958.

Passow, A. H. (ed.) *Education in Depressed Areas.* New York: Teachers College Press, Columbia University, 1963.

Schlatz, D. P. *Sensory Restrictions.* New York: Academic Press, 1965.

Simpson, B. R. The Wandering IQ. *School and Society,* 1939, *50,* 20–23.

Solomon, P., Kabzansky, P. E., Leiderman, P. H., Mendlesohn, J. H., Trumbull, R. & Wexler, D. *Sensory Deprivation.* Cambridge, Mass.: Harvard University Press, 1961.

Straus, A. & Kephart, N. *The Brain Injured Child.* New York: Grune and Stratton, 1955.

Straus, A. & Lehtinen, L. *The Brain Injured Child.* New York: Grune and Stratton, 1947.

Straus, A. & Lehtinen, L. *The Brain Injured Child.* New York: Grune and Stratton, 1950.

Vane, J. The Vane Kindergarten Test. (Manual). *Journal of Clinical Psychology Monograph 24,* 1968.

Wechsler, D. *WISC.* New York: The Psychology Corp., 1949.

Weikart, D. P. & Ericson, M. Cognitively Oriented Follow-Thru Project. Ypsilanti: Eastern Michigan University, 1969. (mimeo).

Witkin, H. Some Implications of Research on Cognitive Style for Problems of Education. In M. Gottsegen & G. Gottsegen (eds.), *Professional School Psychology,* V. 3. New York: Grune and Stratton, 1969, pp. 198–227.

Witkin, H., Dyk, R., Faterson, H., Goodenough, D. & Karp, S. A. *Perceptual Differentiation.* New York: John Wiley and Sons, 1962.

Witkin, H., Lewis, H., Hertzman, M., Machover, K., Meissner, P. & Wapner, S. *Personality thru Perception.* New York: Harper and Row, 1954.

Zimmerman, I. & Woo-Sam, J. Research with the Wechsler Intelligence Scale for Children. 1960–1970. *Psychology in the Schools,* 1972, *9,* 232.

CHAPTER 6

Exploring Cross-Cultural Developmental Skill Differences in Elementary School Children

This study is reported to demonstrate that psychologists committed to serving critical needs of school children can, in spite of the many obstacles placed in their paths, make meaningful research use of the data they collect to gain significant insights into the learning and personality processes of the target populations studied.

SOCIOECONOMIC CHARACTERISTICS OF SAMPLES

The data reported in this study were collected with the help of three school psychologists assigned to schools in Manhattan and Queens, New York, schools in which the traditional roles of the psychologist were expected, in spite of the experimental changes ongoing in the school organizations and staff functions. These psychologists were frustrated under these circumstances, feeling that their traditional services were futile in the changing school scene and the types of problem presenting themselves in these new settings. Each approached the writer, seeking involvement in a challenging research approach to the critical problems of learning among school children. Accordingly, they were invited to collect data using the Vane KT on children in their assigned schools, if their program and time permitted. All three agreed to participate and collected data from four schools, three located in Manhattan and one in Queens. Thus we had data from five schools, the fifth located in the Bronx, where this writer was working on the Model B program described in the preceding chapter.

The socioeconomic and cultural composition of these schools were determined by the ranks of the catchment areas in which they were located. These catchment areas were evaluated for socioeconomic level and sociological and cultural characteristics in the Directory of Needs released in 1968 by the Human Resources Administration of New York City. The data relative to our study schools are presented in Table 1.

These data reveal that all but one of our sample schools were located in below average socioeconomic areas; the one remaining school was located in an upper class area. However, we do have distribution from the very low to borderline average socioeconomic level, permitting comparisons between degrees of milieu deprivation and grade norms on the developmental skills under study. The schools involved were distributed as follows: PSX, very low socioeconomic area; PSM1 and PSM2, low socioeconomic areas; PSM3, upper end of the low area; PSM4, borderline average area; and PSQ, upper socioeconomic area.

Examination of the data in Table 1 reveals a consistent

Table 1. Socioeconomic Characteristics of School Catchment Areas

School* Location Catchment Area	Composite Rank, R	Population Nonwhite Puerto Rican (1965)		Juvenile Offenses per 1000 Youth		Out-of-Wedlock Births per 100 Live Births		Infant Deaths per 1000 Live Births		Financial Aid to Children under 18 per 1000	
		%	R	N	R	N	R	N	R	N	R
PSM1 (39)	6	18.3	6	58	6	14.5	6	23.4	6	119.3	6
PSX (27)	9	87.0	10	107	9	41.0	10	36.0	9	559.0	10
PSM2 (76)	8	49.0	8	64	7	21.0	8	21.0	6	285.0	8
PSM3 (76)	8	Same as above across the board									
PSM4 (66)	7	28.0	7	69	7	23.0	8	37.0	9	298.0	8
PSQ (19.1)	2	3.0	3	13	1	0.2	1	7.0	2	0.7	1

* PS = Public school   X = Bronx
M = Manhattan (four schools)   Q = Queens
The numbers in parentheses designate catchment areas.

decrease in *percentage of nonwhite population* as the composite socioeconomic ranks rise, suggesting a close inverse relationship between percentage of nonwhite populations and negative or deviant socioeconomic characteristics. This relationship suggests that negative deviant social characteristics are a function of the percentage of nonwhites in the populations. However, this inference is invalidated by comparison of statistics reported across the board for populations in catchment areas 6, 7, and 8. Thus when we compare these three areas for percentage of nonwhite populations we find significant differences between rank 8 with 49%, rank 7 with 28%, and rank 6 with only 18%, yet these districts differ little in number of juvenile offenses per 1000, out of wedlock births per 100 live births, and infant deaths per 1000 live births. These data suggest that these social population characteristics are functions of factors other than racial composition of the population, very likely inadequate income, crowding, noise level, neglected, deprived neighborhoods, inadequate and neglected housing, and other correlates of poverty.

On the basis of these socioeconomic data it was expected that significant mean grade differences would be demonstrated between child performances in ranks 9 and 2 schools and between ranks 2 and 7–8 schools. Significant trend differences were expected between ranks 9 and 7–8 school samples since these school populations had pronounced differences on all socioeconomic population characteristics noted above; little difference was expected between grade means in samples from ranks 6, 7, and 8 schools.

STANDARDS OF MEASUREMENT

As indicated earlier, the test battery included the Vane Kindergarten Test, which taps perceptual acuity and differentiation skills, visual motor coordination skill, and expressive verbalizations. These skills were scored against the Standard Vane Mental Age Scales. The third task of the Vane, the Draw-a-Man-Test, was also scored against the Koppitz Emotional Index Scale to gauge level of emotional maladaptation, since such maladaptations produce pressures that impede maturational skill development. The 3DPT Fein Testing of Limits Dependency and Self Image Scales were used to screen dependency and self-image attitudes (Appendix B1 and B2) since these attitudes have significant impacts on school attainments (Fein, 1968).

The Vane Test calls for copying three squares, three crosses, and three hexagons; giving the meanings of nine words presented individually to each child; and drawing a picture of a man. The geometric copying test measures visual activity and motor coordination, the word task measures verbal expressive skill, and the man test measures visual perceptual differentiation skill. Vane notes that this last task, the Draw-a-Man-Test, has been shown to measure both intelligence and adjustment at the preschool and primary grade level (Ames, 1943; Goodenough, 1926; Harris, 1963; Koppitz, 1967; Vane & Kessler, 1964).

The Vane Test was ultimately standardized on 400 children, equal numbers of boys and girls, at each half year level ranging in age from 4½ to 6 years of age. The original standardization procedures involved close to 2000 children aged 4 to 10, drawn from all socioeconomic classes, as measured by the occupation of the fathers, from urban and rural backgrounds and from white and Negro groups in proportion to the percentage of these groups in the general population of children under 10 years of age. Although the percentages were allocated in accordance with the population throughout the United States, the children tested came only from the states of New York and New Jersey. The test-retest reliability of the Vane KT provided a correlation coefficient of +.97.

One might assume that this high level reliability coefficient and the extensive standardization procedures employed would validate the use of these norms against which to measure performances of children from all socioeconomic levels, certainly children from New York and New Jersey. If this assumption is justified, then the performances of the children in the Model B program could be evaluated against these Vane norms without prejudice.

The writer had grave doubts about the validity of using these standard Vane norms as criteria against which to measure the performances of deprived child samples, since the Vane norms increased significantly with each chronological age increase, a phenomenon we did not expect among deprived child samples. Research evidence (Fein, 1968b; Masland et al., 1958; Simpson, 1939) indicates that deprived milieus have a cumulative eroding impact on developmental skills and IQ scores, so that measures of these skills among deprived child samples would be expected to reveal increasing MA:CA lags with increase in age and school grade.

Early evidence of this phenomenon was reported by Simpson in his study of canal boat children in England in 1939, when he tested these children ranging in age from prekindergarten to 14 years. In this study *each older age group of children up to 14 years scored consistently and significantly lower in IQ scores (based on the Binet) than each younger age group studied,* even though all the children in this study were from canal boat families, all exposed from birth to the barren, monotonous canal boat culture. The author concludes that this phenomenon was in great part due to the cumulative impact of the barren, monotonous life on the canal boats, thus the longer the children were exposed to this type of influence the more depressed their intellectual, cognitive, perceptual motor, and verbal skills, as measured by the intelligence test.

More recent evidence of the cumulative impact of eroding milieus was obtained in a pilot study (1968) by this writer using the Vane KT and the Koppitz EI scales in a New York City school. This pilot study was conducted under the cooperative auspices of the Roosevelt Hospital, serving catchment area 39, rank 6 (low average socioeconomic rank), and the New York City Board of Education, for the purpose of developing a valid rapid screening test battery to facilitate identification of elementary school children needing placement in special classes such as junior guidance, half way, and mental retardation classes.

The Vane Kindergarten Test appeared particularly useful to the purposes of this project, since it samples three critical developmental skills and it provides mental age equivalents for each score on each skill scale. In addition, the emotional adjustment level could be tapped by evaluating Draw-a-Man Test performance obtained on the Vane against the Koppitz Emotional Index (1967).

Koppitz reports that the 30 items in her scale differentiate between the drawings of children who are well adjusted and outstanding in school and children identified as psychiatric patients. Further studies by Koppitz disclosed that these emotional index items are associated with specific types of behavior and attitudes in children aged 5 to 12. These measures of adjustment were particularly useful to our study since the purpose of the study was to identify children for placement in classes for emotionally disturbed children. (Koppitz [1968] reports a KEI of 2 points as evidence of emotional disturbance, a norm derived from a standardization sample of more than 2000 children, a sample representative of the population of the United States. She reports score of 1 point as within normal limits.)

ROOSEVELT HOSPITAL PILOT STUDY

On June 26, 1968, four classes of children including 35 first graders and 34 kindergarteners were tested with the Vane Kindergarten Test by this writer, with the help of two graduate students and the classroom teachers whose children were being tested. Analysis of the geometric copying performance data revealed a mean MA lag of 9 months from the grade mean CA on Perceptual Motor Coordination Skills at grade 1. Further, analysis of the word meaning response data revealed a mean MA lag of 15 months from the mean grade CA for the first grade sample. At the kindergarten level the mean MA lags were less, thus the lag on P/M skill was only 2 months and the word meaning lag was only 6 months. These results support Simpson's findings. They also support our expectations that national norms are not valid criteria against which to measure deprived child samples since eroding effects of deprived milieus are cumulative, so that MA lags increase with age and grade increase, in contrast to the positive covariation between MA and CA in the national sample.

On the Draw-a-Man Test, tapping perceptual differentiation skills, the first graders revealed only a 2 month lag from the mean grade CA, which is not significant, and the kindergarteners revealed a mean 6 month MA advance over mean grade CA. These findings suggest that perceptual differentiation skill, as measured by the human figure drawing, is resistive to the eroding impact of deprived milieus but does give way under the cumulative impact of deprivation as evidenced by the fact that a 6 month mean MA advance over mean grade CA at kindergarten was reversed to a 2 month mean MA lag at grade 1. If this process continues, we may expect consistently increasing MA lags from mean grade CA's in performances of deprived children on this test, as they continue up the school ladder each year.

The mean 6 month MA advance among the kindergarteners suggests a precociousness in these children possibly stimulated by the lack of limits and privacy in deprived homes, which exposes these children, early, to intense human events and relationships, exposure that may well overstimulate them to details of body structures. Such perceptual experiences may precipitate emotional reactions with which these children are not yet ready to cope. Such forced emotional experiences may create serious social-emotional problems that impair rather than enhance continuing developmental and school skills. Support for these inferences were provided by the KEI scores. Analysis of the "man" data with the Koppitz Emotional Index scale revealed significant differences between the KEI national norm and the mean point scores of our first graders and kindergarteners. Specifically, a KEI score of 1 point is within normal limits whereas a KEI score of 2 points reflects emotional disturbance, according to Koppitz (1968). Compared to Koppitz norms our first graders obtained a mean KEI of 2.7 with SD of 1.5 and our kindergarteners obtained a mean KEI of 3.5 with an SD of 1.7. These high means, both surpassing the Koppitz critical score for emotional disturbance, suggest that our samples of kindergarten and first grade children are, for the most part, emotionally disturbed. Specifically, if our samples were screened for emotional disturbance against the Koppitz national norms, we would have been obliged to refer 27 of the 35 first graders and 32 of the 34 kindergarteners to special classes for emotionally disturbed children. This was not done, of course, but at the same time these data were distressing. They support our expectations that deprived children, exposed to chaotic milieus, events, and relationships, are more disturbed socially and emotionally than are the same aged children from more stable cultural milieus.

Our results support the findings of the Yale Study in Connecticut (Hollingshead & Redlich, 1958) and the Manhattan Mental Health Study (Remmies et al., 1962), both of which revealed serious emotional disturbances in large segments of families in deprived areas. However, in spite of these findings the majority of these people appeared to be coping, somehow or other, in the open society, suggesting that the middle class norms of adjustment used in these studies were too severe as measures for these populations. Similarly, the majority of our sample children were apparently functioning acceptably or at the least tolerably in their home, neighborhood, and school milieus, suggesting that the Koppitz national norm was too severe a measure against which to evaluate our child samples.

MEAN GRADE CULTURE NORMS

For discriminative screening of our samples for special class placement, mean grade own culture norms were used, with a -2 SD from the grade mean as the index of disturbance. Children who deviate -2 SD from their own grade culture means cannot be expected to adapt effectively to their own culture where they must function within acceptable group tolerances, and they certainly cannot be expected to function appropriately in a regular classroom in public school.

When the first graders in our pilot study were measured against their own culture mean grade KEI score of 2.7, 14 fell within $+1$ SD and 11 fell within -1 SD. Although these 11 children would be viewed as disturbed when measured against the KEI national norms, within their own culture group they fell within normal limits. Thus only 4 of the 35 children in grade 1 obtained scores that fell at or beyond -2 SD of their grade mean and so were viewed as seriously disturbed, even in their own culture group, and needed placement in special classes. Among the kindergarteners, 5 of the 34 children obtained KEI scores that fell at or beyond -2 SD of their grade mean, suggesting serious emotional disturbance and need of placement in special classes.

These data support the practice of evaluating children from deprived cultures against their own mean grade culture norms for realistic class placement and for meaningful prescriptive teaching. Further evidence in support of using in-group culture norms on the KEI is provided in a study by Koppitz and Moreau (1968) on differences between 276 lower class Mexican children from Guadalajara and a matched group of 276 lower class children from a small industrial town of upper New York State. The 276 matched pairs included 176 pairs of boys and 100 pairs of girls.

KEI Differences between Mexican and American Children

Evaluations of child performances against the KEI adjustment variables as reflected in the graphic features of the drawings revealed marked differences in dynamics and behavior patterns between these two child samples. The American children are described by Koppitz as anxious, feeling inadequate, with poor self-concept, pressured for achievement by authority, harboring anger and aggressions, and prone to impulsive acting out. The Mexican children are described, from their drawings, as timid, shy, depressed, feeling unstable, very immature, and concretistic in thinking.

These two very different syndromes of personality from two samples of children matched for socioeconomic level, age, sex, and milieu urbanization yet with different cultural exposures point up the power of culture on developmental attitudes and behaviors and underscore the need to evaluate children against their own culture norms when the purposes of the testing are for class placement, prescriptive teaching, or remedial or compensatory education. Similarly, if the purpose of testing is to determine the adequacy of social and emotional adjustment, the child's own group culture norms are essential to determine whether his behaviors and attitudes are acceptable or at the least tolerable to his home and neighborhood culture.

CROSS-CULTURAL SOCIOECONOMIC COMPARISONS

Samples

The total child population included in the 1970 study was 1021 children from prekindergarten to grade 4, from schools located in four socioeconomic districts, differing significantly in racial composition. Specifically, 565 children were from rank 9 districts with 87% nonwhite population; 206 children were from rank 8 areas with 49% nonwhite population; 76 children were from rank 7 district with 28% nonwhite population; and 35 children were from rank 2 district with 3% nonwhite population. The scores of 39 children tested during the Roosevelt project were also included here for comparative purposes; these children were from rank 6 district with 18.3% nonwhite population. In addition, 47 fourth graders from rank 9 district (tested individually for dependency and self-image attitudes) were included in this total and their test performances were compared to test performances of 50 children from upper middle socioeconomic backgrounds who had been tested in 1970 for dependency and self-image attitudes by Dr. Karl Zucker of Indiana State University during attendance at a children's International Summer Village. This sample of 50 children were from 10 countries of the world, Eastern and Western.

Dependency and Self-Image Scales

Before discussing results of testings in this study, the format, administration, and scoring of the 3DPT Fein Testing of Limits Scales are described for the benefit of those readers who are not acquainted with these scales.

The 3DPT Fein Testing of Limits procedures measure dependency and self-image attitudes. (Fein, 1960, 1968). These tests involve the presentation, in standard design, of three ambiguous plastic forms popularly seen as people. These three forms are part of the Three Dimensional Personality Test materials designed by Doris Twitchell-Allen (1947; originally called the Three Dimensional Apperception Test, 1945).

The 28 forms of the test are numbered so that identification of each form used is easily recorded during testing. The three forms used in the Testing of Limits Procedures are form 21, popularly identified as an adult male; form 12, popularly identified as an adult female; and form 17, popularly identified as a child, an infant, or a little animal of some sort. In both TL1 and TL2 the forms are arranged on a table in a tripod relationship, equidistant and facing a central point, symbolic of mutual acceptance.

In TL1, which is the ambiguously structured situation, the examiner alerts the subject to the forms and directs him to call the forms what he wishes and then tell a story using these test forms in his story. This testing procedure seeks to explore dependency and self-image attitudes, relationships to and between authority figures, and the child's means of seeking gratification of dependency and contact affectional needs under ambiguous circumstances.

In TL2, the role structured situation, the examiner identifies the test forms as follows:

I will begin a story and I would like you to finish my story. This (touching 21) is the father; this (touching 12) is the mother; this (touching 17) is the little boy (if the subject being tested is a male) or "a little girl" (if the subject being tested is female). (With children under age 3 it is wise to identify test form 17 by the name of the child being tested.)

This procedure also seeks to explore dependency and self-image attitudes, relationships, and means of gratifying contact affectional and dependency needs *but* under role structured circumstances. Both steps can be administered comfortably within 15 minutes testing time. Dependency measures are based on test form manipulations and spatial relations of test forms with special attention to uses of test form 17. Performances are scored against an 8 point scale, graphically depicted and defined in the manual in Appendix B1. Self-image attitudes are evaluated by identifications projected onto test form 17 and scored against a 5 point scale detailed in the manual in Appendix B3. Manner of recording is also detailed in the manual. Test form manipulations and verbalizations are recorded by the examiner for both TL1 and TL2.

Within School Mean Grade Differences on the VKT and KEI

Analysis of mean grade differences on perceptual motor skills (copying geometric forms) in rank 9 samples revealed significant differences between prekindergarten and grade 1, grades 1 and 3, and grades 2 and 4. No significant differences were demonstrated between *sequential grades,* that is, between PK and K, K and 1, 1 and 2, 2 and 3, and 3 and 4. Similarly, no significant differences were found on this skill between grade 3 and 4 samples in rank 8 district. These data suggest that in deprived child populations, plateaus develop on perceptual motor skills in alternate years' as if these children from deprived milieus take two years to make one year's significant gain.

Word skill data revealed significant differences between grade means from PK to grade 2, but beyond grade 2 no significant differences were obtained in rank 9 district. Similarly, there was no significant difference between mean grade word scores for grades 3 and 4 in the district 8 samples. These data suggest that deprived children make significant gains in expressive language from PK to grade 2 but then their gains slow up to such a degree that they appear to make no significant gains in expressive language from grade 2 to grade 4.

Analysis of data on perceptual differentiation skills

(Draw-a-Man Test) revealed a steady increase in means from grade to grade up to grade 4 in district 9. These findings support the inference drawn earlier, from the Roosevelt study data, that perceptual differentiation skills as reflected in the Man test are resistive to eroding impacts of deprived cultures.

On the KEI scale mean grade point differences were significant between PK and K, favoring K, and between grades 1 and 2, favoring grade 2. However, no significant differences were demonstrated between mean grade KEI points of K and grade 1; grades 2 and 3; grades 3 and 4 in rank 9. In rank 8 district, though, a significant difference was obtained between KEI mean grade point scores in grades 3 and 4, favoring grade 4. The significance between grades 3 and 4 on the KEI scale in rank 8 is surprising at first glance, since rank 8 population is very deprived, as is rank 9. However, the differences between rank 9 and rank 8 populations on this variable become meaningful when the populations of these two districts are compared on percentage of nonwhite members, aid to dependent children, and number of out of wedlock births per 1000 live births, all indices of disrupted family structure. On these dimensions rank 8 and 9 populations differ markedly, with rank 9 higher on these three dimensions, reflecting a much higher percentage of broken homes and disrupted families than rank 8 population. With the security deriving from more intact family structures, the rank 8 children are apparently better able to develop more effective coping mechanisms by the time they arrive at grade 4 than can children from rank 9 districts, with the insecurities engendered by high incidence of broken homes and disrupted family structures.

Between School Mean Grade Differences

Comparisons of mean grade perceptual motor scores *between schools* in ranks 9, 8, 7, and 2 reveal a fairly consistent positive relationship between perceptual motor skill development and socioeconomic rank, with higher socioeconomic samples on the whole revealing significantly higher mean grade scores than lower ranking socioeconomic samples (see Table 2). Similarly, mean grade differences on word meanings between the schools in different socioeconomic areas disclosed a positive relationship between word mastery and socioeconomic level with higher socioeconomic samples revealing higher mean grade word scores than lower socioeconomic samples (see Table 3).

Comparison of mean grade differences on perceptual differentiation skills between child samples from different socioeconomic levels revealed no significant differences or even trends toward significance at the same grades between the different population samples. These results support the

Table 2. Cross-Cultural Mean Grade Differences on Perceptual Motor Skills

School	Socio-economic Rank	Grade	N	Mean MA *	SD **	Signifi-cance ***
PSX	9	4	67	7–1	8.0	
PSM2						.01
PSM3	8	4	128	7–5	6.5	
PSX	9	3	37	6–11	8.7	
PSM3	8	3	85	7–3	7.6	.05
PSM4	7	3	45	7–3	9.1	NS .05
PSX	9	1	160	6–1	10.3	
PSM4	7	1	31	5–9	11.7	.10
PSQ	2	1	35	6–9	10.9	.01 .01

* In years and months.
** Months.
*** Formula for unequal N's (sigma unknown):

$$t = \frac{\overline{X}_1 - \overline{X}_2}{s_p \sqrt{1/n_1 + 1/n_2}}$$

Table 3. **Cross-Cultural Mean Grade Differences on Vocabulary**

School	Socio-economic Rank	Grade	N	Mean MA *	SD **	Signifi-cance ***
PSX	9	4	67	7–8	11.0	.10
PSM2	8	4	85	7–11	11.0	
PSX	9	3	37	7–5	12.0	.01
PSM2	8	3	85	8–0	11.6	
PSM4	7	3	45	7–3	12.4	.01
PSM4	7	1	31	6–1	10.7	.01
PSQ	2	1	35	7–5	14.5	
PSX	9	1	160	6–2	15.2	.01

* In years and months.
** Months.
*** See formula for t in Table 2.

inferences drawn earlier that perceptual differentiation skill, as reflected in the drawing of a man, develops sequentially, at least up to grade 4, in spite of eroding influences of deprived milieus.

Comparison of KEI mean grade point scores between school samples in different socioeconomic ranks revealed highly significant differences between grade means at grades 3 and 4 between rank 8 and 9 samples, even though rank 8 and 9 populations are both at the low end of the socioeconomic continuum. These significant differences on this dimension become understandable, as was pointed out earlier, on the basis of stability of home milieu; that is, rank 8 population provides a more stable milieu for its children than does rank 9, as measured by the indices of disrupted homes in each district. These findings support the practice of evaluating children against their own culture grade norms on the KEI. They also highlight the dangers of evaluating them against other culture grade norms. For example, if the children in rank 9 population were evaluated on this dimension of adjustment against rank 8 norms, the majority would score as maladjusted or false negatives, and the reverse, rank 8 children evaluated against rank 9 norms would be evaluated predominantly as well adjusted or false positives (see Table 4).

Table 4.   Cross-Cultural Mean Grade Differences on KEI Scale

School	Socio-economic Rank	Grade	N	Mean Scores	SD	Significances
PSX	9	4	67	2.8	1.7	.01
PSM2	8	4	85	1.6	1.3	
PSX	9	3	37	3.3	1.8	.01
PSM2	8	3	78	2.3	1.7	

It is noteworthy that these KEI mean grade scores are substantially greater than Koppitz' national KEI norms where a score of 2 points is indicative of emotional disturbance.

**Cross-Cultural Socioeconomic Mean
Age Lag Differences**

The data in Tables 5 and 6 indicate that mean age lags on perceptual motor skills and word meanings increase significantly with increase in age and grade, from prekindergarten to grade 3 in rank 9 samples. There appears to be a continuous deceleration in the performance of these skills to grade 3, at least in deprived child samples. The mean age lag increase on perceptual differentiation is in contrast to the significant mean grade differences on this variable reported earlier for the rank 9 samples. This contrast suggests that mean age lag is a more sensitive measure of progress than simple mean grade differences. This finding lends further support to the observation made several times earlier

Table 5.   Cross-Cultural Mean Age Lag Differences on Perceptual Motor Skills

School	Rank	Grade	N	Mean Age * Lag	SD **	Significance
PSX	9	4	67	−10.8	8.0	
PSM2						.02
PSM3	8	4	128	−7.5	6.5	
PSX	9	3	37	−12.9	7.9	
PSM2	8	3	78	−9.2	7.6	.02 NS .02
PSM4	7	3	45	−9.1	9.1	
PSX	9	1	160	−11.5	11.2	
PSM4	7	1	31	−12.7	16.8	NS .01 .01
PSQ	2	1	35	−2.0	10.9	

* In years and months.
** In months.

that milieu deprivation has a cumulative impact on developmental skills and consequently on learnings. These findings alert us to the importance of the criterion measures used to evaluate performance of children from deprived cultures as well as the effects of compensatory educational programs on these children's learnings. Measures that tap cumulative decrements and increments are more revealing of true performance than are simple interval measures.

Table 6.   Cross-Cultural Mean Age Lag Differences on Vocabulary (Word Definitions)

School	Rank	Grade	N	Mean Age * Lag	SD **	Significance
PSX	9	3	37	−15.8	12.6	
PSM2	8	3	78	−9.9	12.1	.01
PSM4	7	1	31	−10.0	10.	
PSQ	2	1	35	+5.8	14.7	.01
PSX	9	1	160	−9.2	16.1	.01

* In years and months.
** In months.

Summary of Cross Socioeconomic Comparisons

Comparisons of mean grade perceptual motor scores between schools in ranks 9, 8, 7, and 2 reveal a fairly consistent positive relationship between perceptual motor skill development and socioeconomic rank, with higher socioeconomic samples on the whole revealing significantly higher mean grade scores than lower ranking socioeconomic samples. Similarly, mean grade differences on word meanings between the schools in different socioeconomic areas disclosed a positive relationship between word mastery and socioeconomic level, with higher socioeconomic samples revealing higher mean word scores than lower socioeconomic samples on the whole. On perceptual differentiation skills and on the Koppitz Emotional Index no significant or consistent differences were obtained between the mean grade scores of the different socioeconomic samples. However, when the comparisons were made in terms of mean age lag differences, significant differences were obtained throughout the variables between the samples from the varying socioeconomic levels, favoring the higher socioeconomic levels consistently. Apparently mean age lag is a more sensitive measure of progress than are simple mean grade differences. These results lend support to the thesis that milieu deprivation has a cumulative eroding impact on the development of perceptual differentiation and perceptual motor skills, verbal skills, and emotional adjustment.

CULTURAL DIFFERENCES IN DEPENDENCY AND SELF-IMAGE ATTITUDES AS MEASURED BY THE FEIN SCALES

Dependency and self-image attitudes covary in response to the degree of structure in a given situation. Furthermore, dependency and self-image attitudes facilitate or impede learning. In view of the covariation of dependency and self-image attitudes under varying degrees of structure and the impact of such attitudes on learning, programs to improve school achievement must explore the dependency and self-image attitudes of the children under differently structured settings to identify the degrees of structure that elicit optimal, age appropriate dependency and self-image attitudes in each child. Measures of degree of structure needed by each child for optimal learning, that is, measures of level of dependency of each child, should enable educators to structure school milieus, programs, and methods of teaching to meet the measured dependency and self-image needs of each child for optimal learning. Prescriptions of degrees of structures needed by each child for his optimal learning can be determined by each child's performances in the 3DPT-Fein-Testing-of-Limits procedures (Appendix B).

Examination of the data in Table 7 reveals that deprived child samples experience profound frustrations of infantile, contact affectional, dependency needs (scores 7 and 8), confusion (score 6), and conflict (score 5) as they struggle to establish satisfying and effective dependency relations with authority under both ambiguous and role structured conditions. In contrast, high income level children do not

Table 7. T-A 3DPT Fein Testing of Limits
Dependency Patterns of Deprived and Upper Middle Class
Child Populations

	Deprived $N=47$				Upper Middle $N=50$			
Score	TL1		TL2		Score	TL1		TL2	
Patterns	Freq.	%	Freq.	%	Patterns	Freq.	%	Freq.	%
1–4 to 6–8	11	22	8	16	None				
8–4 to 1–4	5	10	6	12	1–4	5	25	7	14
8–4 to 3–1	18	37	8	16	None				
3–1	15	31	27	56	3–1	17	75	43	86

reveal infantile dependency frustrations (no scores of 7 and/or 8), confusions (no score of 6), or conflict in relations with authority (no score of 5) under either ambiguous or role structured conditions.

On the self-image scale (Table 8) the privileged child sample appeared to resort to denial of identity under ambiguous conditions whereas under role structured conditions more than 85% appeared to accept their reality identities directly and with dispatch (score 1). In contrast 95% of children of the deprived sample expressed complete confusion about their identities under ambiguous conditions but fortunately 65% recovered in the role structured setting, revealing self-acceptance quite readily under these conditions.

In brief these data on dependency and self-image attitudes suggest that deprived children have an urgent need for precisely structured school and home programs and relationships to facilitate learnings, development of ego skills, and self-accepting attitudes and age appropriate autonomy. Our findings strongly suggest that the profound dependency needs and confused identities in these children derive in good measure from the ambiguous chaotic role relations and conditions that characterize so many of the homes and schools in deprived areas. Under such conditions, compen-

Table 8. T-A 3DPT Fein Testing of Limits Self-Image Patterns of Deprived and Upper Middle Class Child Populations

	Deprived $N = 47$				Upper Middle $N = 50$			
Score Patterns	TL1 Freq.	%	TL2 Freq.	%	Score Patterns	TL1 Freq.	%	TL2 Freq.	%
5	4	9	0	0	5	0	0	0	0
3, 4, 5	27	58	7	15	4	14	28	0	0
3, 2, 4	9	19	10	21	3	12	24	6	12
2, 1–4	5	10	4	9	2	12	24	0	0
4–1 or 1	2	4	26	55	1	12	24	44	88

satory and experimental educational and organizational school changes are not sufficient to remediate learning and developmental deficits or facilitate continued learning and skill development. To free these children to profit from innovative school programs, care must be taken to provide clear, meaningful structures in organization of space, time, and materials at home, in the school, and in the community. Care must be taken to mediate the meanings of these structures so that the children may develop a variety of cognitive maps that enable them to impose meaningful structures on new, ambiguous challenges.

IMPLICATIONS

The findings reported in this study imply that negative, deviant, and deficit characteristics of a given population segment are functions of poverty, crowding, noise level, barren cultural experiences, neglected surroundings, inadequate, neglected housing, and other correlates of poverty rather than of racial or ethnic factors. The results also indicate that the impacts of socioeconomic-cultural poverty are cumulative, so that programs seeking to facilitate school learnings are futile unless corrosive and eroding impacts of the many types of poverty are also concurrently attacked. Furthermore, since different socioeconomic-cultures appear to have different expectancies and tolerances of behaviors, the products of these cultures may be expected to function around their own culture means rather than around a national norm on any given behavior. Accordingly, all efforts to evaluate attainment among children from different socioeconomic cultures should use own culture means on any given variable of behavior against which to measure individual children's status on the variable. Measurement of progress among these deprived children is more realistically measured by mean MA/CA lags than by mean grade differences, even when own culture norms are used as standards. The results of this study also point up the significance of measuring self-image and dependency attitudes among deprived children under both structured and ambiguous conditions, to facilitate development of educational interventions that provide degrees and types of structure that release these children for appropriate independent function in the learning situation. Confused, conflicted self-images and profound dependencies seriously impair ability to learn.

Finally, the results of this study suggest that the reported failures of many of the compensatory and experimental programs (reported in earlier chapters) to demonstrate continuing learning after interventions ceased may have been due to eroding impacts of the home and community factors to which these children are exposed daily in heavy dosage. These influences are so powerful that school interventions of limited duration cannot counteract them.

Evidence of these influences was suggested in the DARCEE program where children from deprived milieus whose families moved during the study period to middle class milieus continued to demonstrate achievement gains after interventions ceased, although comparable children who remained in the deprived milieus began to lose their gains as measured against national norms after interventions ceased. These data point up the urgency to counteract the correlates of poverty to which these children are exposed if they are to be free to learn at their optimal potentials.

REFERENCES

Ames, L. B. The Gesell Incomplete Man Test as a Differential Indicator of Average and Superior Behavior in Preschool Children. *Journal of Genetics and Psychology,* 1943, 62, 174–217.

Cowen, E. L. Coping with School Adaptation Problems. *Psychology in the Schools,* 1971, *8,* 323–329.

de Moreau, M. & Koppitz, E. Relationships between Goodenough Draw-a-Man-Test IQ Scores and Koppitz HFD Scores. *International American Journal of Psychology,* 1968, *2,* 35–40.

Fein, L. G. *The Three Dimensional Personality Test: Validity, Reliability and Clinical Implications.* New York: International Universities Press, 1960.

Fein, L. G. 3DPT-Fein Testing of Limits Dependency and Self Image Scales. Norwalk, Conn.: Norwalk Hospital School of Nursing, 1960. (mimeo)

Fein, L. G. Non-Academic Personality Variables and Success at Nursing School. *International Research Newsletter,* Post Graduate Center for Mental Health, Spring 1968.(a)

Fein, L. G. Roosevelt Hospital Screening Program for Junior Guidance and Half Way Classes. New York: Roosevelt Hospital, 1968 (mimeo) (b)

Glass, D. C., Cohen, S. & Singer, J. E. Urban Din Fogs the Brain. *Psychology Today,* 1973, *6,* 94–98.

Goodenough, F. L. *Measurement of Intelligence by Drawings.* Yonkers-on-Hudson, N.Y.: World Book, 1926.

Harris, D. B. *Children's Drawings as Measures of Intellectual Maturity.* New York: Harcourt, Brace and World, 1963.

Hollingshead, A. B. & Redlich, F. C. *Social Class and Mental Illness.* New York: John Wiley and Sons, 1958.

Human Resources Administration. *Directory of Needs.* New York: New York City Administration, 1968.

Klineberg, O. *Negro Intelligence and Selective Migration.* New York: Teachers College Press, Columbia University, 1935.

Koppitz, E. Expected and Exceptional Items on Human Figure Drawings and IQ Scores of Children Age 5–12. *Journal of Clinical Psychology,* 1967, *23,* 81–83.

Koppitz, E. & de Moreau, M. A Comparison of Emotional Indicators on Human Figure Drawings of Children from Mexico and the U.S.A. *International American Journal of Psychology,* 1968, *2,* 41–48.

Machover, K. *Personality Projection in Drawings of Human Person.* Springfield, Ill.: Charles C Thomas, 1949.

Masland, R. L., Sarason, S. & Gladwin, T. *Mental Subnormality.* New York: Basic Books, 1958.

Remmies, T., Srole, L., Michall, S., Lagnen, T. & Ollen, M. K. *Mental Health in the Metropolis, The Midtown Manhattan Study.* New York: McGraw-Hill, 1962.

Simpson, B. R. The Wandering IQ. *School and Society,* 1939, *50,* 20–23.

Twitchell-Allen, D. A. Three Dimensional Apperception Test. *American Psychology,* 1947, *2,* 271–272.

Vane, J. Relation of Early School Achievement to High School Achievement When Race, Intelligence and Socioeconomic Factors Are Equated. *Psychology in the Schools,* 1966, *3,* 124–129.

Vane, J. The Vane Kindergarten Test (Manual). *Journal of Clinical Psychology Monograph 24,* 1968.

Vane, J. Importance of Considering Background Factors When Evaluating the Effects of Compensatory Education Programs Designed for Young Children. *Journal of School Psychology,* 1971, *9,* 393–398.

Vane, J., & David, W. Factors Related to the Effectiveness of Preschool Programs with Disadvantaged Children. *Journal of Education Research,* 1971, *64,* 297–299.

Vane, J. & Kessler, R. T. The Goodenough Draw-a-Man-Test: Long Term Reliability and Validity. *Journal of Clinical Psychology,* 1964, *20,* 487–488.

Witkin, H. A., Lewis, H., Hertzman, M., Machover, K., Meissner, P. & Wapner, S. *Personality Through Perception.* New York: Harper and Row, 1954.

CHAPTER 7

Coping with Multiple Target Populations

In the preceding chapters we focused attention on the massive learning retardation among deprived child populations in the schools, new targets calling for a variety of new services from psychologists. The traditional target populations toward which school psychology training and practice have been directed are exceptional children—the mentally retarded, the minimally brain injured, and the gifted—primarily at the elementary school level. The original targets defined by Witmer when he instituted his training program for the "new profession in psychology" in 1896 also included the mentally retarded and brain injured as well as the "morally" retarded, which no doubt meant children with behavioral deviations. By midcentury, psychologists in the schools had expanded their concerns to all children in the schools with special focus on those with social,

135

emotional, and behavioral difficulties. Attention was also given by MA level psychologists to school failures, dropouts, and reading problem children, while at the doctoral level work with parents and community groups was initiated, primarily to educate them to the family and community factors that operate to impair child development and those that foster good mental health.

During the past decade and continuing with the changes in the school and social scenes, psychologists have been and are confronted with new target populations even as they seek to serve the traditional targets. Thus they are called upon to cope with or devise programs for coping with widespread drug addiction among school children, especially at the junior and senior high school levels, with widespread learning retardation, especially in basic school skills, with aggressive and rebellious children in the schools, with angry parents and community groups demanding effective mental health services, equal to those available to the private sector of the population. In addition psychologists have been given responsibility for training and supervising paraprofessionals with limited educational background, through programs funded by various federal agencies seeking to improve the lot of deprived populations. Of course, psychologists have also been required to participate in a variety of ways in experimental and compensatory programs, as described in earlier chapters of this book.

AUXILIARY STAFF URGENTLY NEEDED

It is at once apparent that psychologists in the schools cannot possibly cope with all the problem populations presenting themselves for attention due to limits of time and energies and also to limits of essential knowhow and skills to cope with these many different types of problem. No one psychologist can possibly be all things to all people. Even if each psychologist served those groups for which his skills are best suited, there are not enough psychologists to turn the tide. Additional staff need to be trained quickly to work in the many programs, with psychologists, to stem the tide, at the least.

This need raises the question of what psychological skills are sufficiently simple to be learned and applied by paraprofessionals, from BA level down to elementary school level backgrounds. Answers may be found if coping approaches, based on sound rationales, are analyzed for their discrete skills and if the relative complexities of these skills are defined. They can then be ranked hierarchically from full professional to mundane routine skills. With such hierarchies professional psychologists could assume the complex skills and assign the simpler skills to lower level staff, training them for the specific tasks to be done. This job analysis approach is commonly used in business and industry and has been used in medicine, dentistry, education, law, and engineering to define roles for subprofessional or paraprofessional staffs within each professional hierarchy.

The skill analysis method calls for definition of the methods of choice in diagnoses, treatments, and interventions appropriate to each of the target population problems; it calls for identification and precise definition of the discrete steps in each process applied, arranging these in sequential order of difficulty for learning and training purposes. The analyses also call for close scrutiny of each function to determine what contents, knowledges, principles, facts are basic to enable meaningful performance and prevent routinized performance.

Approaches to coping with diagnoses and treatment of mental retardation are briefly analyzed next to demonstrate the application of this process.

MENTAL RETARDATION

The first step in approaching the analysis of the coping procedures employed with this target population is to recognize from the start that mental deficiency and mental retardation are different syndromes, derive from different etiologies, differ in diagnostic clarity, in prognosis, social implications, and educational orientation, and call for different research approaches (Masland et al., 1958). All personnel, from professional to paraprofessional, working with these two populations need to know the essential differences cited here. Mental defective or deficient, as a label, has a morbid connotation, implying irreversibility due to underlying central nervous system pathology, whereas mental retardation, as a label, has a benign implication, suggesting that it is a reactive condition and as such is reversible, responsive to appropriate educational and training interventions. Children who are readily identified as mental defectives in the first few years of life generally have related physical anomalies and rarely reach the attention of the public schools as a consequence.

On the other hand children without physical anomalies, who appear normal physically and sensorially, reach the public schools and are identified as retarded learners after repeated failure to learn the expected skills for their age grades. Such children are customarily referred to the school psychologist or psychological examiner for IQ testing with intent to place them in special classes for the educable or the trainable. Mild retardation with IQ range from 50 to 69 (85% fall into this category) are considered educable and moderate retardation with IQ range from 36 to 49 are considered trainable. As indicated earlier, children who are profoundly or severely retarded (IQ score ranges under 35) seldom reach the attention of the public schools and are generally placed in residential institutions.

Training Mentally Defective Children

Over the past several years successful efforts have been made to train mentally defective children in institutions in self-care skills, personal hygiene, handling eating utensils, self-feeding, dressing and undressing, learning their way about in the institution, as well as learning elementary concepts of concrete objects, activities, colors, numbers, and the like. Such programs have been funded by Title I and III compensatory elementary and secondary education. In these settings the roles of diagnostician, intervention designers, developers of procedures and materials and evaluations are carried by psychology and special education experts who also devise and conduct training programs for ancillary and child training staff. Child training staff include special education teachers, nursery school teachers at the BA level, and trainees with less than four years of college down to those with elementary education only. Each level of paraprofessional receives differential training equipping him to train the children in discretely defined and circumscribed skills. Training schedules and procedures are built on learning principles and implemented on reinforcement principles.

Identifying Mental Retardation by IQ Scores

The process of classifying children as mentally retarded within the schools has for many years been considered a routine procedure, easily done through the use of IQ scores. Of course Mongoloids (those with Downe's syndrome, or Trisomy 21) are readly identified by their physical anomalies, but since they differ within their own group in learning potentials and abilities, they are also tested with intelligence tests for IQ scores for placement in educable or trainable classes. Phenelketonuria based mental retardation is not a problem for school psychologists today since PKU tests are administered to all children at birth and interventions are applied to prevent development of retardation. Two common diagnostic labels applied to mental retardation that is identified in the schools through IQ testing are "familial retardation" and "of unknown etiology." Generally, the label "familial retardation" is applied to children from severely deprived families, while "of unknown etiology" is assigned to children from middle- and upper-class families. Both categories are catchalls, masking unknown etiologies.

During the 1960s, however, evidence was accumulated indicating that the widespread mental or educational retardation in school children, particularly in those from deprived backgrounds, are correlates of social, cultural, emotional, physical, sensorial, economic deprivations compounded by educational methods that have little relevance to the needs of these children and attitudes that denigrate the abilities of these children. These insights impose on school psychologists the responsibility for changing their traditional, habitual views and approaches to the identification of mental retardation in the school child population. These insights caution against the view that intelligence testing is a routine process, readily objectified, providing a discriminating score, whether administered by fully trained psychologists or in the hands of paraprofessionals, as is the practice in some schools and clinics today. Even if we assume that the global IQ score is the critical goal of intelligence testing, and that administration is simple, since the directions are explicitly defined and scoring is readily mastered, nonetheless, the IQ scores can be invalid due to *attitudes* and *expectations* communicated by the test administrator during testing, through nonverbal cues for the most part. Attitudes and expectations of test administrators can influence test performance of children tested, just as teacher attitudes and expectations of children in the classroom can influence classroom performance (Rosenthal & Jacobson, 1968). Present widespread expectations of poor performance from children of deprived backgrounds stack the cards against the performances of these children. The influence of examiner's attitudes on children during the intelligence testing was recently demonstrated experimentally.

IQ Scores Vulnerable to Examiner Attitude

In a recent study of examiner influence on children's IQ scores (Thomas et al., 1971) results revealed systematic dif-ferences in IQ scores of two groups of children matched on all significant variables and tested by two examiners matched for age, sex, race, education, and experience. The children were Puerto Rican from working class families and the examiners were also Puerto Rican at doctoral level training. Results indicated that IQ scores attained by children tested by examiner A were consistently higher, by at least 10 points, than the scores of children tested by examiner B. All differences were significant beyond the .001 level of confidence. The distributive scores were also different, with 65% of the children tested by examiner A falling in the average range whereas only 15% of the scores reported by examiner B fell within normal range. Only 5% of the children tested by examiner A were classified as borderline whereas 45% of the children tested by examiner B were so classified. Furthermore, the examiner A sample received higher mean subtest scores throughout, with the greatest differences between groups on vocabulary, comprehension, and similarities. Thus despite the fact that both examiners were equivalent with respect to age, sex, ethnicity, fluency in Spanish and English, level of training, and amount of clinical experience, examiner A was consistently able to elicit a higher level of performance from the children than was examiner B.

To test the reliability of these findings, 19 children were tested by both examiners, half first by A and half first by B. The results supported the findings of the larger study that in every instance the scores attained by the children tested by A were higher than those attained by the same children tested by B.

Exploration of the examiners' attitudes and behaviors during the testing periods (as reflected in the examiners' descriptions of the testing sessions in the psychological reports) revealed that the examiners differed in their approaches to the children and that the children responded differentially to these two adult approaches. Thus examiner A was warm, interested, friendly, and concerned in her behavior and the children responded by similar expressions of interest and enjoyment. In response to encouragement they amplified and elaborated their verbalizations and sought to modify their "I don't know" answers. Examiner B, on the other hand, established a neutral emotional relationship with the children and tried to limit her involvement with them to the test material proper. Furthermore, examiner B did not encourage the children to try again after an "I don't know" response. Her distance in the testing situation, her failure to encourage persistence may well have been experienced by the children as negative feedback to their performances, *as critical of them* rather than as an *objective attitude* which examiner B was presumably trying to maintain. The authors note that these findings are similar to findings by Zigler and Butterfield (1968) where culturally deprived nursery school children were tested by an examiner using "optimizing" procedures and another examiner using "standardized" procedures. Optimizing procedures produced significantly higher IQ scores than did the standardizing procedures.

On the basis of these findings the authors suggest that performance level of disadvantaged children on standardized achievement tests can be raised by employing examination procedures that are congruent with their spontaneous cognitive styles. It is further noteworthy that correlations of achievement scores and IQ scores of these children obtained under the conditions of testing provided by examiners A and B revealed significant correspondence between achievement and IQ scores attained under B conditions of testing but little correspondence between achievement and IQ scores attained under A testing conditions. These results suggest that the neutral atmosphere maintained during achievement test periods in school has the same depressing impact on child spontaneity and performance as did the neutral attitude maintained by examiner B during IQ testing.

Implications for Training Testers

These findings have serious implications for the present training of school psychologists in test administration. Test administration training in school settings has been guided by the misconception that neutrality is equivalent to objectivity, although in reality neutrality of attitude, reflected by blandness of expression, distance, aloofness, strict adherence to test tasks, in machinelike manner, is experienced by the subjects tested as negative reinforcement, which of course inhibits and impairs the child's performance. Such trained and habituated attitudes during test administration may account in some measure for the high percentage of children in deprived areas being identified as mentally retarded on the basis of IQ scores and school achievement. These attitudes compound the penalties of deprivation already eroding the abilities of these children.

These facts highlight the urgency to reexamine the concept of objectivity in test administration, of defining it in terms of attitudes and manner of relating that optimize child performance. These responsibilities belong to university faculty, to supervising and training psychologists in practicum setting, and to all professional psychologists administering psychological diagnostic tests. Once these attitudes are clearly identified and defined operationally and training methods are developed to facilitate transfer of such attitudes, then paraprofessional testers may be entrusted with test administration, of course under supervision of full professionals.

The use of global IQ scores per se, obtained even under optimizing conditions, has questionable value in selection, diagnosis, and intervention designs for educationally or mentally retarded children. The fact that the percentage of children identified as retarded during school attendance is significantly higher than the percentage of adults identified as retarded in the open society (Masland et al., 1958) challenges the significance of the IQ score as a measure of learning potential and ability.

Since psychologists in the schools are required to identify children to be assigned to special classes for the mentally retarded, the evidence of the inadequacy of the standard testing procedures, IQ and achievement, presents the psychologist with a serious challenge. He needs methods to obtain a realistic appraisal of learning abilities and styles which provide detailed insights into the child's functional needs to be met by appropriate, precisely defined prescriptions for teaching. New methods of evaluation and teaching are especially critical for compensatory and continuing education of children from the deprived cultures.

Cole and Bruner (1971) recently explored the problem of "Cultural Differences and Inferences About Psychological Processes" from anthropological, experimental, linguistic, educational, and clinical frames of reference and arrived at two recommendations:

1. There is a need to recognize that educational difficulties do not reflect disease but rather differences in performance which are amenable to change under positive teacher expectations (Rosenthal & Jacobson, 1968).

2. The teacher must stop trying to "create new intellectual structures" in these children and start concentrating on how to get the children to transfer skills already mastered to the tasks at hand.

In brief, these authors state that there are no cultural intellectual differences as such, rather different cultures have different ways of organizing the relation between their hands and minds without assuming superiority of one system over another. They charge the school psychologist to analyze the source of cultural difference so that those of the minority, the less powerful group, may quickly acquire the intellectual instruments necessary for success of the dominant culture, the American Middle Class, should they choose to do so. These recommendations are worthy goals but they fail to indicate how the psychologists are to arrive, currently, at realistic appraisals of child learnings, tasks that confront school personnel daily.

As early as 1949, Jastak (Masland et al., 1958, pp. 153–155) protested the use of the global IQ score on the premise that the intellect is not what is but what could or would be if everything else were equal. Jastak suggested treating intelligence tests as a variety of discrete measures of cognitive, perceptual, motor, verbal skills and identifying the child's potential by his highest subscore, an index he called the *altitude quotient*. This approach is in fact used by some psychologists in school settings and in some training programs. Approaching diagnosis of learning difficulties from the view of special abilities and disabilities is not only a more valid approach to diagnostics in this area but it also facilitates designing appropriate interventions, prescription writing, and implementations. Experts in special education have been using these approaches for some time.

Differential Staff Training

In working with mentally retarded children, analysis of the discrete aspects of diagnosis and treatment would be the responsibility of the professional psychologist. He would also be responsible for training subdoctoral staff in optimizing test administration skills and attitudes, in scoring, in recording, and in identifying special abilities and disabilities as revealed in the test performances and reporting the results to the psychologist. The psychologist would be responsible for designing intervention procedures, most likely in the behavior modification tradition, detailing the contingency schedules for each skill to be taught by the subdoctoral staff, and training staff to implement the programs. Experts in special education would be responsible for selecting and organizing the curricula contents and materials to be used by the teachers. In schools as in residential settings, subdoctoral staff may range from MA level through minimally educated paraprofessionals, carrying out training assignments matched for complexity to their formal educational levels and their learning abilities as demonstrated in action.

In brief, analysis of the approaches to coping with the problems presented by the mentally retarded or defective child populations reveals a variety of tasks and skills at different levels of complexity. Thus defining diagnostic principles, selecting or developing diagnostic approaches, designing interventions, training and supervising subdoctoral staff, and research call for the skills of top level psychology experts; implementing the interventions and evaluating progress can be handled by trained subdoctoral people from the MA level down to staff with minimal formal education, each lower level trainee assigned and trained for sequentially lower skill functions. Furthermore, subdoctoral staff can serve as IQ testers and scorers under supervision of top level psychologists if the training involves not only the "objective" administration and scoring procedures but also deliberate attitude training to ensure optimal facilitating examiner attitudes, which in turn elicit optimal performances from children tested. Differential diagnostic decisions remain the responsibility of fully qualified psychologists.

Learning Retardation is not Mental Retardation

A promising approach to the problem of assessing the retarded performer (deprived child) has been described by Feuerstein and his staff (1972) at the Hadassah Wizo Canada Research Institute in Jerusalem, Israel. The approach is called the Instrumental Enrichment Program. The underlying hypothesis of this new approach to compensatory education posits that the rate of cognitive development in normal individuals is significantly related to the amount and quality of environmental stimulation to which these normal individuals are exposed. Individual cognitive potentialities cannot be viewed apart from the milieu that fosters them, states Feuerstein.

Cognitive growth, Feuerstein believes, is impelled in two major ways. The initial push comes from direct exposure to stimulation. This exposure implies the active principles of assimilation and accomodation dependent on the objects experienced, to the extent that even a person relating to the infant is experienced as an object. The second and more significant impetus to cognitive growth is *mediated* learning.

Mediated learning is the training given to the human organism by an experienced adult who frames, selects, focuses, and feeds back an environmental experience in a way that creates appropriate learning sets. This is accomplished through the stressing or focusing on certain sets which of necessity restrict the field and enable intentional learning processes. Mediation includes orientation, labeling, framing, reevocation, comparison, and selection, all prerequisite to independent use of environmental stimuli and all sensitizing the learner to nonmediated learning.

The focus of this research is concerned with overcoming the difficulties in the task of evaluating the culturally different and the socioeconomically disadvantaged, deprived child. Feuerstein notes that an interpretation of retarded performance which emphasizes sociocultural and other environmental factors will lead to an *active modifiable approach* in contrast to the traditional approach, classified as the *passive-acceptant* approach, which accepts the phenomenon of retarded performance as a fixed and unchangeable condition. The Feuerstein team conceives the development of limited cognitive skill as resulting from inappropriate quality and quantity of the child's interactive experiences with his social environment. In other words, the child has not experienced adequate mediated learning experience, which is essential to favorable cognitive development.

This Israeli team of researchers considers poor performance on IQ tests a reflection of the wide array of cognitive deficiencies characteristic of the culturally deprived. These deficiencies are present not because of genetic lack but because they have not been stimulated in development or have been arrested or impaired. To facilitate cognitive development in children from deprived cultures, this research team suggests that assessment of the retarded performer be made dynamically, that is, in the act of learning and of being taught rather than through the traditional static methods of testing. Through this dynamic evaluation process more precise assessment can be made, which in turn permits more precise prescriptions for learning. The technique developed by this team is called the *learning potential assessment device.*

The learning potential assessment device is composed of problems patterned on Raven's matrices, which are content free yet require for solution such processes as figural analysis, logical evidence, precision in perception, and spontaneous comparative skills.

Through the use of the LPAD as a diagnostic device supplemented by mediation of the critical processes in each task (orientation, labeling, reevocation, comparison, selection, etc.) by an experienced adult, those cognitive skills are facilitated in which culturally deprived children are weak. These weaknesses include blurred and sweeping perceptions, impulsive exploratory behavior, lack of receptive verbal tools, lack of orientation with respect to space, time, size, shape, quantity, lack of precision in data gathering, limited skill in organizing ideas, treating each discretely, in isolate fashion, limited ability to select relevant cues in a given problem situation, episodic grasp of reality, lack of the need for logical evidence, inadequate internalization of solutions to problems, limited inferential hypothetical (i.e., "if-then") thinking, toleration for imprecision, lack of meaningful verbal connotations resulting in insufficient verbal feedback, retardation in perceptual (visual) and auditory skills, and understimulated memory function (Feuerstein et al., 1972, Vol. 1).

This ongoing research in Israel promises to provide critical approaches to teaching/learning/assessment which can prevent cognitive lags from developing and can facilitate assessment and repair of demonstrable lags in masses of deprived child populations.

Staff Training in Use of LPAD

Implicit in the use of the LPAD is the training of teachers and other mature adults (parents and paraprofessionals) in the administration of the tasks, in the cognitive skills demanded by the problems presented, and in the methods of mediating these processes and skills. The staff members are trained to model with precision, intentionally and meaningfully, so that the children, the learners, can grasp the processes cognitively and translate or transfer them to an ever wider variety of problems. This method holds great promise for socioculturally deprived learners but may have limited usefulness with children who are differentially diagnosed "mentally retarded."

MINIMAL BRAIN DAMAGE

In recent years there has been a remarkable increase in the numbers of children referred to school psychologists for testing to verify suspected brain damage as observed by teachers and guidance counselors. The referral slips generally state suspected brain damage along with descriptive remarks of behavior such as short attention span, hyperactive, explosive, emotionally immature, touchy, on a trigger, frequent tantrums, hits other children, doesn't do assigned written work. The referral slip also contains a request to the psychologist for referral of the child to a class for brain damaged (BD), if there is such a classroom available in the school system, or for placement in a room for educable mental retardates EMR if no BD class is available. Implicit in such requests is the assumption that the child with BD is more like the child with mental retardation than like the normal child in response to the demands of the school situation. The facts indicate that the BD and MR children are very different in their reactions to stimuli, the BD child needing minimal stimuli to facilitate his attendance to the situation at hand, whereas the MR child needs a great deal of stimulation to facilitate his attention to the situation at hand. Consequently the classroom milieus and teaching methods essential to learning in BD children are very different from the milieus and teaching methods that facilitate learning in MR children. There is often a hidden motive in the recommendation for placement of the BD child in a special class—removal of the child from the classroom for the comfort and convenience of the teacher.

Diagnosing for Brain Damage

Frequently the psychologist operating within the regularities of the school system administers a Bender and a DAP, examines the performances of the child for signs of brain injury, and offers verification of the diagnostic impression made by the teacher or the guidance counselor. This approach to evaluation of brain injury has little merit, since the most frequent signs of brain injury in children are also signs of emotional disturbance or immature development in the perceptual motor area. To make a differential diagnosis of brain injury with a fairly high degree of validity the psychologist would do well to familiarize himself or herself with the published work of Straus, Lehtinen, and Kephart (Straus & Lehtinen, 1947, 1950; Straus & Kephart, 1955) and with the monograph by Lewis, Straus and Lehtinen (1951) on behavioral characteristics, diagnostic instruments, and management of the brain damaged child.

Differential diagnosis of minimal brain damage by the psychologist calls not only for a fitting test battery but also for focused observational samplings of behavior at home and in the school, playground, neighborhood and the testing situation. (Of course neurological study and an EEG are essential to a definitive diagnosis.) Observational data need to be operationally defined in the critical areas of function: perceptual, conceptual, language, and behavior. Recording observations categorically, such as distractible, irritable, explosive, emotional, aggressive, disruptive, constant movement, stubborn, resistive, is neither meaningful nor helpful, since such behaviors also may characterize an emotionally disturbed child, a behavior problem child, an immature child, or a child experiencing situational threat.

On the perceptual level the brain injured child has difficulty integrating parts into a whole configuration and separating figure from ground. All stimuli have equal valence for him so that he is unable to process, select, and relate critical stimuli in a given task or situation. Often he fixates on a detail like "hairpin" rather than hairdo, "button" rather than coat, "brick" rather than wall (Lewis et al., 1951). This difficulty often is classified as short attention span. Actually the attention of the BD child is attracted to all stimuli in the situation and those extraneous to it including auditory, tactile, thermal, olfactory, and kinesthetic, so that as he fixes on everything he actually fixes on nothing. To gain and hold his attention to a task at hand it is necessary to reduce the possibilities of distraction to absolute minimal essentials, keeping the objects extraneous to the task at hand to a minimum, for example, the colors on the walls, floors, blackboards, bulletin boards, as well as noises.

The brain injured child has difficulty ordering details into meaningful patterns so needs structured tasks if he is to learn to function appropriately and effectively. He becomes confused and threatened by sudden changes, by the unexpected, by surprises, so such events need to be kept at a minimum for this type of child. This child has difficulty shifting his attention from one set of circumstances to another, as is required in testing situations at school and in classroom assignments in elementary grades. Overwhelmed by the changing stimulus situations, he frequently will respond to a new situation with a response that was adequate in a previous situation which has a similar detail in it. Perseveration, which this behavior is called, is generally readily recognized by the psychologist in a testing situation and noted as suggestive of brain damage, but perseverating behavior in the playground, at home, in the classroom is not recognized by teachers, parents, peers, or neighbors as a helpless response of a brain injured child. Instead it is viewed as resistance, indolence, negativism, or stupid, infantile, and arbitrary, intended to provoke others. In such cases the child is chastised in one way or another, treatment that compounds the child's dilemma.

Psychological testing of children suspected of brain injury usually involves a test battery that seeks to tap perceptual motor coordination skills, perceptual differentiation, receptive and expressive language, short term memory, emotional controls, and social adaptation skills. The test battery generally used in schools includes an intelligence test (Binet or WISC), the Bender Gestalt, the Human Figure Drawing, Porteus mazes, at times supplemented with the Benton Visual Retention Test and the Marble Form Board Test (Straus & Kephart, 1955). In recent years some psychologists have added the Wide Range Achievement Test (WRAT) and the Illinois Test of Psycholinguistic Abilities (ITPA) to the test battery.

Research on Contributions of Diagnostic Test Battery

The contributions of these tests to the identification of brain injury to 1955 is reviewed by Straus and Kephart (1955). The literature on test signs of brain injury in children since that time has been reviewed by Koppitz (1964, 1968), with special reference to the Bender and the HFD, and by Tolor and Schulberg (1963) with special reference to the Bender. These sources provide test performance clues to brain injury. Making a differential diagnosis of brain injury on the basis of these tests is a challenging clinical task since no one clue to brain injury appears in the performances of all brain injured children tested. The Marble Form Board Test, used more frequently in clinics than in school settings, does appear to be discriminating (Straus & Lehtinen, 1947, 1950; Straus & Kephart, 1955) when it elicits two incoherent patterns which rarely appear in the performances of nonbrain injured children.

Koppitz has identified on her developmental scale 11 items that appear significantly more often in drawings of (BD) children than in drawings of non-BD children. However, it is important to bear in mind that Koppitz' findings are based on group studies, so the use of her diagnostic signs of BD must be applied with caution to an individual child. Dependence on organic test signs in the evaluation of individual children may identify both false positives and false negatives.

An example of a false negative BD is the case of Sandy, age 7 years, 3 months. He was neurologically identified as brain damaged and placed on Dexadrine. His home and school behaviors were classically characteristic of the brain damaged child, yet his HFD in no way resembled the "characteristic" drawings of brain damaged children. On the basis of the HFD he would have been identified as a false negative. In contrast is Eddie, age 6 years, 9 months. (Both Sandy and Eddie scored in the superior level on the WISC.) Eddie's HFD was replete with Koppitz "organic" signs but the EEG was negative, as were the other tests in the battery. Eddie would be a false positive in diagnosing for BD. Differential analysis of the entire test battery supplemented with developmental, medical, and social history and behavioral observations at home and school indicated that Eddie suffered profound dependency frustrations in relation to the father figure. The father was "forced" out of the home a year before testing was done and Eddie had not been allowed to visit him throughout that year to the time of testing. Eddie's mother "feared father's bad influence on Eddie." Obviously interventions for Eddie and for Sandy were very different.

In an effort to determine whether the Bender Gestalt in whole or part can differentiate BD from non-BD children aged 5–10, and whether age and intelligence are critical factors in such differentiation, Koppitz conducted a study involving two groups of children, one BD sample as determined by neurological, medical, birth, and developmental histories, and one group of non-BD children. The two samples were matched for IQ, age, sex, and socioeconomic backgrounds and the children were predominantly in attendance at the same schools. Koppitz' findings were equivocal. She cautions wisely that a valid "diagnosis" of brain damage, or, better yet, the development of a diagnostic hypothesis when testing children for BD, requires consideration of test results in combination with birth, developmental, medical, health, and accident histories and various family factors critical to child development and behavior. In short, diagnosis of brain damage in a child cannot be made by test signs or behavior alone or by these two approaches in combination. The histories of the child, the family patterns, and events must also be taken into account along with neurological and behavioral studies.

In spite of the complexity of this diagnostic task, school psychologists are faced with such tasks daily and are expected to produce answers on demand.

Task Analysis for Staff Training

In analyzing diagnostic procedures for identifying brain injured children, the psychologist not only needs to define the discrete aspects of psychological testing to determine which aspects to turn over to trained subdoctoral staff, but he must define also the dimensions of behaviors that are critical indices to brain damage in children and train subdoctoral staff in observations of these behaviors and manner of recording the observed behaviors operationally. In this situation the psychologist must also inform parents of the essential needs of the child for simple, structured home milieu and activities and train the parents in observation methods and accurate operational recordings of behavioral progress. Essential facts and knowledges about the behavior and reactions of such children need to be understood by all people involved in working with such children, and all must understand the expected contributions of the interventions in coping with deviant or difficult behaviors, so that interventions are applied meaningfully with understanding and sympathy. Again, differential diagnostic decisions must be the responsibility of the top level psychologist.

EMOTIONALLY DISTURBED CHILDREN

Coping with children with emotional, social, or behavioral disturbances generally calls for the case study approach including detailed studies of the histories (medical, birth, developmental), family constellations, home space, structure, and uses as well as personality studies through projectives as well as observations of behavior in school, neighborhood, and home. Such a clinical approach calls for the skills of an expert clinical psychologist. The psychologist of course must collect data from other school personnel—teachers, social service and special service staff—as well as from parents, siblings, and at times school and neighborhood peers. The expert clinician assumes responsibility for the overall study, diagnostics, and intervention design while subdoctoral staff can be trained in principles and methods of objective and projective testing and in objective scoring systems, when available, so that they may administer and score the test performances, leaving interpretations of the data and synthesis of all data to the expert clinician. Intervention designs can be analyzed into discrete steps and hierarchically arranged so that clearly defined structured aspects can be turned over to trained subdoctoral staff under supervision of the clinician.

The use of subdoctoral staff and paraprofessionals is fairly common practice today when interventions are based on behavior modification principles, techniques, and schedules. As this approach to child treatment becomes the treatment of choice among school psychologists, paraprofessionals will become critical members of the intervention teams. Where dynamic psychotherapy with individual children is the method of choice, the psychologist must again analyze the particular approaches he uses, assuming full responsibility for interpretations and dynamic explorations, turning over to the trained subdoctoral staff responsibility for structured observations, recordings of play sessions, conduct of structured play sessions, and supervision of activity and remedial sessions where these are assigned interventions. Progress reports of observed behaviors can also be made by trained auxiliary staff. However, the psychologist has the ultimate responsibility of critically reviewing the staff reports and determining progress from these combined with clinical observations made on his own. Where interventions call for family therapy, the trained aide can serve to record interactions, "play a role" in a psychodrama, serve as a role model in some situations, keep records, record appointments and contact any agencies that are involved with the family when their cooperation is needed to facilitate progress.

NEW TARGET POPULATIONS

In dealing with the new target populations noted earlier, the psychologist is confronted with so many subjects at one time and with such urgent problems of emergency proportions that few considerations have been given to the use of diagnostic testing as a first approach to coping with such problems. The urgent nature of these emerging problem target populations has forced direct action interventions. School psychologists have joined other professionals and laymen in launching group modality programs intended to dissuade children and high school students from their destructive behaviors such as drug addiction, delinquency, violent rebellion, and disruptive behaviors in school and community. School dropouts or potential dropouts have been persuaded to remain in school by a few psychologists with the help of paraprofessional aides through behavior modification, commitment, and reality group therapy methods. Confrontation methods like those employed at Synanon have been tried with school children and high school students with little benefit. Although these group approaches seem to be effective in the Synanon settings, they do not work in public school settings. Perhaps their failure in school settings is due to the fact that school programs do not offer the fully structured controlled milieu offered in Synanon residence facilities. The failure of these school efforts with drug addicted children was recently reported by the New York State Commissioner of Education (Nyquist, 1972). He noted that after all the efforts to cope with these problems, about 45% of today's high school students are on drugs, and 20% of the junior high school students are addicted. The report also notes that little change has been made in the percentage of school dropouts, in the lags in basic school skills, and in violence and rebellion; furthermore, gifted children generally are being ignored, so that their talents dry up and they give up trying, joining their peers in the dangerous destructive patterns noted previously. In other words, seeking to cope with dangerous disruptive problems of epidemic proportions in the school population through group modalities appears to be futile in the school setting and the open community, although some of the group procedures do seem to work in closed settings. It is likely that these group methods fail for still other reasons beyond the open school structure and its limited controls, such as poorly equipped leaders and group methods that are inappropriate to the target population needs, having been applied for arbitrary reasons, on the basis that any group approach is better than none, rather than on sound principles of behavior change.

Drug Addiction in School Children

What can psychologists contribute to solving these overwhelming problems among school children? First they might consider setting up in the school the equivalent of the hot line used in the open community and the universities and maintain a walk-in clinic manned by trained counselors (professional if available or mature paraprofessionals with training). Furthermore and of utmost importance, psychologists must become fully acquainted with the early signs of drug involvement, in children at all school levels, so that such children can be identified and treated early, before they become trapped by addiction. A network to identify early signs of addiction can be set up and maintained by training school staff, students, parents, and community groups to recognize early signs of involvement or signs of vulnerability. Ultimately psychologists must return to their special instruments and skills, to diagnostic tests, seeking to identify personality variables that are common to drug addiction. If such a syndrome can be identified, then nonaddicted children can be tested diagnostically and vulnerable children identified before they become involved. Interventions then may be designed to counteract these dispositions.

It is likely that such diagnostic clues would now be available for use had psychologists not scrapped their professional diagnostic testing procedures for the panacea of "group treatment modalities" over the past decade. This diagnostic approach calls for extensive and intensive research, which in turn calls for a large number of research staff, a lot of time, facilities for the research, and of course funding. Government funds have been made available for all types of remedial, compensatory, and experimental educational and mental health programs. Such funds often are dissipated by programs arbitrarily designed and applied. Perhaps such funds should be assigned discriminately to psychological experts with research skills who are committed to scientifically based approaches to exploring the epidemic proportions of drug addiction afflicting the masses of our child populations.

Operation Future

One research project using a group survey approach to drug abuse control was recently reported by the director of Operation Future, a program ongoing in California (Clark, 1972). This research team hypothesized that an individual with a weak system of personal values will abuse drugs. Further, this team hypothesized that if these values are strengthened, a reduction in drug abuse would occur.

Since sets of values vary from culture to culture, the members of the research team avoided the task of defining desirable values. Instead they identified certain character traits that, when exhibited frequently, indicate a lack of personal values. These negative character traits are apathy, uncertainty, flightiness, drifting, role playing, dissension, inconsistency, and overconformity.

Selecting a pilot study group of 851 school age children in grades 5 to 10, they administered two simple survey questionnaires, one asking the children to list the frequency of their use of nonprescribed drugs, the other asking them to indicate the frequency with which they felt apathetic, uncertain, and the six other traits. Coefficients of correlation between use of nonprescribed drugs and the negative traits averaged .95. Next they exposed these school children to a 5 month period of detailed experience with self-actualization or value clarification activities, repeating the testing procedures at the end of the training period. Results were highly encouraging. All groups of school children reduced their drug intake. In some cases the reduction was dramatic. On the basis of this study the researchers conclude that drug abuse can be prevented through value clarification as the psychological method.

This research is continuing in efforts to answer other critical questions such as Are there drugs of abuse that correlate with particular character traits? Is there an optimum time that value clarification training will prove most effective? Is there any correlation between traits and juvenile crime—and if so which ones? Why do certain traits appear at certain chronological ages and not at others? (Clark, 1972). If successful, these studies will provide useful clues for preventing and eliminating drug addiction among school children, but such hope is limited unless similar personality research explorations are multiplied tenfold.

SUMMARY

To recapitulate, psychologists in the schools are overwhelmed by the variety of target populations confronting them, populations in urgent need of psychological services over and beyond the need of the traditional child targets. Presumably psychologists in the schools are trained to cope with the traditional target populations such as mentally retarded, brain injured, gifted, emotional, social and behavior disturbances. but limits of time, staff, and facilities prevent them from coping even with these populations in a discriminating, effective manner. Obviously there is a need for many trained auxiliary staff to carry some of the simpler discretely defined testing and intervention procedures to release the psychologists to provide the complex professional services involved in differential diagnostic testing, designing interventions appropriate to each type of target, writing individualized prescriptions, and carrying on research, staff training, supervision, and consultation.

Psychologists now confronted with the challenges presented by the new target populations have scrapped their professional approaches, that is, diagnostic testing and case studies, and have joined the public in enthusiastic support of a large variety of group approaches to the treatment of these psychological epidemics. Evidence has been released attesting to the futility of these global approaches to the awesome problems affecting our youth and society today. It is essential that psychologists return to their diagnostic instruments and procedures, to explore the dynamics and milieu conditions underlying the problems of the new targets and the conditions precipitating the development of these problems in children and youth. Perhaps then psychologists could design interventions to reverse the processes and prevent them.

To permit such widescale testing and treatment of multitudes of children psychologists must analyze the discrete steps in each process used, ranking these steps in terms of complexity and assigning them hierarchically to subdoctoral and paraprofessional staff, properly trained in short term programs to cope with these discrete skills under professional supervision. Psychologists must also study the proposed changes in school and community organization and programs to determine whether these programs are based on sound behavioral, learning, developmental, and interrelational principles and provide guidelines where needed.

These critical contributions to the school and community problems can be made only if psychologists are committed to diagnostic research approaches to the ailments afflicting our children and if they are given the essential cooperation from school administration and staff, parents, and community and government leaders. Obviously psychologists undertaking such extensive studies of the burgeoning problems must be ready to acknowledge the limits of their critical skills and be ready to consult colleagues expert in the essential skills they themselves lack or have not fully mastered.

REFERENCES

Apgar, V. (ed.) Down's Syndrome: (Mongolism). *Annals of the New York Academy of Sciences,* 1970, *2,* 303–688.

Bender, L. A Visual Motor Gestalt Test and its Clinical Use. *Research Monograph 3, American Journal of Orthopsychiatry,* New York, 1938.

Benton, A. *The Revised Visual Retention Test,* 3rd ed. New York: The Psychology Corp., 1963.

Clark, J. *A Kings-Tulare Drug Abuse Control Project. Drug Abuse Can Be Prevented.* Visalia, Calif.: Operation Future, 1972.

Cole, M. & Bruner, J. Cultural Differences and Inferences about Psychological Processes. *American Psychologist,* 1971, *26,* 867–786.

Feuerstein, R., Shalon, H., Hoffman, M., Kiram, L., Narrol, H., Schachter, E., Katz, D., & Rand, Y. *Studies in Cognitive Modifiability: The Dynamic Assessment of Retarded Performers: The Learning Potential Assessment Device, Theory, Instruments and Techniques,* 2 vols. Jerusalem: Hadassah Wizo Canada Res. Institute, 1972.

Gottsegen, M. & Gottsegen, G. (eds.) *Professional School Psychology,* Vol. 3. New York: Grune and Stratton, 1969.

Jastak, J. A Rigorous Criterion of Feeblemindedness. *Journal of Abnormal and Social Psychology, 1949,* 44.

Koppitz, E. *The Bender Gestalt Test for Young Children.* New York: Grune and Stratton, 1964.

Koppitz, E. *Psychological Evaluations of Human Figure Drawings.* New York: Grune and Stratton, 1968.

Lewis, R. S., Strauss, A. & Lehtinen, L. *The Other Child.* New York: Grune and Stratton, 1951.

Masland, R. L., Sarason, S. & Gladwin, T. *Mental Subnormality.* New York: Basic Books, 1958.

Nyquist, E. B. Master's Level Programs Hit by State as Product of "Collusive Mediocrity." *NYSPA Newsletter,* 1972, *24,* 1–9.

Rosenthal, R. & Jacobson, L. *Pygmalion in the Classroom.* New York: Holt, Rinehart and Winston, 1968.

Straus, A. & Kephart, N. *The Brain Injured Child,* Vol. 2. New York: Grune and Stratton, 1955.

Straus, A. & Lehtinen, L. *The Brain Injured Child.* New York: Grune and Stratton, 1947.

Straus, A. & Lehtinen, L. *The Brain Injured Child.* New York: Grune and Stratton, 1950.

Thomas, A., Hertzig, M., Dryman, I. & Fernandez, P. Examiner Effect in IQ Testing of Puerto Rican Working Class Children. *American Journal of Orthopsychiatry,* 1971, *41,* 809–821.

Tolor, A. & Schulberg, H. *An Evaluation of the Bender-Gestalt Test.* Springfield, Ill.: Charles C. Thomas, 1963.

Wechsler, D. *Wechsler Intelligence Scale for Children.* New York: The Psychology Corp., 1949.

Zigler, E. & Butterfield, E. Motivational Aspects of IQ Test Performance of Culturally Deprived Nursery School Children. *American Journal of Orthopsychiatry,* 1968, *34,* 1–14.

Zimmerman, I. & Woo-Sam, J. Research with the WISC: 1960–1970. *Psychology in the Schools (special monograph supplement),* 9/3, 1972.

CHAPTER 8

Gifted Children in the Schools: Targets

In the United States of the 1960s educators concentrated on efforts to change the schools to meet the learning needs of retarded learners, leaving gifted children in public schools pretty much to their own devices to cope with the challenges of their school experiences. Indifference to the special needs of the gifted not only traumatizes and penalizes these children but also denies society the benefits gifted children can contribute to social progress if their talents are appropriately cultivated.

The inclusion of gifted children in the category of exceptional children along with mentally retarded and brain injured may appear as an inappropriate classification to many, since the gifted are seen as the fortunate "who have what it takes to succeed at school," in contrast to the other

164

two categories of children who in varying degrees lack the essentials to school success under normal teaching and administrative school procedures. However, it is common experience that gifted children, meaning here intellectually gifted as measured by intelligence and aptitude tests, are often resented by their classmates, who assign to the gifted in their midst nicknames they consider derogatory, such as Einstein, brain, bookworm, egghead, greasy grind (Raph et al, 1966).

Many gifted children, needing to be liked and accepted by their peers, unfortunately give up striving and soon become identified as the "underachieving gifted." Others who do not respond to the group pressures, who have high achievement motivation and firm positive self-regard, may continue to strive for achievement in their regular grades but their strivings often go unrewarded. In fact, they are often penalized by the democratic teaching process and philosophy characteristic of most schools which require equality of education for all children in a given classroom, regardless of natural differences in rates of learning and motivations. Under the banner of equal education for all, equal or the same assignments are given to all children in a grade class, so that many gifted children highly motivated to learn at their own speed are discouraged and frustrated by the slow pace set in the regular classroom, a pace that caters to the needs of slow learners.

In short, whether the gifted child gives up striving for achievement in order to be liked by his peers or whether he is cut to size by the requirement to "keep down" with the rest of the class, it is apparent that the gifted child is a misfit in a regular classroom and as such may be seriously traumatized by continued exposure to the restrictions of the regular classroom. To facilitate optimal development of the gifted child, he needs special educational programs, teaching, and learning opportunities, as much as do the children with learning deficits.

GIFTED UNDERACHIEVERS

Interest in the gifted child was stimulated in the United States in the 1920s with the publication of Terman's *Genetic Studies of Genius* (1925). This study revealed in no uncertain terms that the popular conception of the gifted as psychically and sensorially weak was false. The Terman studies revealed the opposite fact, that intellectually gifted children are actually superior physically, sensorially, and socially and are emotionally more mature than the average (Terman & Oden, 1947, p. 452). Terman is also responsible for calling widespread attention and stimulating widespread interest in the phenomenon of underachieving gifted children, for in the followup study of his original gifted children (1947) he discovered that many of those children functioned at or below average at college, dropped out of college after two years, or flunked out of college. Since this publication, extensive research efforts have been invested in studies of underachievement of gifted children in efforts to find the "causes" of underachievement (Raph et al., 1966; Getzels & Jackson, 1962; McClelland et al., 1958).

Review of the research on underachievers by Raph et al. reveals that self-concept attitudes of gifted children were significant factors in underachievement, that is, when the self-concept is poor, gifted children do not achieve to potential. Parent attitudes and ethnic values also interfere with full development of gifted potential (McClelland et al., 1958). Studies of various groupings for teaching did not provide consistent results with underachievers (Raph et al., 1966). A study conducted by this writer in 1960–1963 (Fein, 1963) on the relationship of anxiety as measured by the IPAT Anxiety Scale (Cattell, 1961) to achievement at nursing school revealed a curvilinear relationship between IPAT anxiety and school achievement, that is, very high and very low anxiety levels operate against academic achievement, despite IQ scores. A second study by this

writer, seeking to identify factors operative in the high
dropout rate among nursing school students (50% dropout rates were common in the late 1950s and early 1960s)
(Fein, 1968), revealed no relationship between intelligence
level and school dropout rate. The factors that were significantly related to dropout from nursing school included very
high or very low anxiety levels as measured by the IPAT
Anxiety Scale, very severe feelings of maladjustment (scores
over 155) as measured by the Rotter Incomplete Sentence
Stems (Rotter, 1950), profound dependency needs in either
structured or unstructured (or both) settings as measured by
the Fein Dependency Scales (Fein, 1960, 1968), rejection
of the self-image or denial of body problems as measured
by the Fein Self Image Scales (Fein, 1960, 1968), denial of
personal associations to stories told to the Testing of Limits
Productions (Fein, 1968), and undifferentiated, incon-
gruent, conflicted, or confused goals as revealed in responses to the Fein Identity Questions (Fein, 1968, Appendix C). These findings support some of the reported findings
by Raph (1966), notably poor self-concept, incongruence
between self-concept and occupational aspirations, and
feelings of poor adjustment. The fact that in our study students with profound dependency needs dropped out of
school whereas those with age appropriate independence
did not drop out suggests that family attitudes and relationships are critical factors in underachievement and school
dropout, facts identified in studies reported by Raph (Raph
et al., 1966) and McClelland (McClelland et al., 1958) and
their co-workers.

The factors identified above as critical to underachievement are predominantly deep seated personality factors that
generally are not responsive to changes in class groupings
or varying group teaching methods. To change such attitudes that operate for underachievement in bright and
gifted children, it seems essential to use the individual case
study approach combined with teacher and parent coopera-

tion. This method permits development of individual prescriptive interventions to meet the specific needs of each student.

The case study approach with teacher and parent cooperation was used by this writer in an elementary public school in an upper middle socioeconomic area during 1957 and is presented here briefly to demonstrate the program design, procedures used, and results obtained. The rationale underlying this program was that *learning is aggressive* and *underachieving children are passive, defensively* (Fein, 1958).

PRIVILEGED GIFTED UNDERACHIEVERS

A common challenge to the school psychologist servicing upper middle class schools is assisting school staff with ways and means of motivating underachieving gifted children to full use of their learning potentials. Confronted with this challenge by the principal of an eight grade elementary school in a privileged suburban community, I suggested weekly meetings with the staff to orient them to the dynamics of underachievement in gifted children. Further, I proposed to study a few children intensively, clinically, to obtain insights into the factors underlying their passivity with the expectation that the insights derived would serve as guidelines to home and school management to free these children for learning.

With parent approval and agreement to ongoing involvement, four boys were selected for study. The boys were observed in their classrooms, in the playground, in the gym, and on the school grounds before and after school. Their cumulative records were studied as were the guidance counselor's reports and the birth and developmental histories compiled by the social worker. The children were tested with the WISC, DAP, Rorschach, Twitchell-Allen Three Dimensional Personality Test, Fein Testing of Limits Procedures, and the Wide Range Achievement Test. Each child was then seen in weekly therapy sessions at school and their parents were seen twice a month for a three month period. Family sessions were held as need indicated. The school staff was oriented at weekly staff meetings to the thesis that *learning is aggressive* in the following terms.

Learning Is Aggressive *

Only as we understand the dynamics of achievement can we plan to break through the defenses against learning in underachieving gifted children. Learning is aggressive and the underachieving child cannot learn because he is unable to accept his aggressive feelings. He dare not admit he has such feelings, so he must suppress them, deny them, and thus he cannot learn. To effectively inhibit and deny aggressive feelings and urges to action, the child must reduce his actions to minimal essentials As he reduces his actions to the minimal essentials of living, he appears passive and dependent. His energies are consumed by his efforts to control his destructive action urges and so are not available for constructive aggressive action, which is required for school learning.

It is common experience for teachers to ask: Do you *get* my meaning? Do you *get* the point? Do you *grasp* the significance of what I say? Did you *gain* insight? Did you *master* the technique? In each case the words grasp, gain, get, master, imply an aggressive act, suggesting that to learn we must have control over our aggressive urges so that we may direct them into the constructive acts of mastering the learning materials and solving the ever more challenging problems presented by sequentially higher stages of learning.

* Abridged from "Learning is Aggressive," Lëah Gold Fein, in The Gifted Child Quarterly, Vol. 2, 1958. Permission of editor.

The underachieving child has learned to fear his aggressive feelings; he views them as "bad feelings" that must be denied as well as inhibited. *Thus he must first be helped to accept his aggressive urges to action before he can use his aggressive urges in constructive ways.* To accept his aggressive urges to action he must know that his aggressive feelings are acceptable to his significant authority figures, both parents and teachers. This means that the child must feel free to tell the authority how he feels about the authority, about the rules and regulations, about the behavior of peers and siblings, about himself. The child must feel safe when he experiences resentment, hurt, anger, and fears. His safety can derive only from the knowledge that his feelings are not abnormal, that his feelings are natural reactions to threatening or frustrating situations. When he knows that he may tell the authority about these feelings and still be loved and accepted, he will then be ready to learn how to express those feelings in safe and constructive ways and he will be free to learn.

Underachieving children are filled with anxiety about themselves and fear their social environment. They do not know what to do about these anxieties and fears, they dare not move out for fear of bumping into an unseen enemy, so they reduce their actions to a minimum, presenting a passive, dependent, resistive adjustment.

What threatens these children who come from well ordered homes, free of *open* conflict, free of the threats of poverty, free of devastating illnesses, free of violent punishments, free of *open disdain* for social, secular, and religious laws? What threats do children experience in homes that are considered the backbone of society? What hidden threats exist in these fine families that make it necessary for the gifted child to inhibit his aggressive urges to action by regressing to an infantile level of adjustment, to passivity and dependency?

The factors, in such fine families, that are conducive to the development of passive resistance and underachievement are not readily observable, for they are masked by learned, proprietary, stereotyped attitudes and actions. However, close clinical scrutiny of the attitudes and actions of the parents reveals subtle clues to existing conflict, disdain, fears, and anxieties. Parents may differ in attitudes toward child rearing, discipline, expectations, and goals, in values—socioeconomic, social, religious, physical—or one or both of the parents may suffer from personally frustrated goals or from suppressed fears or vague, free-floating anxieties. Still other parents may be working against each other's goals in subtle, furtive ways. These suppressed and denied feelings cause the parents to suffer guilt and tensions which are drained off furtively, in hardly perceptible doses, in their relations to their children and to each other.

These subtle conflicts between parents (usually described by parents laughingly as healthy differences of opinion), these denied, frustrated ambitions in parents, these *suppressed* fears, anxieties, and conflicting goals within and between parents are experienced by the child as mysterious tensions. The child is frightened yet he does not know what he fears. The child's fears are further aggravated by the overprotective and/or overindulgent treatment accorded him by his guilt-laden parents. Overprotection and overindulgence are *not mutually exclusive* behaviors. They are part of one pattern. Both techniques of manipulation are methods of control, both serve to relieve the parent of the responsibility of making judgments about child guidance, both relieve the parent of guilt feelings, both serve to mask fears, anxieties, and aggressions.

Overprotection frustrates a child's natural drive toward attainment and thus fills him with hostile tensions. The child is made to feel worthless, inadequate, helpless, untrustworthy, by overprotective devices. He feels worthless for he is denied the chance to prove his ability, his prowess, his stamina. These denials of opportunity for expression enrage him but he dare not give expression to these feelings; in fact, he dare not tell his parents how he feels for they will tell him that he has no right to feel this way "after all they do for him." This reprimand impresses the child with the fear that if he expresses his feelings of resentment to the parent, the parent will resent him as unappreciative and may stop doing for him, stop protecting him, in short may reject him. The child, needing his parents' acceptance and love, feels guilty about his feelings and begins the process of suppressing and denying his unacceptable feelings. Thus slowly but surely he manages to suppress his aggressive urges to action, limiting himself to passive dependent behavior, conforming to the manipulations of his parents.

It is noteworthy that the parents sincerely feel that they are doing what is best for the child. They manipulate him and control him either by cautions such as You can't do this yet, you are too small! You don't know how, you'll spoil it or spill it! Watch out! Be careful! Don't do that! Look out! Stop it! These and similar vague cautions frighten the child but do not teach the child how to cope with the situations. Parents also may let the child try his hand at the tasks and then interfere with the child's efforts, saying he is too slow, too sloppy, too careless, or they just take over the task, redoing what the child did, improving on the child's efforts, and finishing it, thus indicating their superiority and his inferiority. These parents do not take the time to let the child do what he can within his limited development, nor do they credit what he does at his various developmental levels.

Not only parents but teachers too are often guilty of overprotecting and overindulging children. "Don't tax the child with homework!" is one form of overprotection. The following incident dramatically portrays overindulgence by the school. A young man aged 13 was told that he had to stay after school to make up homework that he had failed to bring in at the required time. He agreed shame-facedly and remained in his seat after the others left the room. When he was alone with the teacher, the teacher said to him: "I hate to do this to you, especially today, when the big league game is on. Suppose we stay after school tomor-

row instead of today so you won't miss the game on TV."
This overindulgence left the boy with conflicted feelings.
He reported to me the next day that he felt insulted because
the teacher considered the game more important than his
need to learn. He felt that the teacher probably doubted his
ability to do the work but didn't want to say so and got
around it by letting him off for the ball game; that adults
are softies; they want "kids" to have a good time instead of
working. He concluded that baseball is more important
than school work.

These two school procedures, no homework and administering punishment when convenient, are not justifiable in
terms of the needs of the children, *rather they are rationali-
zations masking hidden needs and urges of the adults.* No
homework means no extra papers to correct. No punishment when indicated but postponed until convenient reflects rationalized resistance on the part of the teacher to
staying on at school, giving extra time to teaching, time for
which he is not paid.

Overindulgence cheats the child of normal frustrating experiences that are essential to serve as propellers toward
more mature actions and higher goals. Overindulging parents and teachers satisfy infantile whims and appetites of
the child, thus reinforcing a passive dependent adjustment.
The overindulged child, like the overprotected child, wants
to please authority. Discovering that the authority derives
pleasure from overindulging or protecting him, the child
gives up his striving for growth, sits back, passively gorging
himself with overindulgence while the adult beams and the
child sickens. For even as he submits to the overindulgence,
hostilities and resentments rise and fill him so that he is
forced to become ever more passive the better to prevent
his aggressive urges from spilling out.

All goes well until the school and the home are shocked
by the degree of underachievement in the child. The authorities soon find that force, threats, punishments are to no
avail. The more the child is upbraided, the more resistive

he becomes. When he is asked why he does not do his work and why he does not ask for help, he answers: "I don't know. I don't remember. I forget." Here they are, the underachieving children, wanting to achieve but not daring for fear of their own aggressions and rejection by their significant authorities. As they resist action, they feel stupid, unworthy, inadequate.

What can be done to free such children of their feelings of unworthiness, stupidity, and guilt? How can they be helped to regain their self-respect, to free themselves of the passive dependent defenses against their own aggressive urges, so that they can express their aggressions in constructive ways, expressing their needs without fear of ridicule and feeling free to learn, to move out, to grasp meanings and master skills?

Freeing Bright Underachievers for Learning

As indicated earlier four children were selected for special study to obtain insights into the factors underlying their passivity and underachievement in school. Analysis of the case studies revealed some common factors and dynamics, personal, interpersonal, and intrafamilial. The four children selected were all boys, since there were many more gifted underachieving boys in this school than girls, a phenomenon reported in most studies on gifted underachievers.

The presenting problem in each case, as defined by the teachers, was "underachieving, day dreamer, detached, indifferent, pleasant, smiling, hypersensitive, shy." RM was 10 years old in fourth grade, the elder of the two boys in a family where the father was a high school teacher and the mother managed a summer camp training horseback riders. TE was an 11 year old boy in the sixth grade, the elder of two boys in a family where the father and mother came from Holland some years back and were developing a business, "hopefully to gain a monopoly in the field," said mother. MG was a 12 year old boy in the seventh grade, the second eldest of four siblings in a family where the father inherited great wealth, which freed the father and mother for extensive traveling, leaving the care of the children to servants. GF was a 14 year old boy in the eighth grade, the younger of two boys in a family where the father and mother came from Germany. They were developing a business "to get rich quick," boasted the mother.

Although all four sets of parents presented smiling, gracious facades and spoke in tempered tones to the school staff, to neighbors, and to members of the community with whom they had contact, in confidential conference they all revealed underlying hostilities toward others. RM's parents maintained a truce in an armed camp, each striving for attainment of his personal ambitions, the father for a Ph.D. degree and the mother for her camp, even as each "laughingly" claimed interest in the other's ambitions. TE's parents harbored furtive disdain for democratic ideals and institutions including the school and school staff, cautiously guarding against exposing these feelings in public but indulging these attitudes in the privacy of their home, in the presence of their boys. MG's parents gave lip service to the virtues of work and democracy when in public but expressed open disdain for democracy and work in the privacy of their home, in the presence of their children. Their disdain and ridicule were expressed in laughing tones, as if the laughter softened the impact of their aggressions. GF's parents harbored hostility toward their neighbors, "who had no respect for their property," toward the school where their boy was mistreated "because he came from German parents," toward the police "who did not protect them" from the intrusions of the neighbor's children in their yard or lawn. GF's parents harbored suppressed fears and guilt developed during their experience in Hitler Germany. Their guilt stemmed from their failure to assist Jewish neighbors when the Gestapo came for these people. Their fears stemmed from the ever present threat of being accused of helping the enemy of the German state.

In all four families *overprotection, overcontrol, and/or overindulgence* characterized the patterns of socialization, defined and implemented for the most part by the mothers. Thus RM's mother dressed him in the same type of clothes as his brother on the premise that "it is simpler to pretend to have one child, for then you buy one set of clothes and order a larger size for the older child." RM had to play with his brother in the family yard, no other children were allowed into the yard; the boys played with the same toys, neither was allowed "to own private property," explained the mother. Both boys were bathed together and had to be in bed at 7:30 PM. This mother brooked no deviations and called on the father to punish the boys if they deviated in any of her limits. She was proud of her rigid organization, of her "tight ship" at home and her efficiency. RM did not dare resist his mother's orders, limits, directions. He gave up his strivings for maturity, assumed a passive conforming role, releasing his aggressive urges only for absolute minimal essentials.

TE's mother also ran a tight ship. The boys shared a bedroom while the mother and father used the third bedroom as their private sitting room from which the boys were barred. The boys got to bed at 8 PM; they played in their yard together; no neighbors were allowed in "because the neighbors have no respect for property and use dirty language and the parents are low level socially." The children remained in the yard until their mother called them for supper. When they came in they left their shoes in the hall, a Dutch custom. The boys were expected to be clean at all times in case their mother wished to take them along shopping; also this saved her the extra work of washing and pressing clothes. Their father did not mix in the upbringing of the boys, explaining "laughingly" that this is a mother's job. The overcontrolling pattern in this household is clearly apparent. TE like RM dared not deviate from his mother's established routines and limits and dared not reveal his feelings under these restrictions. He, like RM, assumed a passive conforming role releasing his energies only for absolute minimal action essentials.

MG's parents were overindulgent and overcontrolling to an extreme degree. The children were encouraged to drink as much milk as they wished, in fact to drink milk rather than water when they were thirsty. MG consumed four quarts of milk each day. This mother served a variety of home baked pies at each dinner, urging the children to eat to their heart's content. MG accommodated her by consuming the equivalent of a full pie each night at dinner. He was allowed to go to the movies after school and weekends and to spend his allowance of $10 a week any way he chose. On the other hand, MG and his siblings were not allowed to play actively on the family grounds because "they might injure mother's magnificent flowers," which her gardener nurtured for flower shows. MG was in bed at 8 PM along with his two younger siblings, aged 9 years. He was not allowed to mow the lawn "because he is careless, doesn't do a good job," said his father; he was not allowed to use the tool shop in the basement for the same reasons. (Furtively MG mowed lawns for neighbors, earning $6 weekly, and helped a bicycle repair shop owner, free of charge.) MG felt stupid, unworthy, distorted, and unloved, complaining that his parents wanted him to lose weight and ridiculed his large size, yet urged him to eat all kinds of fattening foods. MG conformed to his parents' expectations and limits, assuming a passive dependent role to retain their affection and protection.

GF's parents imposed rigid controls over GF, expecting him to be in bed by 8 PM, assigning him to the attic room while they maintained the third bedroom on the second floor for their own comfort. GF was not allowed to work in the factory in spite of his fine technical skills, "because he might spoil something"; he was limited to his own backyard and required to come into the house if the neighbor children engaged him in conversation. The urge for quick wealth was so intense in this set of parents that the mother baby sat for families living at some distance from their home. In spite of her rigid rule that GF be in bed by 8 PM every night, she took him along when she baby sat for others, keeping him up until midnight and at times into the early morning hours, without any apparent guilt over this manipulation of GF. GF responded to these rigid controls and manipulations by withdrawal from contact, assuming a passive, conforming dependent role characteristic of a young child. He was completely obedient so that his parents described him as "a wonderful boy, so good, we never have to punish him." Little were they aware of the grandiose destructive fantasies GF indulged as he quietly lived up to their rigid limits and accepted their arbitrariness.

Therapeutic Strategy

Intervention designs were based on the premise that the boys developed passive dependent conforming patterns of behavior in defense against their frustrated aggressions generated by the rigid controls set by their parents, by the arbitrary indulgences, and by the confused standards, values, and goals engendered by the contradictions between the parents' overt and covert behaviors and attitudes.

It was postulated that these dependent passive adjustments could be dissipated and the boys could be released for learning by a program that was based on clearly defined standards, values, limits, activities, and goals suited to the age and development of the boys and by freedom to express their honest feelings in safe ways.

Beginning in the home setting the boys were given differential treatment in terms of their age and developmental level in all areas of function, such as food, bed time, play time, play areas, peer relations, and responsibilities. Reasoned and clearly defined limits were set up with the help of each boy in terms of where, when, how, and what to study, play, and do chores; in terms of cleanliness and privacy. Within these limits each was given freedom to try his abilities and test his own judgments. Goals were set high enough to develop a degree of frustration that could be relieved through attainment, which was within reach with a little extra effort. Daily sessions of homework were set up for each boy under tutelage of his father. The schools cooperated by assigning homework to be returned to school the next morning, when the teacher was to review and correct it in the boy's presence. Teachers were informed that the boys needed firmness but kindness; that the boys were to be kept after school if they did not finish class work during class period. Parents and teachers were helped to understand the needs of the boys to express their feelings about directives, orders, assignments, and restrictions and to respect the boys' views and suggestions for change, and where indicated to institute suggested changes. Parents were helped to understand the destructive impact of their furtive disdain for neighbors, school, and democratic institutions on the character development and behaviors of their children.

Structured programs for each day of the week were prepared by the writer with the help of each boy and were submitted to the parents and teachers for approval and acceptance, since full cooperation by both types of authority was needed to carry the plans through effectively. The boys, protected by the well defined limits and standards of these programs, were freed to function independently and released for aggressive attacks on their school work.

Teacher reports at end of three months found all the boys doing good work in school, gaining mastery of their school subjects and skills, relating well to their school peers, participating in the physical activities at school. All were well on their way to using their fine potentials for success at school. The parents of these boys worked hard to help the boys grow toward their potentials, as difficult as this challenge was for them.

DISADVANTAGED GIFTED UNDERACHIEVERS

Disadvantaged gifted children cannot be treated by the case study approach as a general rule, since parents in disadvantaged situations are too burdened with the overwhelming challenges of supporting the basic essentials of life to spare time, energy, and attention for the benefit of one child in the family. Educational programs to facilitate the unique development of disadvantaged gifted children have not been too successful, as evidenced in the report by Witt (1965) on the results of LEAP (the Life Enrichment Activity Program), a program he conducted in Hamden, Connecticut. Witt reports that "we had nothing but trouble at first. The kids teased and berated each other." He reported that one little girl looked at her reflection in the mirror the first day and said: "You're nothin' and nobody, and you're always gonna be nothin' and nobody." In a review of the LEAP program in 1967, Golden noted that most of the 16 children originally selected for the program had dropped out. As LEAP continued, Witt recognized that these children need the support of a stable creative family to facilitate their efforts to use their fine potentials through the special school program provided them. Accordingly he sought out creative families to sponsor each child, with the result that many exciting and worthwhile outcomes were attained. The use of creative sponsors (as parent surrogates) for gifted disadvantaged children is now spreading to many metropolitan areas of the nation. In New York City, members of the Avon Corporation and the Gift Industry are serving as sponsors to selected gifted children from Harlem (personal communications). Although this approach is effective, it does not scratch the surface in terms of the numbers of gifted children that are lost in the disadvantaged segments of our society. Torrance notes (1968) that "there are many problems involved in implementing implications concerning creatively disadvantaged children. There are many problems of identification." Gowan (1968) notes that several significant issues must be studied before we can help the disadvantaged gifted fulfill their creative potentials: How do we determine that these children are really gifted? Do disadvantaged gifted differ from other gifted children? At what age is intervention most effective in reversing the deficiencies imposed by the erosion of the deprived experiences? In short, research is needed to help the disadvantaged gifted children develop fully their talents and creative potentials.

The few efforts to provide enrichment for gifted children in New York City inner schools during the past several years were of limited value, since the designs of these programs ignored the dynamic factors that prevent gifted children (advantaged and disadvantaged) from profiting from enriched curricula. Designs for facilitating learning in the gifted must include psychological along with educational considerations. Psychodiagnostic testing needs to be included in such programs to provide guidelines to learning interventions and to the types of behavioral, milieu, home, school, and larger community modifications needed to motivate each gifted child in his unique way toward his highest potentials.

The psychologist in the schools faces a critical challenge as he tries to cope with this target population, the gifted, especially the disadvantaged. Gifted children "have more talent to reward society if it nurtures them, and more to oppose society if it neglects them" (Gowan, 1968). *We dare not neglect them.*

SUMMARY

In the last two chapters an effort was made to analyze the dilemma confronting the psychologist in the schools over and beyond the challenges presented by the educational innovations and the masses of retarded learners. Psychologists in the schools are still expected to provide stereotyped services to the traditional target populations—the exceptional children—even as they are expected to provide diagnostic judgments and design interventions for new types of target populations including drug addiction, violence and rebellion, and school dropouts.

Psychologists have tried various group approaches to many of the epidemic problems afflicting the child populations, but these methods have failed to turn the tide. It was suggested that psychologists return to their specialized skills of differential diagnostics and case study methods to identify the dimensions of the various behavioral syndromes of these target populations and facilitate intervention designs that would reverse the malignant trends in these children. It was also suggested that psychologists must train paraprofessional aides who can provide the simple mundane services to these target populations, freeing the top level psychologists for diagnostic designs and decisions, development of intervention designs, and evaluative procedures along with supervision of the paraprofessionals. Special consideration was given to means of coping effectively with mentally retarded, brain injured, educationally retarded, and gifted children.

The following two chapters focus on behavior modification approaches to coping with behavior and learning problems in the classroom, methods that can further facilitate psychological services to critical child target populations through cooperation of teachers and paraprofessionals under supervision of psychologists. Through the application of behavior modification principles and methods psychologists in the schools can reach masses of children who cannot be accommodated by individual therapeutic approaches and who do not respond to arbitrary group action techniques.

REFERENCES

Cattell, R. *IPAT Anxiety Scale*. Champaigne, Ill.: Institute for Personality and Ability Testing, 1961.

Cattell, R. & Scheier, I. H. *The Meaning and Measurement of Neuroticism and Anxiety*. New York: Ronald Press, 1961.

Fein, L. G. Learning is Aggressive: Case Study Analysis of the Defenses Against Learning in Underachieving Gifted Children. *The Gifted Child Quarterly, 1958, 2.*

Fein, L. G. *The Three Dimensional Personality Test: Validity, Reliability and Clinical Implications.* New York: International Universities Press, 1960.

Fein, L. G. Promoting the Gifted Child's Awareness of his Creative Potentials. *The Gifted Child Quarterly, 1962, 6.*

Fein, L. G. Evidence of a Curvilinear Relationship Between IPAT Anxiety and Achievement at Nursing School. *Journal of Clinical Psychology, 1963, 19.*

Fein, L. G. Non-Academic Personality Variables and Success at Nursing School. *International Mental Health Research Newsletter,* 1968, *10.*

Getzels, J. & Jackson, P. *Creativity and Intelligence.* New York: John Wiley and Sons, 1962.

Goldberg, M. L. *Research on the Talented.* New York: Teachers College Press, Columbia University, 1965.

Golden, T. LEAP An Experiment in Creativity for Gradeschoolers. *New Haven Register,* Feb. 19, 1967, 6–9.

Gowan, J. C. Issues in the Education of the Disadvantaged Gifted Students. *The Gifted Child Quarterly, 1968, 12,* 115–119.

Jastak, J. F. & Jastak, S. *The Wide Range Achievement Test.* Wilmington, Del.: Guidance Associates, 1965.

McClelland, D. C., Baldwin, A., Bronfenbrenner, U. & Strodbeck, F. *Talent and Society.* New York: Van Nostrand, 1958.

Raph, J. B., Goldberg, M. & Passow, H. *Bright Underachievers.* New York: Teachers College Press, Columbia University, 1966.

Rotter, J. *Incomplete Sentence Stems. College Form.* New York: The Psychology Corp., 1950.

Terman, L. M. *Genetic Studies of Genius,* Vol. 1. *Mental and Physical Traits of a Thousand Gifted Children.* Stanford: Stanford University Press, 1925.

Terman, L. M. & Oden, M. *Genetic Studies of Genius,* Vol. 4. *The Gifted Child Grows Up.* Stanford: Stanford University Press, 1947.

Torrance, E. P. Creativity and Its Educational Implications for the Gifted. *The Gifted Child Quarterly,* 1968, *12,* 67–78.

Witt, G. P. *The Life Enrichment Activity Program: A Community Children's Culture Center,* Hamden, Conn.; 1965.

CHAPTER 9

Behavior Modification: Principles and Methods

Behavior modification methods are viewed today as the treatments of choice in coping with child learning and behavior problems at school and in the home in contrast to the psychodynamic methods that held sway from the 1940s to the mid-1960s. The present focus on behaviorism is a revival of interest rather than an innovation, though of course many present day methods for modification of varieties of learnings and behaviors are innovative.

LEARNING THEORIES

Behavior modification principles date back to John B. Watson, who at the turn of the century protested the European concern with the study of consciousness as an approach to

185

the study of human psychology. Watson insisted that the study of consciousness initiated by Wundt and his colleagues in 1879 was impractical, unreliable, and not amenable to validation and that only the study of actual behavior is real, objective, practical. With the publication of his paper "Psychology as the Behaviorist Views It" in *Psychological Review* (1913), Watson ignited the American psychological "revolution of behaviorism," which focused on observable, measurable phenomena. Watson's behaviorism of necessity rejected all subjective views, such as those postulating innate mental characteristics, innate personality characteristics, native talents, and even predispositions to emotions. Watson was an environmentalist, like Locke, who postulated that the mind is a blank slate upon which is recorded all experience, and like Pavlov he viewed all behavior as reactions to conditioning. Watson's views were timely, for they fed into the American faith in education for all and in the American belief in the equality of opportunity for all. Watson's theory and methods had great impact on child rearing, education, advertising, and social organization (Hill, 1963).

Watson explained learning and behavior change on the basis of two principles from classical conditioning, the law of frequency and the law of recency. The law of frequency states that the more often the practice, the better learned; the law of recency states that the most recent experience practiced is best learned. In short, Watson's learning theory is based on the contiguity of events. Guthrie supported Watson's theory of contiguous experience—that is, what happens together, most recently, is learned—but he ruled out the need for practice. He viewed learning as an all or nothing experience. Guthrie made a contribution in three practical methods of modifying behavior, the *threshold method,* the *fatigue method,* and the *incompatible stimuli method.*

Behavior theory was further expanded by Thorndike (1898) through his precise work in animal experiments. He accepted the law of frequency, which he called the law of exercise, but he introduced a more basic law, the law of effect. This law states that a response that is followed by satisfaction is learned and one followed by annoyance is avoided. Later Thorndike recognized that satisfiers or rewards are more potent learning reinforcers than are annoyers or punishments. Thorndike's laws of learning are encompassed in Skinner's reinforcement learning theory, which postulates that learning results from positive reinforcers and is inhibited by negative reinforcers. Skinner, like Thorndike, may be called a connectionist theorist, emphasizing reinforcement as the basic factor in learning.

Skinner differs from other learning theorists in that he recognizes two types of learning, respondent learning, which is elicited by a specific stimulus, and operant learning, which the organism emits spontaneously, or so it appears to the observer. Respondent learning follows the pattern of classical conditioning, although Skinner does not call it that. Operant learning is much more common than respondent, for it is behavior that is emitted by the organism at will. No doubt operant behavior is emitted in response to stimuli also, but these are generally complex and not necessarily available to direct observation and identification. Skinner has no concern for the stimuli that elicit operant behaviors in organisms; he is concerned with methods of modifying operant behavior. Most of his methodology in behavior modification is concerned with developing ever more complex operant behavior repertoires in animals and humans, which in essence means ever more complex learnings.

It is noteworthy that although Skinner recognizes both positive and negative reinforcers, he views negative (aversive) reinforcers as basically ineffectual, as a poor method of controlling behavior. For one thing he points out that it does not have a lasting effect, since when the punishment is ended the undesirable behavior generally returns. Second, the emotional responses it produces are likely to spread to neutral stimuli present in the situation, including the administrator of the punishment, so that the administrator may become the aversive stimulus and elicit the undesirable crippling emotions by his mere presence. Third the emotional behavior it produces may be undesirable from other points of view such as replacing crying or anger for the misbehavior that was being treated.

SCHEDULES OF REINFORCEMENT

Through his research and work on operant conditioning Skinner has identified the various schedules of reinforcement that are effective behavior modifiers, and he has demonstrated the relative effectiveness of each schedule for motivating productive activity. The simplest schedule of reinforcement for teaching a subject to emit a discriminating response to a given stimulus is *continuous reinforcement* in which every appropriate response to a given stimulus is rewarded. This schedule generally is used when the subject is learning to respond in a discriminating manner to a given set of stimuli. After the response is established to the critical stimulus, that is, after the subject has learned to discriminate the correct stimulus, the schedule is shifted to some form of intermittent reinforcement schedule in which only some of the responses are reinforced. There are two types of intermittent reinforcement schedule, the *ratio schedule* and the *interval schedule* and each of these may be administered in either a fixed or a variable pattern.

A ratio schedule presents reinforcements for a given frequency of response whereas an interval schedule simply reinforces responses after passage of time. In a fixed ratio schedule the subject is reinforced after every given number of responses established at the start of the training, so that a reinforcer may be given after every third, seventh, tenth response, whichever ratio has been established. A variable ratio schedule presents reinforcers after a different number of responses rather than after the same number each time, but it is controlled by the fact that reinforcers are given for an average number of responses. For example, on a variable schedule of 3, reinforcement may be given after two responses at one time but at another time the subject is reinforced only after giving five responses, thus averaging 3. The avariable ratio schedule of reinforcement stimulates high productivity, apparently setting up a winning expectancy in the subject which keeps him working at a fast pace on the chance of winning a payoff characteristic of gambling situations.

On a fixed interval reinforcement schedule the payoff is generally given at a fixed time interval, such as every minute or hour, no matter how many times the subject responds appropriately. Thus the subject need not work consistently or diligently since he will receive only one reward in a given time segment no matter how much he produces. This schedule is typical of salary schedules when the payoff is given at the end of a specified time interval, like the end of the day, week, or month. This schedule operates against productivity since it pays off as much for minimal production as for optimal production.

Generally subjects will make more responses per reinforcer on any kind of intermittent schedule than on a continuous or fixed schedule. Furthermore, when reinforcement is finally terminated, resistance to extinction is greater after intermittent than after continuous or fixed reinforcements. It is noteworthy that these schedules are not intended to teach subjects new material; rather they are designed to motivate speed of production or response once the response has been learned under continuous reinforcement. For the purpose of facilitating new and complex learnings Skinner has developed a method of "operant conditioning" he calls *shaping*.

SHAPING

Through the technique of shaping, Skinner trained animals to perform complex acts that are outside their normal range of behavior. The behavior is shaped by selectively reinforcing responses that are increasingly closer approximations of the desired behavior and ignoring other behaviors unrelated to the goal. This method of "teaching" or "conditioning" has been widely applied to the treatment of withdrawn patients in hospital wards (Skinner, 1957b), the training of mental retardates, autistic children, and even normals where "verbal conditioning" sought to modify language patterns (Greenspoon, 1955; Verplanck, 1955; Skinner, 1957a).

It is noteworthy that Skinner rejects the assumption that behavior disorders are a reflection of some internal conflict or sickness, that motivation resides in the person, that insight, making the unconscious conscious or lifting repressions, are necessary for behavior change. He does not accept the dictum that people learn what they want to learn, what interests them; rather he believes that people learn and do what their reinforcing environment maintains.

Other leading behavior theorists and therapists agree with Skinner in their rejection of the traditional psychodynamic personality theories and seek to demonstrate that the application of the principles of modern learning theory is the approach of choice to modification of learning and behavior. (Eysenck, 1960; Bandura, 1969; Wolpe, 1958). However, since different behavior theorists often use different terms to describe similar procedures in behavior modification, behavior modification presentations can be confusing. For example, Skinner's method of "negative reinforcement" is called "aversion therapy" by Eysenck, "counterconditioning or punishment" by Bandura, and "conditioning avoidance response" by Wolpe. Bandura's method of eliminating an undesirable response is called "extinction," while this same method is called "negative practice" by Dunlap, "conditioning inhibition" by Eysenck, and "reactive inhibition" by Metzner. Skinner's concept of "operant conditioning" is called "reward" by Bandura and "positive conditioning" by Eysenck. Wolpe's "systematic desensitization" is called "counterconditioning" by Bandura, "reciprocal inhibition" by Eysenck, "graded stimulus situations" by Metzner, and was originally called "threshold" method by Guthrie.

COMMON USES OF REWARDS AND PUNISHMENTS

Some of the foregoing behavior modification methods have been and are still being used by the socializing authorities in our society, home, school, community, government agencies, although inconsistently and without awareness of the need for precise control of administrations to insure success. Thus parents, teachers, and society administer aversive stimuli—punishments—to subjects who display maladaptive, undesirable, destructive behaviors, in the hope of extinguishing such behaviors. Empirical experience reveals the futility of many of these efforts. Operant conditioning or *rewarding developing behaviors* is also common practice in school, at home, and in society but here again the administrations are inconsistent and often the specific behavior being modified is not clearly defined and the timing is not controlled, so that success with this method depends on chance.

Extinction or *withdrawal of rewards for misbehavior* is also a common practice in school, home and society. Here again success in modifying the undesirable behavior depends on chance since the administrators of "punishment" are not alert to the needs for consistency and for precision of definition of the undesirable behavior, nor are they alert to the need to control the multiplicity of variables in the learning milieu which may be rewarding the undesirable behavior in subtle ways. For example, a teacher may send a child out of the room for misbehaving and unwittingly reward him by this "punishment" for the child may have wanted escape from the classroom; or the child is rewarded by having an opportunity to relate to other children out in the hallway. A more subtle reward to a misbehaving child being thus punished may be the attention he receives from the teacher even at the cost of punishment or the approval he reads in the faces of his classmates for being a "toughy."

Negative practice as a means of modifying undesirable behavior is not as common as those cited, but it has been used occasionally in the classroom where the child who cannot remain in his seat is told to stand up near the window for the morning or afternoon session. This practice seldom works, for the child is rewarded, unwittingly, by serving as a distractor to other children, being the center of attention, or having an opportunity to watch the world outside the classroom. A common practice in schools in the past that is still ongoing in some schools is the requirement to write, 100 or more times, a promise not to misbehave in school in the particular manner of which the child is guilty. Although this practice is not precisely the same as negative practice, as defined by behavior modifiers, nonetheless it is intended to work the same way. The child is required to repeat, until fatigued and bored, the essence of his misbehavior. The value of such "negative practice" is questionable for changing the misbehavior, but it might have unexpected side effects: it might dampen the child's interest in writing.

PREMACK PRINCIPLE

One behavioral modification procedure that derives from operant conditioning and is receiving widespread attention and application in schools (and industry) is called *contingency management*. This method is based on the simple principle that the likelihood of behavior recurring depends on its consequences. This principle has been translated into a very workable simple formula for behavior modification by David Premack (1965) as follows: For any pair of responses, the more probable one will reinforce the less probable one. Concretely this means that if a child prefers to do art work to arithmetic, he can be induced to work at arithmetic if he has the promise of working at art when he finishes his arithmetic.

MODELING

Another behavior modification procedure that is receiving wide attention today is called "modeling" or "vicarious processes" by Bandura (1969), "imitation" by Miller and Dollard (1941), "identification" by Freud, "copying," "contagion," or "role playing" by Moreno, and so on. Modeling is not a new method or principle of teaching; in fact modeling appears to be a natural teaching method used by subhumans and humans, primitive and civilized, to transmit species-specific survival behaviors. The effectiveness of learning through modeling and observation depends on the subject's possession of the essential "sensory capacities for receptivity of modeling stimuli, the motor capacities necessary for precise behavioral reproduction, and the capacity for representational mediation and covert rehearsal, which is crucial for successful acquisition and long term retention of extended complex sequences of behavior" (Bandura, 1969, p. 148).

Modeling or learning through vicarious experience has received extensive attention from social learning theorists in laboratory settings. Their research findings suggest that "virtually all learning phenomena resulting from direct experiences can occur on a vicarious basis through observation of other person's behavior and its consequences for them." For example, "one can acquire intricate response patterns . . . by observing the performance of appropriate models; emotional responses can be conditioned . . . by witnessing the affective reactions of others undergoing painful or pleasurable experiences; fearful and avoidant behavior can be extinguished through observation of modeled behavior toward feared objects without harm accruing to the performer; deviant behavior can be inhibited by witnessing the behavior of others punished; and learned responses can be strengthened and socially regulated through the actions of influential models" (Bandura, 1969, p. 118).

Numerous explanations have been offered by the various social learning theorists (Humphrey, 1921; Allport, 1924; Holt, 1931; Miller & Dollard, 1941; Mowrer, 1950), about the dynamics or mechanics of learning from modeling, imitation, role playing, contagion, and the like. However, the potentials for learning from modeling are not sufficient conditions for learning, since such learning is determined in good measure by the status and attributes of the model which have high valence for the learner. (Miller & Dollard, 1941). Research reveals that the attributes of models that facilitate learning from a model include high competence, expertise, celebrity status, power status, and other self-enhancing qualities. Other distinctive characteristics such as age, sex, social power, ethnic status also influence the degree to which models will be selected for emulation (Bandura, 1969, p. 136). Furthermore, our own valued group affiliations and living circumstances affect our preferences and determine in great measure the types of model that are significant for us and accordingly the modes of behavior that we will learn thoroughly.

The fact that we learn from models, from vicarious experience of models, is both a boon and a tragedy, a blessing in the fact that cultures are transmitted both wittingly and unwittingly through this modeling process, and a tragedy in the fact that negative and destructive attitudes and behaviors are also transmitted wittingly and unwittingly to the members, especially the young members, of the culture. For example, the work of Kurt Lewin and his students at Iowa demonstrated that prejudice against minority groups, against people who differ from the self-group image, is learned from significant home models. Generations of juvenile delinquents, incarcerated for minor acts of defiance of law, have come out of jails and prisons with destructive skills, motives, and attitudes of hardened prisoners to whom they were exposed while incarcerated. How to extinguish delinquent behavior and replace such behavior with positive constructive behavior and how to replace prejudicial attitudes with attitudes of respect for those different from the self are challenges still confronting our society today.

Personal characteristics can impede or facilitate learning from modeling; these include dependency needs and attitudes (Fein, 1968; Jakubczak & Walters, 1959; Kagan & Mussen, 1956; Ross, 1966), self-image attitudes (Fein, 1968; de Charms & Rosenbaum, 1960; Gelfand, 1962; Lesser & Abelson, 1959), level of felt competence (Kandareff & Lanzetta, 1960), and socioeconomic and racial status (Beyer & May, 1968). In addition, motivational variables and transitory emotional arousal may facilitate, impede, or channel observing responses (Bandura, 1969). Haphazard observations of modeled behavior lead to haphazard reproduction of the behavior observed, whereas deliberate intent to teach by modeling can insure precise learning. The ability of the observer to discriminate, identify, and isolate subtle attributes of the modeling stimuli also affects the learner's ability to imitate modeled behavior accurately. This problem is common to many school teaching and learning situations.

Although the process of modeling as it operates in the socialization process of children in both subhuman and human cultures appears, at superficial glance, to facilitate learning by contagion, at closer look it becomes apparent that the adult socializers of the young facilitate the learning from modeling by shaping, reward, and punishment, that is, by both positive and negative reinforcements and even by aversive conditioning. Modeling, then, like contingency management, effects learning by the principle of consequences and consequences may be positive or negative. If positive, the learning will be repeated and if negative, the learning may extinguish.

In brief, it appears that the basic law or principle of learning underlying behavior modification methods is the law of consequences or, in Thorndike's terms, the law of effect. In turn, effect is determined by the principle of reinforcement, positive or negative, extrinsic or intrinsic (Skinner, 1957a). Although the basic principle of learning in behavior modification is common to all methods, nonetheless not all the methods can be effectively applied to all types of learnings. It is essential that the method of modification employed fit the sensory, motor, and cognitive needs and the emotional capacities of the learner as well as be adaptable to the milieu in which the learning must take place.

SOME APPLICATIONS OF BEHAVIOR THERAPY

There are many published reports on the application of behavior modification methods to a variety of deficit and maladaptive behaviors in both children and adults (Yates, 1970; Bandura, 1969; Rachman & Teasdale, 1969; Wolpe, 1969; Fargo et al., 1970; Ullman & Krasner, 1965). Child studies have focused on stuttering, phobias, autism, and mental deficiency with some attention to reading difficulties, hysterias, tics, delinquency, and emotional outbursts in children, and more recently on the management of maladaptive classroom behavior.

Stuttering (stammering and cluttering), a speech disorder affecting about 4% of the school child population (Andrews & Harris, 1964), has been treated by a variety of behavior modification methods including "shadowing" (which appears to be similar to modeling), "negative practice," (which is the same as Guthrie's fatigue method), rhythmic and syllable timed speech, and operant procedures.

In the treatment of fears and phobias the most popular method has been systematic desensitization as developed by Wolpe (1939) or variations of this method. More recently

Bandura has provided convincing evidence that modeling, both direct and symbolic, is a faster and more effective method for eliminating fears and phobias in children. Bandura and his co-workers (1967) report a series of experiments where strong avoidance behavior (fear) of long standing was extinguished by modeling, real, direct, and symbolic, through observance of vicarious behavior.

Tics have been successfully treated by Yates (1970) and others through the method of negative (massed) practice. A few studies indicate that delinquent adolescents respond with improved behavior to negative reinforcement in the form of "time out" of the group setting, that is, time out in isolation, but they do not respond to verbal reprimands (Tyler & Brown, 1967). Other studies indicate that prison inmates respond positively to contracts based on the Premack principle, that is, they will work at a low probability activity that is contingent upon availability of a high probability activity. These studies suggest that contingency management is a promising approach to delinquency modification.

Extensive research on the application of behavior modification methods to the training and teaching of autistic and mentally deficient children has been widely reported. For detailed descriptions of the variety of methods used in approaching modification of the multitudinous maladaptations of behavior in these groups, the reader is referred to Yates (1970), Lovaas (1966) and his co-workers (Lovaas et al., 1965, 1967), Hewett (1965), Bandura (1969), Bijou (1965, 1966; Bijou & Orlando, 1961), and Lindsley (1964).

Extensive studies on the training of mentally retarded and deficient children have been widely reported in the literature during the past decade (Bijou, 1965, 1966; Lindsley, 1956, 1960, 1964; Barrett & Lindsley, 1962; Denny, 1966; Bijou & Orlando, 1961; Orlando, 1965; Sidman & Stoddard, 1966; Friedlander et al., 1967; Spradlin & Girandeau, 1966). Operant techniques have been applied not only to teaching, training, and behavior modification of mental defectives but also to the diagnosis and assessment of mental deficiency. One of the most important contributions made through the use of operant methods of training and teaching mental defectives (Bijou & Orlando, 1961; Ellis et al., 1960; Orlando, 1961, 1965) relates to the assumption that defective performance does not necessarily represent inability, rather that failure by a mental defective in a given task indicates that the experimenter has failed to analyze the task sufficiently, precisely, discriminately. Mental defectives have been trained in self-care and social skills through the use of successive approximation techniques, that is, shaping; disturbing behaviors have been extinguished by the method of time out (isolation) and positive reinforcement for social interaction with peers.

The use of programed instruction methods to teach high grade mental defectives the basic school skills of reading, writing, arithmetic, and spelling has been detailed (Bijou, 1966) in a review of three years of work.

In brief, since behavior is governed largely by its consequences, differential reinforcement has been widely applied both singly and in combination with other behavior modification methods to overcome behavioral deficits, alter deviant behavior, and maintain constructive patterns. The successful work done with autistic and mentally retarded children in groups has led to serious consideration of applying these methods to learning and behavior problems within the normal classroom. Application of behavior modification methods to normal classroom are examined in the next chapter.

REFERENCES

Allport, F. H. *Social Psychology*. Cambridge: Riverside Press, 1924.

Andrews, G., & Harris, M. *The Syndrome of Stuttering*. London: Heineman, 1964.

Bandura, A. *Principles of Behavior Modification.* New York: Holt, Rinehart and Winston, 1969.

Bandura, A., Grusee, J. E. & Menlove, F. L. Vicarious Extinction of Avoidance Behavior. *Journal of Personality and Social Psychology,* 1967, *5,* 16–23.

Barrett, B. H. & Lindsley, O. R. Deficits in Acquisition of Operant Discrimination and Differentiation Shown by Institutionalized Retarded Children. *American Journal of Mental Defects,* 1962, *67,* 424–436.

Beyer, N. O. & May J. G., Jr. The Effects of Race and Socioeconomic Status on Imitative Behavior in Children Using White Male and Female Models. Unpublished manuscript, Florida State University, 1968.

Bijou, S. W. Experimental Studies of Child Behavior, Normal and Deviant. In L. Krasner, & L. P. Ullman (eds.), *Case Studies in Behavior Modification.* New York: Holt, Rinehart and Winston, 1965, pp. 56–81.

Bijou, S. W. A Functional Analysis of Retarded Development. *International Review of Research in Mental Retardation,* 1966, *1,* 1–19.

Bijou, S. W., Birnbrauer, J. S., Kidder, J. & Tague, C. Programmed Instruction as an Approach to Teaching Reading, Writing and Arithmetic in Retarded Children. *Psychological Record,* 1966, *16,* 502–522.

Bijou, S. W. & Orlando, R. Rapid Development of Multiple Schedule Performances with Retarded Children. *Journal of Experiments in the Analysis of Behavior,* 1961, *4,* 7–16.

de Charms, R. & Rosenbaum, M. E. Status Variables and Matching Behavior. *Journal of Personality,* 1960, *28,* 492–502.

Denny, M. R. A Theoretical Analysis and Its Application to Training the Mentally Retarded. *International Review of Research in Mental Retardation,* 1966, *2,* 1–27.

Ellis, N. R., Barnett, C. D. & Pryer, N. W. Operant Behavior in Mental Defectives: Exploratory Studies. *Journal of Experiments in the Analysis Behavior,* 1960, *3,* 63–69.

Eysenck, H. J. The Effects of Psychotherapy. In H. J. Eysenck (ed.), *Handbook of Abnormal Psychology*. London: Pittman, 1960.

Fargo, G., Behrns, C. & Nolen, P. *Behavior Modification in the Classroom*. Belmont, Calif.: Wadsworth, 1970.

Fein, L. G. Non-Academic Personality Variables and Success at Nursing School. *International Research Newsletter, New York: PGCMH*, 1968.

Friedlander, B. A., McCarthy, J. & Safarenko, A. Z. Automated Psychological Evaluation with Severely Retarded Institutionalized Infants. *American Journal of Mental Deficiencies*, 1967, *71*, 909–919.

Gelfand, D. M. The Influence of Self Esteem on Rate of Verbal Conditioning and Social Matching Behavior. *Journal of Abnormal and Social Psychology*, 1968, *65*, 259–265.

Greenspoon, J. The Reinforcing Effect of Two Spoken Sounds on the Frequency of Two Responses. *American Journal of Psychology*, 1955, *68*, 409–416.

Greenspoon, J. Verbal Conditioning and Clinical Psychology. In A. J. Backrack (ed.), *Foundations in Clinical Psychology*. New York: Basic Books, 1962.

Guthrie, E. R. *The Psychology of Learning*, (rev. ed.) New York: Harper, 1952.

Hewett, F. M. Teaching Speech to an Autistic Child through Operant Conditioning. *American Journal of Orthopsychiatry*, 1965, *35*, 927–936.

Hill, W. *Learning*. San Francisco: Chandler, 1963.

Holt, E. B. *Animal Drive and the Learning Process*, Vol. 1, New York: Holt, 1931.

Humphrey, G. Imitation and the Conditioned Reflex. *Pedagogical Seminary*, 1921, *28*, 1–21.

Jakubczak, L. F. & Walters, R. H. Suggestibility as Dependency Behavior. *Journal of Abnormal and Social Psychology*, 1959, *59*, 102–107.

Kagan, J. & Mussen, P. H. Dependency Themes on the TAT and Group Conformity. *Journal of Consulting Psychologists*, 1956, *20*, 29–32.

Kandareff, V. T. & Lanzetta, J. T. Effects of Task Definition and Probability of Reinforcement upon the Acquisition and Extinction of Imitative Responses. *Journal of Experimental Psychology,* 1960, *60,* 340–348.

Lesser, G. S. & Abelson, R. P. Personality Correlates of Persuasibility in Children. In C. I. Hovland & I. L. Janis (eds.), *Personality and Persuasibility.* New Haven: Yale University Press, 1959, pp. 187–206.

Lindsley, O. Operant Conditioning Methods Applied to Research in Chronic Schizophrenia. *Psychiatric Research Reports,* 1956, *5,* 118–139.

Lindsley, O. Characteristics of the Behavior of Chronic Psychotics as Revealed by Free Operant Conditioning Methods. *Diseases of the Nervous System Mongraph Suppl.,* 1960, *21,* 66–78.

Lindsley, O. Direct Measurement and Prosthesis of Retarded Behavior. *Journal of Education, 1964, 147,* 62–81.

Lindsley, O. Operant Conditioning Methods Applied to Research in Chronic Schizophrenia. *Psychiatric Research Reports,* 1956, *5,* 118–139.

Lovaas, O. I. A Program for the Establishment of Speech in Psychotic Children. In J. K. Wing (ed.), *Early Childhood Autism.* Oxford: Pergamon Press, 1966, pp. 115–144.

Lovaas, O. I., Freitag, G., Gold, V. J. & Kossaria, I. C. Experimental Studies in Childhood Schizophrenia. Analysis of Self Destructive Behavior. *Journal of Experimental Child Psychology,* 1965, *2,* 67–84.

Lovaas, O. I., Freitag, L., Nelson, K. & Whalen, C. The Establishment of Imitation and Its Use for the Development of Complex Behavior in Schizophrenic Children. *Behavior Research and Therapy,* 1967, *5,* 171–181.

Miller, N. E. & Dollard, J. *Social Learning and Imitation.* New Haven: Yale University Press, 1941.

Mowrer, O. H. Identification: A Link between Learning Theory and Psychotherapy. In O. H. Mowrer (ed.), *Learning Theory and Personality Dynamics.* New York: Ronald Press, 1950, pp. 573–615.

Orlando, R. Shaping Multiple Schedule Performances in retardates, Establishment of Baselines by Systematic and Special Procedures. *Journal of Experimental Child Psychology*, 1965, *2*, 135–153.

Premack, D. Reinforcement Theory. In D. Levine (ed.), *Nebraska Symposium on Motivation, 1965*. Lincoln: University of Nebraska Press, 1965, pp. 123–180.

Rachman, S. & Teasdale, J. *Aversion Therapy and Behavior Disorders*. Coral Gables, Fla.: University of Miami, 1969.

Ross, D. Relationship between Dependency, Intentional Learning and Incidental Learning in Preschool Children. *Journal of Personality and Social Psychology*, 1966, *4*, 374–381.

Sidman, M. & Stoddard, L. T. Programming Perception and Learning for Retarded Children. *International Review of Research in Mental Retardation*, 1966, *2*, 151–208.

Skinner, B. F. *Science and Behavior*. New York: Macmillan, 1953.

Skinner, B. F. The Experimental Analysis of Behavior. *Scientific American*, 1957, *45*, 343–371. (a)

Skinner, B. F. *Verbal Behavior*. New York: Appleton-Century-Crofts, 1957. (b)

Skinner, B. F. Teaching Machines. *Scientific American*, 1961, *205*, 90–102.

Spradlin, J. E. & Girandeau, F. L. The Behavior of Moderately and Severely Retarded Persons. *International Review of Research in Mental Retardation*, 1966, *1*, 257–298.

Thorndike, E. L. Animal Intelligence: An Experimental Study of the Association Processes in Animals. *Psychology Review Monthly Supplement*, 1898, *2*, 8.

Tyler, V. O. & Brown, G. D. The Use of Swift, Brief Isolation as a Group Control Device for Institutionalized Delinquents. *Behavior Research and Therapy*, 1967, *5*, 1–9.

Ullman, L. P. & Krasner, L. *Case Studies in Behavior Modification*. New York: Holt, Rinehart and Winston, 1965.

Verplanck, W. S. The Control of Content of Conversation Reinforcement of Statements of Opinion. *Journal of Abnormal Social Psychology*, 1955, *51*, 668–676.

Watson, J. B. Psychology as a Behaviorist Views It. *Psychology Review*, 1913, *20*, 158–177.

Watson, J. B. *Behaviorism,* 2nd ed. Chicago: Chicago University Press, 1930.

Wolpe, J. *Psychotherapy by Reciprocal Inhibition.* Stanford: Stanford University Press, 1958.

Wolpe, J. *The Practice of Behavior Therapy.* New York: Pergamon Press, 1969.

Yates, A. J. *Behavior Therapy.* London: John Wiley and Sons, 1970.

CHAPTER 10

Behavior Modification in the Classroom

Over the past decade behavior modification principles have been introduced into some public school systems through programed instruction materials designed to facilitate learning and development of basic school skills or remediate such skills and help pupils master course content. Whether these programs are presented with the aid of technological hardware or through software only (texts and booklets), the essential format of presentation of the material is the same. The format is based on the principle that learning is facilitated when it is presented in precise minute sequential steps and immediate feedback is given the learner on his progress.

CLASSROOM HURDLES TO BEHAVIOR MODIFICATION

However, to date there is limited evidence supporting the applicability of behavior modification procedures to entire classrooms of children with disruptive behavior patterns. Efforts in this direction have been hampered by problems of control, where one teacher must affect the behavior of large numbers of children, where hurdles exist in the physical settings, by curricular requirements, by teachers' resistances and their limited skills in applying relevant techniques for optimal learnings and behavior changes in all classroom children. Thus disruptive classrooms persist in spite of accumulating evidence that a large variety of behavior deviations have been eliminated through use of behavior modification contingency management methods under controlled conditions with high teacher/pupil ratios, about 1:5 (Ayllon & Azrin, 1965; Birnbrauer et al., 1965; Homme, 1966).

Many school psychologists recognize the potentials of these methods in facilitating their efforts to cope with heavy service demands, for through classroom management with behavior modification methods many children can be affected at one time, with the help of teachers and paraprofessionals trained to implement and maintain the programs in the classroom, relieving the psychologist to design programs for other classrooms and provide other critical professional services where needed in the system.

CONTINGENCY MANAGEMENT

Research to date indicates that contingency management is probably the best behavior modification method for use in disrupted classrooms. Contingency management procedures are based on the simple principle that recurrence of behavior depends on its consequences. This view of behavior change and behavior development has been implicit in the traditional practices of socialization in our society as reflected in the widespread use of rewards and punishments to motivate learning, to eliminate undesirable behaviors and habits, and to facilitate development of appropriate behaviors and habits.

However, the use of consequences is ineffectual unless the consequences are related to the needs of the child, that is, have high preference value for any given child, so that he is motivated to strive for the particular consequences, contingencies, or reinforcements. In addition, the contingencies (consequences) must be controlled, applied early in the game, when the child first makes an attempt at an approximation of the desired behavior, and they must be consistently applied to sequentially closer approximations of the desired behavior to the final achievement of efficiency. Traditional efforts to modify behavior in terms of its consequences used absolute standards against which to measure the child's performance, so that rewards, reinforcements, and consequences were given as an end product, that is, for full attainment of the desired behavior. Many children could not attain this goal without benefit from reinforcements for successive approximations of the ultimate standards.

In our traditional socialization process common rewards (i.e., contingencies or reinforcements) used to motivate appropriate behavior and inhibit inappropriate behavior include candy, cookies, other sweets, boys, prizes, games, trips, gold stars, marks, and highly valued activities as well as verbal and nonverbal cues of approval or disapproval. Similar contingencies or rewards are used in the process of contingency management, but here again the traditional differs from the present method in the respect that in the traditional process the awards are not controlled but often are administered inconsistently, many times giving contradictory messages. In contingency management, rewards or contingencies are administered in a deliberate consistent pattern that ensures continuing development of the desired behavior to efficiency.

Contingency management makes use of tokens (poker chips, varieties of small disks, stars, check marks, or other symbols) to reinforce learning through sequential steps. These tokens are exchangeable for high probability activities or highly valued objects, much as money is used in the open society, in exchange for goods or services. Through graded token systems children learn to tolerate increasing amounts of frustration and so are better able to work at ever more challenging tasks before receiving the reward they are striving for. Through studies with contingency management, researchers have discovered that reinforcement possibilities are unlimited if the manager is alert to cues communicated by the subjects under study. This discovery offers great promise for the application of contingency management even in large classrooms, if the teachers are alert and sensitive to the cues released by the children.

As noted earlier, Premack (1965) demonstrated a contingency principle that has substantially simplified the process of structuring contingency schedules. He noted that for any pair of responses, the more probable one will reinforce the less probable one. Probability of occurrence is defined here in a nonrigorous sense. The psychological manager or teacher can determine the relative frequency of occurrence of two activities by simple observation of the subject's behavior for a brief period of time. Preschool and primary school children generally announce what they want to do, and this clues the teacher to the high probability activity useful as a contingency at the given moment. For example, if a child announces on entering the classroom that he is going to work with the paints, the teacher is in a position to use this activity as a contingent upon which the child will first work at the class assignment set by the teacher and then be rewarded with freedom to paint for a few minutes. Of course the teacher must reward the child for his first approximation of attending to the class assignment and reinforce with painting activity consistently for each closer approximation of the assigned task to completion of the assignment. This differential probability hypothesis appears to work with all children whatever their socioeconomic, cultural, or ethnic backgrounds (Homme, 1966).

EXPERIMENTAL APPLICATIONS

Adolescent Dropouts

Homme reports on the application of the Premack principle with 23 adolescents who were contemplating leaving school. "They spoke a hip jargon, some of them were discovered to be carrying knives, some of them wore their sun glasses at all times and so on." The low probability program for these subjects was completing programed instruction material in math and reading. The high probability behaviors, used to reinforce the low probability behaviors, were conventional rewards like coffee breaks, smokes, and sodas. To the surprise of the experimenters, studying Russian proved to be a reliable high probability behavior for most of these students. When this fact was discovered the contracts read as follows: "Do 20 frames of arithmetic, then you can work on Russian for 10 minutes." Results of this program after only one week revealed high motivation for learning with 100% school attendance daily and no fights, which was a high probability activity before the study was undertaken.

Preschoolers

Haring et al. (1969) reported effective use of a contingency management program to accelerate appropriate behavior in a class of preschoolers in a Head Start program. The program included 12 children who had demonstrated severe social, emotional, and/or language deficits as identified by classroom teachers and the research staff. The length of assignment of the children to the behavioral modification program varied with the needs of each child so that length of stay ranged from 3 to 33 sessions. In short, when the children demonstrated consistent appropriate behavior in the demonstration classroom they were returned to their home classroom with recommendations for continuing the *individual structure* essential to their continued learning.

The teaching staff in this study included two assistant teachers-in-training and a coordinator, who not only structured the program but advised the teachers and trained them toward the master teacher level. Observations of the children at the start of the program were made at 15 second intervals and prepared blanks were checked + or − for attendance to motor and verbal teacher cues. The global goal of the program was to develop the social and preacademic skills needed in kindergarten. Language goals for children with speech were specified sequentially as an imitative response, a fully prompted response, a partially prompted response, a one word new response, and a sentence response employing subject, verb, and modifiers sequentially in appropriate stages and at appropriate times. For example, if a picture of a boy running was presented to the child, he would be reinforced sequentially for successive approximations as follows: in answer to the question "What is the little boy doing?"

run
boy runs
boy running
boy is running
boy is running in street
boy is running in the street
the little boy is running down the street

To ensure that the task was seen as a teaching situation rather than a testing situation, care was taken to cue any oral response correctly and to repeat it immediately afterward with the key word or words missing, to give the child a model for his language behavior (Fargo et al., 1970, p. 96). Number concepts and discriminations of form, color, and letters were taught through sequential programing from concrete experience to representational.

From the outset very short periods were scheduled with play period participation dependent upon the successful completion of the work task, which of course was very simple at the start. For example, a child might be asked to work a puzzle and be rewarded with a play period after placing one piece of the puzzle correctly; another child might be assigned to find a specific colored circle from a box full of colored geometric forms. It is noteworthy that for many children teacher attention and approval were reinforcing from the start, resulting in measurable increases in social and preacademic skill attainment, for other children task effectiveness seemed more reinforcing than social approval, and some children refused the contingency play periods, preferring to continue with work activities. This discovery that some children responded with increased learning and behavior change to teacher attention and approval, others to task effectiveness, or to continued work as against play opportunities while some continued to respond to the play contingencies is not surprising. These differential response patterns are expected in view of differential need levels in children deriving from their socialization experience from infancy. Moreover, there are differential learning rates among children, and in this situation there are differences in learning to make the transition from simple concrete contingencies like play activities to social verbal and nonverbal cues of approval to intrinsic gratifiers like skill mastery.

Emotionally Disturbed 9 Year old Children

Many studies have demonstrated that these principles and methods can be applied effectively to special population classes like adjustment classes (O'Leary & Becker, 1967), emotional disturbed classes (Hewett et al., 1969), out of control classes (Orme & Purnell, 1970), and mental retardation classes (Birnbrauer et al., 1965; Quay et al., 1966). In the majority of these studies token reinforcement methods proved effective; however, in all cases the teacher/pupil ratio was small, one teacher to four or five children, a very extravagant pattern for general public school education.

O'Leary and Becker (1967) sought to apply a token reinforcement program to an average classroom under the direction of one teacher to test whether token reinforcement could be withdrawn gradually without disruption of behavior, by transferring reinforcement power to teacher cues such as praise (verbal or nonverbal) or marks. This study included 17 nine year old children identified as emotionally disturbed. IQ measured by the Kuhlman-Anderson ranged from 80 to 107. The children had been placed in this special class because they disrupted the regular classroom with crying, tantrums, uncontrollable laughter, fighting, and so on. Observations and recordings of deviant behaviors by two students in training between 12:30 PM and 2:10 PM revealed the following types of deviation: pushing, talking out of turn, chewing gum, eating, name calling, making disruptive noises. Each student observer attended to four children in random order. Observations were made on observation sheets, on a 20 second observe/10 second record basis. The observations were made during structured sessions when the children were expected to be quiet and in their seats. Base data were obtained by observations and recordings over a 3 week period during which time the teacher handled the class in her regular manner. The average interobserver reliability for individual children ranged from 75 to 100%.

The psychological experimenter placed the following directions on the board the first day of the token period:

In seat, face front, raise hand, working, pay attention, desk clear.

The experimenter informed the children of the token procedures, tokens being in the form of ratings from 1 to 10, reflecting the extent to which the children followed directions. The points or ratings could be exchanged for a variety of backup reinforcers, none costing more than 29 cents, including candy, peanuts, comics, and kites. Each day for one week at the beginning of the token period the experimenter repeated the directions and rated the children, to provide a norm for the teacher. The teacher recorded the ratings in each child's booklet during the short pause at the end of a lesson period. Ratings were given for approximate behaviors listed on the board. To facilitate development of tolerance for delay of gratification and to transfer token control to teacher praise and attention the number of ratings decreased from five to three a day, the number of points required to obtain a prize gradually increased, and the number of days delay for redeeming points earned increased from immediate redemption privilege, to one, two, and finally four days delays. It is noteworthy that time out from classroom was also used to eliminate unacceptable behavior in cases where the behavior was particularly disruptive. Results were very promising in view of the percentage of deviant behavior that declined for all the pupils from the ease period to the token period.

Disruptive Classroom in Ghetto School

Orme and Purnell conducted an experiment with a group of 18 children from grades 3 and 4 in an urban ghetto area. The children were disruptive, impulsive, aggressive, and destructive, taking apart their slotted wooden desks, running out of the room, tearing up classmates' work papers, throwing books, yelling, singing, making noise that could be heard throughout the school building. To provide total control of the milieu the classroom was divided into two smaller rooms, A and B, where room B was the experimental room in which behaviors were modified by conditioning and modeling. Experimental conditions were structured so that behavior produced in room B could be expected to transfer to room A. This transfer of control hypothesis was the basic experimental aim of this study. The study ran for more than 6 weeks and included, in addition to token reinforcement, teacher training in the manipulation of surrounding conditions and curricular variables and videotape in training as well as measurement and analysis.

Both teachers received training in verbal, nonverbal, and token reinforcement procedures and in addition they were trained in basic questioning procedures (probing) and methods of varying the stimulus situation. In a sense these instructional strategies were really "shaping" methods translated into concrete teacher behavior. For a full description of this challenging study the reader is referred to the original report by Orme and Purnell (1970). The results of the study were promising, revealing relatively stable and desirable modification in child behavior and indicating that such improved behavior is transferable from one classroom to another and to a different teacher.

Educable Retardates

Sulzbacher and Houser report a simple experiment using *group contingency consequences,* that is, for deviant behavior displayed by one child the entire class forfeits a portion of the "treasured" or high probability experience. The study included 14 educable retardates aged 6 to 10.

The behavior that was disrupting the classroom procedures was the use of the "naughty finger," verbal reference to it, and tattling or other disrupting reactions on the part of children other than the child who used the naughty finger.

After a baseline frequency of occurrences of these three behaviors was obtained, a calendar bracket with 10 cards numbered 1 to 10 was mounted in front of the room and the children were instructed as follows:

From now on there will be a special 10 minute recess at the end of the day. However, if I see the naughty finger or hear about it I will flip down one of these cards and you will have one minute less of recess whenever this happens. Remember, every time I flip down one of these cards, all of you lose a minute of your recess.

The results revealed immediate deceleration of the undesirable behaviors when the contingency was in force and a gradual rise when the contingency was removed. However, the only behavior that gradually returned was the raising of the naughty finger, rather than talk about it, giggling, or gesturing, so that classroom procedure was not noticeably disrupted. This procedure had significant impact on the group's response to the misbehavior of one member of the group, that is, where before the program was instituted the class members reinforced the naughty finger behavior by responding actively to it with words, giggling, gestures, after the study was instituted class members did not respond to the child exhibiting the naughty finger behavior. These findings emphasize the power of peer reinforcement of deviant behavior and reduction of deviant behavior.

This method of contingency management—that is, applying decelerating consequences to a group of children, contingent on the deviant behavior of one child in the group—is very simple and convenient, requires no extra equipment, little classroom change, and little investment of teacher time. The use of group contingency conditions in settings where the peers are reinforcing deviant behavior of an individual by giving it critical attention, verbal or non-verbal, makes good sense, since the deviant behavior is not limited to any one member but all members or most members of the group are participating by attending to it and making a stir about it. However, this method can be destructive when a whole class of attentive children are penalized for one child's misdeeds. This group contingency method lends itself to misuse by teachers who have little patience with any misbehavior or deviance and are angered and punish the whole class for the misdeeds of one member. Such class punishments were very common in public schools during the early years of this century and unfortunately are still prevalent in many classrooms today. Used in anger, these contingencies do not work. If anything, they compound the disturbances.

CRITICAL COMPONENTS OF CONTINGENCY SYSTEMS

Kuypers, Becker, and O'Leary (1968) report an experiment using token systems in an effort to clarify the important components of such modification systems. This study demonstrates the pitfalls of behavior modification procedures when the teacher is uninvolved and participates resistively or mechanically; when tokens are given only for attainment of absolute standards of behavior rather than for successive approximations of the behavior in question; when the teacher fails to systematically apply differential social reinforcements between token periods or at other times of the school day; when the teacher is too lenient or too tolerant of deviant behaviors, that is, when the teacher has a permissive attitude, perhaps feeling that "after all they are only children, so what do you expect of them." This study reveals the futility of using tokens per se or inconsistently. The token system to be effective is designed to make reinforcers commonly used in school more effective for children, and it is intended to lead to substitution of concrete reinforcements, tokens, with verbal and nonverbal social cues and ultimately with intrinsic motivations.

The use of differential social reinforcements appears to be essential at all times, meaning that teachers need to be alert to give praise and privileges for improvements and ignore deviant behaviors unless the deviancies are dangerous. When the undesirable behavior does not stop after exposure to controlled contingency treatment, or when it is ignored by teacher and peers, then time out of the classroom technique, isolation, withdrawal of all social contact is the treatment of choice. Improved behavior needs to be shaped successively by approvingly acknowledging positive change even in minute degree, and care must be taken to define and reward sequential steps toward ever closer approximations of the goal behavior desired.

SUMMARY

In this brief examination of the application of behavior modification methods to regular classrooms, the focus was deliberately centered on methods and techniques that are readily recognized as appropriate by psychologists of varying persuasions, and are not likely to elicit strong resistances among selected school staff, parents, and community leaders with traditional orientations. Behavior methods that are not readily applicable to classroom management include negative practice, aversive therapy, or conditioning, reciprocal inhibition, and relaxation/hypnotic modification. Not only are these methods difficult to apply in the classroom, but many psychologists in the field of behavior modification consider these methods less effective than those described above. Moreover, the latter techniques may provoke angry protests and resistances from teachers, parents, and community leaders as well as from professional psychologists aware of the potential dangers of these methods of treatment in the hands of people with less than expert clinical skill.

In short, psychologists in the schools can turn to behavior modification methods in efforts to cope with classrooms full of children who are so disruptive that the teacher cannot teach anything. Fortunately these methods have already been systematized so that hierarchically arranged skills can be directly taught to teachers, teacher aids, parents, and other ancillary staff available as needed, who then assume the responsibility of implementing and conducting the programs in the classrooms. Psychologists expert in these procedures and principles must train the school personnel to establish baseline behavior by appropriate observations, recording baseline behaviors, identifying the critical behaviors to be modified, preparing schedules for recording change, setting up reinforcement schedules appropriate to the developmental levels of the children involved, and identifying emerging intrinsic contingencies in individual children in the process of change.

When psychologists have mastered these behavior modification methods and their application and implementation to disruptive classrooms, they are far better equipped to cope with the overwhelming service needs in present day school systems.

REFERENCES

Ayllon, T. & Azrin, N. *The Token Economy*. New York: Appleton-Century-Crofts, 1965.

Barrett, B. H. & Lindsley, O. R. Deficits in Acquisition of Operant Discrimination and Differentiation Shown by Institutionalized Retarded Children. *American Journal of Mental Deficiencies,* 1962, *67*, 424–436.

Birnbrauer, J., Bijou, S. W., Wolf, M. & Kidder, J. Programmed Instruction in the Classroom. In L. P. Ullman & L. Krasner (eds.), *Case Studies in Behavior Modification*.

New York: Holt, Rinehart and Winston, 1955, pp. 358–363.

Birnbrauer, J., Wolf, M., Kidder, J. & Tague, C. Classroom Behavior of Retarded Pupils with Token Reinforcement. *Journal of Experimental Psychology*, 1965, *2*, 219–235.

de Charms, R. & Rosenbaum, M. E. Status Variables and Matching Behavior. *Journal of Personality*, 1960, *28*. 92–502.

Fargo, G., Behrns, C. & Nolen, P. *Behavior Modification in the Classroom*. Belmont, Calif.: Wadsworth, 1970.

Haring, N., Hayden, A. M. & Nolen, P. Accelerating Appropriate Behavior in the Head Start Program. *Exceptional Children*, 1969, *35*, 10. 773–784.

Haring, A. & Philips, E. L. *Analysis and Modification of Classroom Behavior*. Englewood Cliffs, N. J.: Prentice-Hall. 1972.

Hewett, F. M. Teaching Speech to an Autistic Child through Operant Conditioning. *American Journal of Orthopsychiatry*, 1965, *35*, 927–936.

Hewett, F. M. *The Emotionally Disturbed Child in the Classroom*. Boston: Allyn & Bacon, 1968.

Hewett, F. M., Taylor, F. D., & Anfuso, A. N. An engineered classroom design with emotionally disturbed children. *Exceptional Children*, Mar. 1969, pp. 523–529.

Homme, L. E. Contingency Management. *Clinical Child Psychology Newsletter, 1966, 11.*

Kazdin, A. E. *Token Economies: An Annotated Bibliography*. Journal Supplement, Abstract Service Catalog of Selected Documents in Psychology. Washington, D.C.: APA, 1971.

Kuypers, D., Becker, W. & O'Leary, K. D., How To Make a Token Systey Fail. *Exceptional Children*, 1968, *35*, 101–108.

O'Leary, K. D. & Becker, W. C. Behavior Modification of an Adjustment Class: A Token Reinforcement Program. *Exceptional Children*, 1967, *33*, 637–642.

O'Leary, K. D. & O'Leary, S. G. *Classroom Management: Successful Use of Behavior Modification*. New York: Pergamon Press, 1972.

Orme, M. E. & Purnell, R. F. Behavior Modification and Transfer in an Out-of-Control Classroom. In G. Fargo, C. Behrns, & P. Nolen (eds.), *Behavior Modification in the Classroom*. Belmont, Calif.: Wadsworth, 1970, pp. 116–138.

Premack, D. Reinforcement Theory. In D. Levine (ed.), *Nebraska Symposium on Motivation*. Lincoln: University of Nebraska Press, 1965, pp. 123–180.

Quay, H., Werry, J. S., McQueen, M. & Spraugue, R. Remediation of the Conduct Problem Child in Special Class Setting. In G. Fargo, C. Behrns, & P. Nolen (eds.), *Behavior Modification in the Classroom*. Belmont, Calif.: Wadsworth, 1970, pp. 201–210. (Reprint from *Exceptional Children*, 1966, 32.)

Sulzbacher, S. I. & Houser, J. E. A tactic to eliminate disruptive behaviors in the classroom. Group contingent consequences. *American Journal of Mental Deficiency*, July 1968, pp. 88–90.

Woody, R. H. *Behavioral Problem Children in the Schools*. New York: Appleton-Century-Crofts, 1969.

CHAPTER 11

Paraprofessional Training Trends

The last few chapters have made clear the urgent need for trained paraprofessionals to assist psychologists in the schools with delivery of services for the welfare of the various child target populations. Training of paraprofessionals, however, has received little attention in the majority of our undergraduate and graduate psychology programs. If effective services, equal to those available to the private sector of our population, are to be made available to deprived segments of our child populations, psychology must develop such programs within the psychology training hierarchy.

STAFF TO FILL GAP IN DELIVERIES OF SERVICES

It is apparent to all enlightened observers of the national, state, and urban scenes that there is a need for the training of paraprofessionals to supplement the services provided by professionals to the myriad problem target populations in schools, day care centers, clinics, hospitals, community service centers, the labor force, the unemployed, the welfare families, the prisoners, and so on. Huntington (1972) presents data attesting to the critical need for preparation of paraprofessional child care workers. This need is urgent when measured in terms of the increasing numbers of working mothers of children under 18 years of age; this number has grown from 1 out of 10 in 1940, to 3 of 10 in 1960, to 4 of 10 in 1970, and the trend continues.

The need for day care workers and facilities is not only the need of the poor, notes Huntington, but of families at all socioeconomic levels, since handicapped children cut across all levels of income. It is estimated that there are 450,000 children under 21 with cerebral palsy; 2,600,000 mentally retarded children; 3,200,000 children with speech impairments; and 5,000,000–10,000,000 emotionally disturbed (one in four families of the nation). In terms of services now available, facilities are so limited in number that "babies are cared for by 3 year old siblings; children are locked alone in apartments; neighbors care for five or six children who sit on the sofa all day watching TV. The latch key children care for themselves. According to the latest estimate, day care in licensed homes and centers is available for only 640,000 children" while "several million children need such services" (Huntington, 1972, pp. 13–14).

Zigler (1972) notes that early childhood education programs suffered from inadequately trained staff assigned to assist professional staff in Head Start programs. He observes that the nation moved into the practice of hiring poor, unskilled community residents to work in child care settings on the naive notion that "if you are poor yourself or have a good heart or some combination of the two you are ideally suited to train young children" (p. 6). What we need, says Zigler, is "to develop an entirely new cadre of child care workers," trained and certified for delivery of specific skills in child care much like the children's nurse in Denmark, the upbringer in Russia, and the childrens' house worker in Israel.

The training of child care workers ongoing today is one of the more recent categories for which paraprofessionals are being trained. Paramedical, paradental, and paranursing staff have long existed while paraprofessional teaching aides have been with us at least since the early 1960s.

PARAPROFESSIONAL TRAINING CENTERS

The training of paraprofessionals in the early 1960s was conducted, for the most part, on the job. Thus members of the communities were canvassed and assigned to work as aids to teachers, special service staff, psychologists, administrators, social service staff, and so on. These approaches to training paraprofessionals were soon recognized as inadequate in terms of the mounting need for more *skilled* staff to cope with the burgeoning problems in emerging target populations. By the mid-1960s community colleges began to offer 2 year training programs leading to the Associate of Arts degree in Human Services, Human Relations, and psychological skills. At the same time various institutes outside university walls were established under private auspices to provide human relations skills to members of deprived populations. Community college programs were funded by universities, the National Institute of Mental Health, and the Department of Health, Education and Welfare while the private institutes were funded partly privately and partly federally, by the U.S. Department of Labor committed to development of work skills among indigent populations, by HEW committed to improving the welfare of deprived children, and by the Office of Economic Opportunity. These special institutes have since organized and established the Accrediting Board for Specialized Schools and Colleges, specifically the American Association of Specialized

Schools (AASC) and the National Association of Specialized Schools (NASS). A fourth approach to training is developing within agencies and institutions under state, city, and community auspices.

Unique Features of Paraprofessional Training Programs

The curricula of the community college programs in human relations and of the specialized schools differ significantly from traditional curricula in university psychology programs, in methods of teaching/learning/evaluating products (students), and in the thrust of the teaching. Thus in traditional curricula content receives major focus whereas in the paraprofessional programs the vehicles include discussion groups, group dynamic sessions, seminars, T groups, sensitivity training, confrontation procedures and a variety of other group modalities. In addition to these experiential modes of teaching, field experiences are provided to students from the start.

What knowledges and skills are offered these students in the community colleges and what positions are they filling? In a survey of community colleges in 1970, Simon reports that the curricula generally consist of three categories: general education including the humanities, physical sciences, and social sciences; a second series of courses in mental health related areas such as psychology and social work; and the third includes the mental health practicum aspects of the program. Although the amount of field experience varies from school to school, every program provides some kind of work involvement with agencies before graduation. A survey of the jobs graduates are filling indicates that these paraprofessionals from community colleges are working in community mental health centers, psychiatric hospitals and clinics, speech and hearing centers, institutions for the mentally retarded, school systems, rehabilitation institutions for the blind, nursery schools and child care centers and residential centers for disturbed children. In these settings, these paraprofessionals conduct intake interviews, take medical histories, do counseling, apply behavior modification schedules, conduct psychodrama sessions for role training and conflict resolution, assume responsibility for general management of hospitalized patients, follow up discharged patients in the community, and supervise new trainees. In a few cases these paraprofessionals have been "trained" to administer and score intelligence, achievement and aptitude tests and participate in case study conferences.

Whether all these skills and their application to the large variety of target populations can be mastered sufficiently within a two year training program to permit effective function remains to be seen. However, as long as these paraprofessionals serve under the supervision of professionals in each of the settings where they are employed, the responsibility for their functions falls on the shoulders of the professionals, a circumstance that should ensure quality professional services to the public being served.

Dangers of Autonomous Practice by Paraprofessionals

Threats to the public become critical if and when these paraprofessionals seek to deliver "professional" services to the public, autonomously, independent of professional supervision. This danger is apparently imminent, judging from the goals set by the Southern Regional Education Board at its 1970 conference (Simon, 1970). The goals included: "A working knowledge of basic data gathering techniques" (research skills), "evaluation procedures including basic competencies in interviewing, administering, scoring and screening psychological tests, conducting and reporting mental status examinations and social and medical histories and basic competence *in at least one method of psychotherapy.*" At no point did the conferees indicate that the paraprofessional will conduct these activities under professional supervision.

The omission of "professional supervision" suggests that these subprofessionals are being encouraged to view themselves as autonomous workers in the mental health service field. This inference is supported by the fact that a large group of paraprofessionals, graduates of community college programs, met with representatives of other paraprofessional "psychotherapists" and psychiatric technicians in Atlanta in 1970 to organize nationally as an independent profession. Further evidence of the trend toward autonomy is reflected in the fact that paraprofessionals are being employed in programs to train and supervise new trainees. Since these community college programs are multiplying rapidly, with a new program opening each week (Simon, 1970), the likelihood of damage to the public through services rendered by superficially trained persons is extreme.

The trend toward autonomy by paraprofessionals will negate any gains made in delivery of psychological services since the mid-1950s, when the conferees at the Thayer Conference noted that poor services by inadequately trained school staff threaten the welfare of children and the public and impair the credibility of fully qualified psychologists. The trend toward autonomous function by paraprofessionals presents a serious challenge to the profession of psychology, which has struggled for the past 25 years to establish high standards for the practice of psychology, primarily to protect the public from unqualified persons. If paraprofessionals insist upon working without full professional supervision, they will vitiate any good that they are prepared to provide to the variegated needs of our many target populations. This caution applies to all mental health paraprofessionals, whether they are trained in community college programs, independent specialized programs, community sponsored programs, universities, or professional schools of psychology.

The training offered in the member schools of NASS and

AASC generally includes a large variety of group modalities, such as group dynamic methods, art, music, play, family, rehabilitative, physical, dance, and hypnotic therapies, as well as psychodrama, sensitivity, and confrontation approaches. In some settings, reality, commitment, bioenergetic and humanistic therapies are offered, as are psychoanalytic principles and methods, principles of diagnosis, and conflict resolution methods. The dangers of application of some of these techniques by paraprofessionals operating autonomously in institutions or the open community are obvious.

The training programs offered in community sponsored programs are too diverse to summarize. One of the best such programs is described below.

SAMPLE TRAINING PROGRAMS

Community Sponsored Program

The *Illinois Mental Health Generalist Worker Series* (Hadley, True, & Kepes, 1967) was implemented in the state of Illinois August 1971 under the aegis of the Department of Mental Health by Executive Order No. 50 and was approved by the Illinois Department of Civil Service as a major step in providing manpower to meet the mental health needs of Illinois citizens (personal communication from Dr. Parrish, July 12, 1972, and mimeographed release July 30, 1972, Department of Mental Health, Illinois, Albert Glass, Director).

The impetus to the reorganization of State Mental Health Training and Service programs came from certain communities and professionals cognizant of the changing population needs emerging during the second half of the 1960s and the inability of the established system to meet these urgent mental health needs.

Aware that the State Mental Health Institutions up to the mid-1960s were treating their target populations much like a "merchandizing company sees its market or an entertainer sees his audience . . . that is, . . . as an essential but dehumanized mass which had certain tastes and styles of behavior," these community and professional leaders sought to assist the State Department of Health in new approaches to delivery of "services which could be tailored to the changing needs of communities . . . small enough that they could understand and perceive the origins of their own delinquencies, illnesses, accidents, etc." (Parrish, 1972).

Communities set up their own programs, and many taxed themselves to implement these programs for their own populations. A community representative board was empowered within each community program to hire and fire the managers of the program. Neither universities nor government arms regulated these programs; however, the state did provide grants in aid, consultation, and at times free working personnel for these programs:

Often the chief of a program and his entire staff were themselves citizens of the community they served. Their children had to go to the community schools, suffer from the community delinquencies, etc. This, combined with the small size of the community concerned, tended to RE-HUMANIZE the people served. In fact, the people were serving themselves to a large extent, or else were responsibly hiring others to help them. The tendency now was to budget, programs and projects, and not institutions. . . . The programs were usually run by teams. Part of a team would work on an inpatient aspect of the program, another part on an educational aspect, another on a rehabilitation aspect in the community.

Since the primary purpose of the Department (now) was to serve communities and to develop programs, there was no further need to retain discrete disciplinnes, e.g., chief psychologists, chief nurses, etc., in the institutions nor was it necessary in the general offices and headquarters. The personal identity and image of an Illinois Mental Health Professional seems to come, now, more directly from his own personal doings, his own behavior and not from his class nor his guild. (Parrish, 1972).

The training of workers in this Generalist Series is built into the actual functioning programs, that is, much of the training is on the job and the rest is in-service didactic training given by state or community professional staff or university staff from program-affiliated university departments. This approach to training is justified on the premise that the Department of Mental Health can be more readily responsive to the ever changing needs of each specific community than can university based and controlled training programs. It is noted and emphasized that although the "state guidelines suggest a kind of standardized core of training, the quality of that training in each region is tailored to the particular needs of that region. Each community program develops its own kind of continuous training" (Parrish, 1972). It is further noteworthy that each regional director may invite specific departments of universities to participate, cutting across departmental lines in the universities as the needs of training require, and only those programs involved are funded, whereas the university per se is not.

By Executive Order No. 50 entry into the Generalist Mental Health Series is through the trainee classes, except for appointments to the Mental Health Administrator IV and V positions. Examinations for all trainee classes are on open continuous call. An important feature of this program is the opportunity for advancement up the career ladder through experience and special training. The four steps in this hierarchy are, from lowest to highest, Mental Health Technician, Mental Health Supervisor, Mental Health Specialist, and Mental Health Administrator. The specific entry requirements, experience, and functions of each of these levels are defined briefly below. First the essential components of the training program include the following:

1.   Orientation to the job (12 hours) to acquaint the trainee with the philosophy, policies, objectives, and programs of the Department of Mental Health and the critical aspects of the immediate work sit-

ᴧuation; with the personnel system and conditions of employment; with the training, treatment, and rehabilitative functions and practices of the program in which the trainee is involved and the kind and nature of special services that are offered adjunctive to the program.

2. Skill training (30 hours), consisting of supervised training in human relationships and other "technical" skills essential to the performance of the duties of the trainee's role in the mental health program.

3. Study in humanistic attitudes and values (20 hours), which seeks to develop in the trainees understanding and practice of those attitudes and values relevant to working with and serving people.

4. Theory underlying practice (20 hours), designed to instruct the trainee in the fundamental conceptualizations, principles, and ideas that make practice meaningful.

5, 6. Work problem solutions, both technical and human relations (15 hours each or 30 hours combined), to provide opportunities to explore problems arising in the application of training methods to work practice and the problems arising from interactional experiences at all levels, patient, peer, authority.

7. On-the-job-training (400 hours) is given in the treatment program to which the trainee is assigned under supervision of the appropriate level supervisors.

8. Elective time (8 hours) is devoted to individual consultation of trainee with supervisors, training coordinator, training peers for purposes of remedial learning and enrichment of experiences.

A critical provision permits a trainee to submit either inservice or formal academic training or relevant experience as equivalent to parts of a training program, "making it possible for a trainee to 'proficiency-out' of any aspect of the training program." Evidence of equivalency of training must be fully documented and evaluated before accepted. Such equivalency offerings may allow for a reduction in the amount of calendar time spent in a training unit but under no conditions may training time be cut to less that three months.

Entrance and Experiential Requirements for Each Mental Health Job Level

The technical series moves from Mental Health Technician Trainee I or II to Technician levels I, II, III, IV, sequentially on to the level of Mental Health Supervisor I, II, III. Supervisor level III is the highest step in the nonprofessional hierarchy. Admission to this nonprofessional hierarchy requires no basic formal education, but simply the ability to learn to care for mentally ill or retarded *under supervision* and the ability to acquire necessary skills to provide basic personal and nursing care services and participate in a program of care, treatment, and development of the patients. The Technician Trainee II level calls for knowledge, skill, and mental development equivalent to two years of college with courses in the behavioral sciences and the ability to acquire the skills to apply basic therapeutic techniques in the treatment of the mentally ill and retarded.

The second hierarchy leads up the professional ladder and begins with the Mental Health Specialist trainee, requiring the equivalent of knowledge and skill at the Bachelor level in the behavioral sciences with ability to acquire skills to evaluate treatment and needs of mentally ill or retarded and to design appropriate intervention programs. This training leads to Mental Health Specialist I. Mental Health Specialist II calls for the equivalent of a Masters degree and successful completion of an approved training course at the Mental Health Specialist Trainee level. The highest level in the Mental Health Specialist series is the Specialist Level III. In the administrative hierarchy admission is open to trainees with skills, knowledge, and development equivalent to completion of a Masters degree in administration, education, or the behavioral sciences, ability to administer training programs, coordinate a variety of educational and training activities, develop curricula and materials, and evaluate training programs. This training, with successful and appropriate experience, leads to the Mental Health Administrative levels I to V.

The responsibilities of the members of the nonprofessional ladder are basically concerned with the physical care, safety, comfort, and recreational and social activities of patients as well as assisting professional staff in planning, coordinating, and implementing treatment and development programs. In contrast, the focus of the duties of the members of the professional ladder at the specialist levels is supervision of the workers at the nonprofessional levels, participation in diagnostic and therapeutic activities *under direction of senior specialists,* carrying a psychiatric case, serving as skilled consultant on training, implementing and conducting training programs, acting as assistant to a major unit administrator, and assisting in development of program policies and procedures.

It is noteworthy that an incumbent at Mental Health Specialist III may move into the next professional hierarchy, Mental Health Administrator, and on up through the five administrative levels to the IV and V levels where they function autonomously, though with administrative approval (State of Illinois Department of Personnel, Mental Health Generalist Series, 7/12/72).

All training in these hierarchies appears to involve a combination of didactic, experiential, and practicum training in contrast to traditional didactic approaches at college and graduate schools. This combination of didactic, practicum, and experiential, in proper ratio, should prove more effective in the training for human services than the traditional didactic curricula or the pure experiential practicum approaches of some paraprofessional training programs.

This program, as defined in the official release, appears to provide effective vehicles for delivery of essential services on a community level to the large variety of target populations present today in our open societies, particularly in the inner cities and deprived rural areas of the nation.

Protection of the public served by these mental health generalists is provided by the requirement that the members of the Illinois Mental Health Hierarchies work *within the confines of community agencies "supervised by professionals."* Presumably these workers may not move out of the civil service umbrella into independent practice. Whether the paraprofessionals in this series are cautioned or limited by explicit policy to keep out of independent practice is not indicated in the report on hand. What controls have been established in the event some of the generalists do move out into independent practice to supplement their incomes is not indicated in the present report. Such limits seem urgent, since experience in psychology to date reveals that many noncertified psychological personnel, employed in "umbrella settings, during the day, open private offices to serve the public during evening and weekend hours without benefit of license or professionally licensed supervision (communications from certified colleagues, uncertified practitioners, and personal direct observations).

Bronx Community College: Psychological Generalist

At the Bronx Community College of the City University of New York a paraprofessional program within psychology is ongoing under the direction of Dr. Herbert Robbins. Robbins notes that his program seeks to prepare "a generalist" in human services psychology, apparently modeled on dimensions of the Purdue program (Hadley et al., 1967).

The Bronx program seeks to "professionalize" the training of paraprofessionals, upgrade in-service training, and establish career ladders for these paraprofessionals within the profession of psychology (Robbins, 1972). These AA graduates are trained in administration, scoring, and interpretation of "simple" psychological tests such as IQ tests, administration of diagnostic learning tests, interview techniques, research methods, and group therapies. Such functions are traditionally viewed as skills required by school psychologists at the MA level and in some cases by clinical and school psychologists at the doctoral level. A few skills listed derive from the repertoire of social workers, guidance counselors, and counseling psychologists. These "parapsychological" personnel are expected to function under direct supervision of certified professionals just as traditionally noncertified psychological personnel at the MA and BA level are expected to function under supervision of qualified professionals. Here again, as in the programs described earlier, the danger that these paraprofessional personnel will move out into autonomous practice is a serious threat to the public and a challenge to the traditional mental health professions and to the certification boards.

The Bronx Community program is just a two year curriculum, without a built in ladder to the BA and higher degrees. However, the graduates of this AA program may enter the regular academic classes in the City University BA program if they decide to continue their education. This process may well create problems for them and for the college staff who are following the traditional college curriculum and teaching in traditional ways. As one professor in psychology at CUNY put it, "it is like baking a cake under a mound of whipped cream." Obviously, if many of these AA graduates plan to continue their education toward professional status, serious collaboration must be established between administration and staff of this paraprofessional program and City University administration and staff to integrate the diverse teaching and training procedures for effective continuation of the development of these paraprofessional students.

Cuyahoga Community College (Kulik et al., 1973)

The Cuyahoga Community College was organized in 1963 with an enrollment of 3000 students and grew by 1970 to 15,000 students on two campuses. Cuyahoga's open-door policy attracts a wide range of students from 18 to over 30, from those with good academic skills to those who can barely read. Of the students at the Metropolitan campus 60% are studying part time rather than full time. The course offerings include a two quarter general psychology sequence, child growth and development, educational psychology, and dynamics of human behavior. In addition to its psychology program this college offers a program in human services which emphasizes response to local community needs. Students work in different ways on problems related to crime, welfare, mental illness, neighborhood services, urban housing, and so on, in such diverse settings as the public schools, hospitals, and residential settings for a variety of problem target populations.

The program emphasizes a systems approach, that is, awareness of the total field of influences on behavior and these interactions. Behavior modification techniques are viewed as particularly effective for changing specific behaviors. Services provided by these students include activity therapy with problem children in the schools, crisis intervention between children and teachers and/or principals, work with families of prisoners and with prison administration aimed at modifying the limits so that families may visit their imprisoned relatives, acting as curbstone counselors appearing at the same place each day in a kind of client finding approach. Students work with a full time ombudsman of the campus to discuss and examine problems and interventions.

The college is working on plans for placement of the graduates of the program certified as Health Service Technicians. At present they are placed in state positions only, but plans are being made for their placement in nonstate settings. Credits obtained in this junior college program are at present transferable to the nearby Cleveland State University on an informal basis. It is hoped that a formal coordination of programs between these two institutions will soon be developed.

Human Relations Work Study Center: The New School for Social Research (1972)

This program was organized at the New School in New York City to provide opportunities to the multitude of persons without traditional credentials seeking skills in the human services or helping professions. The program offers a year's training in such roles as social work assistants, counselor assistants, school psychology assistants, early childhood education interns, mental health workers, community health interns, and community planning aides. The program combines classwork and field work. Classes meet once a week for 15 weeks each semester. This program certifies students for work in a given health or education setting and also provides a few college credits acceptable by the New School toward the BA degree.

Bowling Green University Behavior Analyst Program (Keeley et al., 1973)

The paraprofessional training program recently introduced at Bowling Green University, Department of Psychology, is based on the philosophy that one means of handling the "numbers game" is to train community agents who are in direct contact with those in need of services, and that adequate training of sufficient numbers of such agents can be greatly facilitated by use of trained subprofessionals. At Bowling Green undergraduates are trained as behavior analysts who serve as intermediaries between consulting professionals and mediators. The behavior analysts work with teachers in the classroom, parents in the home, in tutorial modeling roles, and as consultants to Head Start classrooms as part of the training program for teachers and other staff. These paraprofessionals are expected to play a critical role in a variety of mental health centers, public schools, community agencies, hospitals, and the like. These behavior analysts provide a large reservoir of staff for training large forces of community people in critical behavior change skills essential to the improvement of work and life in urban centers.

SCHOOLS OF PROFESSIONAL PSYCHOLOGY PARALLEL CURRICULUM / CAREER

Ladder (Potthurst, 1970)

Concurrent with the development of paraprofessional training programs in human services by private agencies, community colleges, and state, federal, and civil service boards are programs at the paraprofessional (AA) level being developed in newly organized schools for professional psychology. The model for the professional schools in psychology was developed by the California Association of Psychology. The CSPP program is a radical departure from all previous programs for the professional training of psychologists. CSPP is not university affiliated, admits a different breed of student selected by unorthodox methods, by administrators and faculty who are predominantly in private practice rather than in "academic ivy covered towers." The program is designed to allow the student flexible exit and reentry from school to job and job to school with maximum credit for courses completed. It is of critical note that this professional school has just been approved by the state of California as qualified to award degrees from the associate to the doctoral level.

The CSPP curriculum provides the following:

1. A sequential program of six trimesters (90 units) including six months of supervised work experience in a selected specialty, leading to an AA degree. The graduate of this program is seen as qualified to function as a skilled paraprofessional in one of a number of speciality fields.
2. A sequential program of nine trimesters (135 units) including practice but no professional work experience leads to the BA degree.
3. The MA degree can be earned by continuing the sequential program and completing 180 units, with practice, internships, a research project, and professional work experience in one area of specialization.
4. Finally, continuing the sequential curriculum, completing 270 units, practice, internships, professional experience in one major and two minor specialties, and completion of a doctoral thesis leads to the Ph.D. degree.

The California School of Professional Psychology represents the first organized efforts within the field of professional psychology to carve out of the professional knowledges, skills, techniques, title roles, and functions a sequential training and career ladder within the profession of psychology and under the direct supervision and monitoring of fully qualified professional psychologists. This model is unique in its aim to eliminate the "caste system" in psychology by integrating the psychological "vocation" with the profession of psychology through a curriculum ladder that parallels the career ladder. This program reflects unique respect for the members of the deprived segments of the population of the United States who too long have been imprisoned at the lowest level of the manpower scale. This program provides a model for other professional state groups seeking to develop professional schools in various parts of the nation including New Jersey and New York.

The newest program addition to the California School for Professional Psychology is a doctoral program in School Psychology sponsored by the joint action of the California Association of School Psychologists and Psychometrists (APA Monitor, 1973, p. 10). Dr. Cummings, president of the CSPP, hailed this collaborative endeavor as a giant step in healing the widening breach between school and clinical psychology in the United States. Minimum requirements for admission include a masters degree in school psychology, a state school psychologist credential, and at least three years of experience as a school psychologist at the journeyman level. The program will take three academic years (two calendar years) to complete. Working school psychologists will be able to take a leave of absence for school attendance or will work on a half time basis so they will not need to leave their jobs to obtain their doctorates.

GRADUATE TRAINING PROGRAMS ADAPTABLE TO PARAPROFESSIONAL TRAINING

Innovative graduate psychology programs with sequentially graded knowledges, skills, and functions from year to year of training can be adapted easily to the preparation of differentially trained paraprofessional staff in psychology.

The Doctor of Psychology Program at Illinois (Peterson, 1971)

In the Illinois program students are expected to participate in five years of laboratories in Clinical Psychology Experience, under continuing direction of experts in each of these clinical specialties. The laboratory experiences begin with training in systematic desensitization and the single subject behavior modification procedures and go on to individual psychotherapies, group therapy modalities, initiation and management of residential treatment programs, community interventions such as consultations with staff at a day care center for disadvantaged children, and training paraprofessional black mental health workers.

The sequential introduction of various skills in the clinical laboratory settings suggests that students develop high level skills that are sequentially graded according to complexity, so that as students master the simpler skills, like behavior modification skills, they are able to provide such services to appropriate target populations even as they continue study and training in more complex skills such as individual psychotherapies.

Rutgers Doctoral School Psychology Program (Bennett, 1971)

The Rutgers School Psychology Program at the doctoral level is based on the assumptions that the schools are a unique social entity, that knowledge of psychology per se does not equip a psychologist to work effectively within the schools, and that the integration of psychological knowledge with a thorough knowledge of education is essential, since the training of a professional psychologist must be within the context of his future practice (Bennett, 1971).

The Rutgers program has as its goal the training of high level professional psychologists who are also expert in education.

The program is basically four years long, three at the university and the fourth year in an internship setting. The students range in age from 21 to 44 years, from recent BA college psychology majors to those who have been teachers for several years and others who have been school psychologists at the journeyman level with an MA degree.

This program is housed in the Graduate School of Education within the Department of Psychological Foundations rather than in the Department of Graduate Psychology. The Department of Psychological Foundations consists of 23 faculty, specialists in areas of counseling, developmental and educational psychology, special education, measurement and statistics, and school psychology. The Department of Psychology in Arts and Sciences offers a wide range of graduate courses that are available to the students in the School Psychology program according to their needs and goals. The focus of the Psychology Department in the Arts and Sciences is experimental with emphasis on behavior modification principles and methods as the approach to treatment.

Along with regular coursework students are assigned to co-operating school districts their first year of training and perform according to their level of training. Third year students in advanced practicum receive training in supervision of junior students. Beyond the prerequisite core program students may specialize in one of four areas of work: high level general school practice working with children, teachers, and parents; administration of special or pupil personnel services in the schools; research methods as applied to solving school problems; college teaching in teacher institutes or in university school psychology programs. Bennett notes that by the time a student is ready for internship placement, the fourth year of graduate study, he is usually ready for state certification as a school psychologist in most states of the nation.

These types of innovative program with their graded coursework and practicum experiences from the first year, operationally defined, under direct personal supervision by professional psychologists, each with his unique specialty, appear to have structures that can be easily adapted to the preparation and certification of paraprofessionals for differential levels of service in the schools and communities.

NASS AND AASC PROGRAMS: GROUP RELATIONS
ONGOING WORKSHOPS INSTITUTE

One of the member schools of the NASS and AASC is the GROW Institute in Manhattan. This school was opened in 1968 with private funds under private auspices to provide training to deprived members of our society in an effort to meet some of the urgent needs of inner city residents for human relations skills. GROW also responded to the urgent demands of governmental and social service agencies seeking training for their staffs and for new staff to cope with rehabilitation, with prevention of drug addiction, delinquency, violence, unemployment, and welfare dependency, and with care of mentally retarded, children, the elderly, and the like. These agencies funded study scholarships for their own staff and for many newly hired staff members.

In July 1971 the GROW Institute was approved by the University of the State of New York, State Department of Vocational Education, to train students toward one or more of five group worker certificates; from lowest level to highest, these are Group Worker, Group Leader, Group Counselor, Group Psychotherapist, Training Group Supervisor (Official Record of the State Board of Education, July 1971 and December 1971).

Admission requirements to the Group Worker and Group Leader programs call for no formal educational background, simply for "empathetic capacity for relatedness, emotional stability, general intelligence and strong positive motivation to work with people" (GROW, 1971).

The Group Worker certificate calls for 27 weeks or 324 class hours of training in group relations techniques; the Group Leader certificate calls for 36 weeks or 504 class hours of group relations/dynamics training. Graduates of these programs are prepared to work under professional supervision as interviewers, case aids, ombudsmen, and prison and offender counselors; they may work in child day care centers, mental health community clinics, mental hospitals, mental retardation centers, public and parochial schools, and prisons.

The Group Counselor Certificate calls for a high school diploma or its equivalent (or Worker and Leader certificate) plus 54 weeks or 684 class hours. These group workers also work *under professional supervision* in settings cited above. Admission requirements to the Group Psychotherapy and Training Supervisor Certificate programs include two years of graduate training in psychology social work or one year psychiatric residency or psychiatric nursing or the Ph.D. or its equivalent. Also required are 150 hours of personal group psychotherapy and 774 class hours for the certificate in Group Psychotherapy and 300 hours of personal group and individual psychotherapy plus 1170 class hours for the Certificate in Training Supervisor. These last two roles represent top level professional group leadership training and status entitling the holders to independent practice and/or supervisory roles in the settings cited above. Here again caution is called for to protect the public against independent practice (without supervision by qualified professionals) by holders of the GROW Worker, Leader, and Counselor certificates. These paraprofessionals, like those from other types of training programs, may seek to establish themselves as independent practitioners unless clearcut licensing precautions are taken.

In its four years GROW has awarded six Leader, seven Counselor, fourteen Psychotherapist, and one Training Supervisor certificate along with countless Worker certificates to students without high school education, employed by federal, state, city, county, and community agencies serving deprived populations of our inner cities.

Although GROW was originally intended to provide training in human relations and social service skills to members of deprived segments of our population, it has attracted a great many students with accredited degrees from other universities, graduate and undergraduate students who leave accredited programs in midstream, seeking more relevant training, and large numbers of certified professionals in the mental health fields seeking to upgrade or learn new skills relevant to coping with the new target population problems.

The GROW program, like other paraprofessional programs, employs experiential teaching/learning approaches at the expense, for the most part, of critical contents. When this program combines experiential process with critical knowledges, scientific contents, theories, and principles throughout all its courses and when courses of study are evaluated and arranged in sequential hierarchies of difficulty and content with parallel curricula and career tracks, the skills of these GROW graduates will be assured more substance. This modification is particularly essential for the training of students seeking certificates in the three lowest categories (worker, leader, counselor) and for candidates for the top level certificates who lack systematized knowledges and skills in a traditional mental health profession.

GROW graduates, like those from community college programs cited earlier, are eager to establish their profession as a new profession, paralleling psychology, social work, psychiatry, and the like. Unfortunately, such efforts will and have alienated large segments of the established professions in New York and other states. Continued efforts by these paraprofessionals toward this goal may well damage the image of paraprofessionals whatever their training, place serious obstacles to the continuing development of such training programs, and reduce the opportunities of these paraprofessionals for employment in professional settings.

ARBITRARY CAREER LADDER CRITERIA

A caution is urged about these paraprofessional programs that allow students to accumulate credits without a clearcut rationale for the sequence of courses, and to those institutional programs that provide movement up the career ladder simply on the basis of work time invested—seniority.

Recently proposals were submitted to the Bureau of Child Guidance of New York City by the New York State Civil Service Commission requesting staff review and discussion of such program proposals. In one proposal, the Mental Health Worker Series, incumbents in institutions could earn the title Mental Health Worker after two years on the job, Senior Mental Health Worker after two more years, Supervisor with two more work years, and finally Principal Mental Health Worker with two additional years. No mention is made in this proposal of academic training or of supervision by professionals, except that the top level worker would have *general professional supervision*. The most startling aspects of this proposal are the job descriptions, which assign to these workers responsibility for the whole gamut of professional psychology skills.

Such programs can only compound the problems afflicting our deprived populations, failing to deliver critical services equal to those available to the private sector of our nation. It is common knowledge that workers promoted on the basis of "time worked" and secured by tenure become sterile, even if they were well qualified at the start of employment. Furthermore, where little formal training is required or provided, or where workers are promoted on the basis of collection of credits for course work, arbitrarily selected, such workers are motivated simply toward self-advancement rather than by concerns for the quality of services they are delivering.

A case in point was recently reported in the *NYSPA Newsletter* (1972). A study by the College Evaluation Board released by the Commissioner of Education notes: "It would seem that an attitude of collusive mediocrity has been adopted among students, faculty and administrators at the Master's level. . . . Statistics compiled during 1969–1970 showed that 90% of the students studying for the MA degree at schools *that do not offer doctoral programs are not seriously interested in academic aspects of their programs*. They are more interested in merely accumulating credits for the sake of bettering themselves professionally, often taking whatever is offered at a convenient time and place." (p. 1). The majority of such students are seeking promotions in their job hierarchies, obtainable on the basis of additional college credits, whether these credits are at continually higher levels of learning or simply repetitions of work done before.

If teachers and other school staff seek advanced credits, often at their own expense, to better themselves professionally and economically, look to gain such credits "the fast and easy way," what may we expect from paraprofessional workers whose training is paid for, who are minimally exposed during their training to the critical knowledges in the behavior and psychological sciences, and who are almost certain of promotions after completing a given period of work, on the basis of evaluations by paraprofessionals who went the same route? The dangers of using years of service as a criteria for promotions and of awarding tenured security (even when the incumbents are required to submit evidence of having earned additional professional credits over a period of time are well documented in the final volume of the three part report of the city and state school systems released by the Commissioner of Education of the State of New York (*New York Post,* 1972). The study committee noted that seniority promotions and tenure systems also provide "swollen pension systems" for the privileged incumbents who pursue their own economic interests even as they protest responsibility for their failures to provide effective education to the school child populations. Similar failures may be expected in government sponsored mental health programs that institute similar patterns of seniority privileges and tenured invulnerability against accountability.

SUMMARY

This brief examination of the training trends of paraprofessionals reveals characteristics that clearly distinguish these programs from traditional college curricula. Differences are apparent in admission requirements, selection procedures, evaluations of attainment, completion of requirements, and time elements and in philosophy of education, methods of teaching, training, and learning theories. The best models of paraprofessional programs today require minimal educational credits for admission, accept experience that can be demonstrated as equivalent to formal courses of study, provide parallel career/curricular ladders, work study opportunities, experiential/didactic teaching versus didactic, theoretical, research emphases. No time limits are set for completing a given course of study and movement from job to school and the reverse is free and open. The thrust of these programs is toward development of high level skills useful in coping with the critical target populations of our present day society. The most promising programs today are the California School for Professional Psychology and the Illinois Mental Health Generalist Series. Other programs would profit from using these two programs as models to guide their program development.

This writer hopes to discover the degree to which psychology departments in universities are adapting their programs to prepare their students for coping with the emerging problems of critical populations in our society through analysis of responses to a questionnaire to department chairmen of graduate programs in psychology, and other clinical, counseling, school, and educational programs. Results of this survey are presented in the next chapter.

REFERENCES

Albee, G. W. *Health Manpower Trends.* New York: Basic Books, 1959.

APA Monitor. School Psychologists join CSPP. *American Psychologist,* 1973, *4,* 10.

Bennett, V. Doctoral School Psychology Training Program at Rutgers. *Professional Psychology,* 1971, *2,* 298–300.

Bevan, W. Higher Education in the '70's. *American Psychologist,* 1971, *26,* 537–545.

Carr, E. F. Evaluation Report on Group Relations Ongoing Workshops. Albany, N.Y., 1972. (mimeo)

Conference of Graduate Students on Clinical Training. New York State Psychology Association, 1969.

Fish, J. Continuing Education in the Midwest Region. *Newsletter, American Association of State Psychology Boards,* 1973, 8.

Glass, A. J. Executive Order No. 50. Department of Mental Health, State of Illinois, *Mental Health Generalist Series.* July 30, 1971.

GROW (Group Relations Ongoing Workshops Institute). *Course Catalogue.* New York: GROW., 1971.

Hadley, J. M., True, J. E. & Kepes, S. *An Experiment in the Education of the Paraprofessional Mental Health Worker. The Purdue Program.* LaFayette, Ind.: Purdue University Press, 1967.

Henry, W. E., Sims, J. H. & Spray, S. L. *The Fifth Profession.* San Francisco: Jossey-Bass, 1971.

Huntington, D. Program of Child Care: The United States Need and What Should Be Done. *Journal of Clinical Child Psychology,* 1972, 1, 12–15.

Keeley, S. M., Shemberg, K. M. & Ferber, H. The Training and Use of Undergraduates as Behavior Analysts in the Consultation Process. *Professional Psychologist, APA,* 1973, *4,* 59–63.

Kulik, J. S., Brown, D. R., Vestieg, R. E. & Wright, H. *Undergraduate Education in Psychology.* Washington, D.C.: APA, 1973.

Kurz, R. B. *Proposals for a National Conference on Levels and Patterns of Training.* APA Committee on Professional Training of the E & T Board and Board of Professional Affairs. APA, 1969. (mimeo)

Kurz, R. B. New Committee on Professional Training. *Professional Psychologist, APA,* 1971, *1.*

May, R. *The Work and Training of the Psychological Therapist.* Washington, D.C.: Psychological Service Center Press, 1950.

New School for Social Research. *Human Relations Work Study Center.* New York: 1972.

New York Post, Oct. 18, 1972, pp. 1, 66.

New York State Psychological Association. *NYSPA Newsletter,* 1972, *24/2,* 1, 9.

New York State Psychologist. Master's Level Programs Hit by State as Product of Collusive Mediocrity. New York, 1972, pp. 1, 9.

Parish, M. D. Written communication. Department of Mental Health, State of Illinois, July 12, 1972.

Peterson, D. R. Status of a Doctor of Psychology Program, 1970. *Professional Psychologist,* 1971, *2,* 271–275.

Potthurst, K. To Renew Vitality and Provide a Challenge in Training. The California School of Professional Psychology. *Professional Psychologist, APA,* 1970, *1/2.*

Robbins, H. *Developing a Clinical Field Work Experience for the Human Services Psychology Program at the Bronx Community College.* New York: CUNY, 1972. (mimeo).

Simon, R. The Paraprofessionals are Coming! *The Clinical Psychologist,* 1971, *24/3.*

Steisel, I. M. Paraprofessionals—Questions from a Traditionalist. *Professional Psychologist, APA,* 1972, *3/4,* 331–334.

Stollak, G. E. An Integrated Graduate-Undergraduate Program in the Assessment, Treatment and Prevention of Child Psychopathology. *Professional Psychologist,* 1973, *4,* 158–169.

Zigler, E. Children's Needs in the 70's: A Federal Perspective. *Journal of Clinical Child Psychology,* 1972, *1,* 3–6.

CHAPTER 12

Training Trends in Psychology To Meet Current Needs

As described earlier, the challenges in the changing schools and communities have imposed a large variety of demands on psychologists, who are viewed as the guardians of mental health of the nation and thus are held responsible for coping with the conditions threatening the mental health of our population. For the past decade psychologists in the schools have struggled with these challenges, some trying to be all things to all people and of course falling far short of expectations; some trying to limit their services to those skills for which they were trained, and again falling far short of the demands and expectations; some protesting the heavy demands and seeking to influence the systems to add more staff, activities that consume time at the expense of critical services. Whatever school psychologists do or did they can change little unless supported by the schools, communities, organized psychology, and the university training programs.

APA TASK FORCE ON TRAINING, ROLES, FUNCTIONS

The challenges of the changing scene were accepted by the APA in 1969 with the appointment of a Task Force on Standards for Psychological Services and Facilities (APA No. 3130) to define roles and functions of psychologists at appropriate levels of training from Ph.D. to AA degree. In a recent issue of the *APA Monitor*, Kenneth Little (1972), Executive Officer of APA, charged "responsible" psychologists to upgrade, expand, and refine their training, teaching, research, and service goals to meet the expectations of society, to design vehicles for delivery of services to the deprived segments of our population equal to those available to the private sector. To date, efforts to define titles that reflect the roles and functions of psychological staff at different levels of training have contributed little that is innovative since the Thayer Conference at midcentury.

The most recent approach to role definition by the Board of Professional Affairs of the APA (1972b) suggests the following ranking: psychologist = doctoral level; associate psychologist = BA + 30–60 hours; psychological assistant or technician = BA level; AA and untrained are not yet identified. Bardon (1968) suggested school psychologist at doctoral level; psychological role I at the BA plus 2 years; psychological role II at the special BA or the BA plus 1 year graduate study. Division 16, Subcommittee on Education (APA, 1970) also suggested level titles: level 1 at the doctoral (APA approved); level 2 at BA plus 60 hours; level 3 at BA plus 30 hours; and level 4 or psychological assistant at 30 hours undergraduate credit in psychology.

STATE TRAINING LEVELS FOR PSYCHOLOGICAL WORKERS

The Conference of Psychology Directors (Center, 1971) has published titles and salaries of psychological workers in many states of the nation, titles that are descriptive of training levels in installations and are suggestive of the hierarchical functions of each title role. They include such titles as psychometric technicians, psychological technicians, psychological assistants, interns, residents, and associates. Reference has already been made to the title roles designed by the Illinois State Mental Health Generalist Series, which describes paraprofessional and professional ladders, each beginning with trainee levels and moving up to administrative levels. Although these title roles are not directly geared to the training at universities, they are suggestive guidelines to definitive titles in psychology. These titles operationally differentiate skills, roles, and functions, whereas numerical titles, I, II, III, IV per se tell us nothing about skills, training, roles, and functions of the carriers. Meaningful differential training and functions in psychology call for task and skill analysis, hierarchical grading of the many tasks and skills, and assignment to appropriate training levels which are operationally defined so that levels and skills are readily inferred.

SURVEY OF TITLE ROLES IN TRAINING AND SCHOOL PRACTICE

In an effort to arrive at psychological title roles that reflect training levels and functions, the problem was approached from the psychological service needs in our society as revealed in the literature of the past decade on compensatory and experimental education, on the new approaches to learning and behavior change, and on the critical problems affecting the changing school and social scenes. Examination of the literature in these areas provided a plethora of title roles and functions augmenting traditional psychological roles defining the variety of discrete services essential to coping with the critical target populations in our society today. Review of the literature provided 44 title roles and 23 target populations, all of which were included in a questionnaire (Appendix D) sent to chairmen of university training programs in clinical, counseling, school, and educational psychology and to school psychology practitioners. This survey sought to explore the roles for which each training program seeks to prepare its graduates, at each degree level, and what title roles practicing psychologists in the schools are assuming or are expected to assume.

For the survey 250 questionnaires were mailed, including 103 to APA approved clinical and counseling programs (83 clinical and 20 counseling), 35 school psychology programs, 10 educational psychology programs including 2 in special education, 2 AA programs. In addition 100 were sent to members of Division 16 of APA, presumably practicing school psychology according to the 1970 *APA Directory*. Of 79 questionnaires returned, 11 were not usable. Of the 68 usable forms, 20 were from APA approved clinical programs, 7 from APA approved counseling programs, 24 from school training programs, 2 from educational programs, and 15 from practicing psychologists. The only AA program response received is described in Chapter 8, so it is not included in this analysis.

It was gratifying to learn that only four respondents had some question about the meaning of title roles. Thus one asked, "What does prescription writer mean?" Another asked the meaning of "psychosocial evaluator." A third asked the meaning of "milieu curricular modifier." The fourth stated he had difficulty distinguishing between the titles, having no frame of reference. Even though the title roles are operational, they are here briefly defined to ensure consensual understanding.

Title Role Definitions

1. IQ tester/scorer/interpreter: Administration of intelligence tests like the Binet, WISC, WPPSI, WAIS; scoring responses; interpreting scores in terms of the normal curve of distribution and standard deviations.

2. Group tester/scorer: Administration and scoring standardized group achievement, intelligence, and aptitude tests and the Draw-a-Person Test scored against an objective scale of intelligence or adjustment.

3. Educational tester/scorer: Administration of standardized individual educational tests for tapping special abilities and disabilities and scoring these according to manual directions.

4. Test result evaluator/interpreter: Qualitative evaluations of test responses and behaviors during testing and identifying conditions that precipitated interferences.

5. Psychological examiner/evaluator: Evaluating a presenting problem in terms of psychological instruments to be administered to obtain data on variables essential to solving the problem; evaluating the test results, that is, scoring and assessing the significance of detailed results relative to the presenting problem.

6. Psychoeducational evaluator: Clinical observations of child behavior in the classroom during the subject matter learning periods and during activity periods, with intent to evaluate the psychological factors interfering with the child's school function.

7. Psychosocial evaluator: Clinical observations of child behavior in school, on school grounds, in neighborhood, and in home milieu to assess the social conditions that trigger disturbed learning and/or behavior in the child.

8. Psychodiagnostician: Skilled clinical approach to a

presenting problem involving study of birth, medical, health, developmental, family, socioeconomic histories and conditions; operational descriptions of behaviors at home, school, and neighborhood under clearly defined physical and social milieu conditions; school attainment reports, intelligence, aptitude, and achievement test results, depth personality testing results, and behavioral, neurological, medical, and physiological reports and writing diagnostic statement.

9. Psychological consultant: Assessing presenting problems, chronic or acute, developing tentative hypotheses, making recommendations for "holding" the situation until it is studied in detail and appropriate interventions are planned and implemented.

10. Educational diagnostician: Similar to psychodiagnostician except that the psychologist must be expert in learning principles, methods, styles as well as skilled in administration of diagnostic educational instruments relevant to the needs of the subject under study, and skilled in interpretations of such test results.

11. Educational consultant: Assessing presenting problems in a classroom, school, or school system, relative to learning, teaching methods, subject contents and materials, teacher/pupil ratios, size of class, roles of paraprofessionals, and the myriad factors that operate in the school and classroom that affect teaching and learning. Making recommendations to ease the situation and studying the situation in detail to guide development of intervention designs.

12. Prescription writer: Identifies precise gaps in learning a skill or content and writes directions, in detail, to remediate each gap sequentially. Prescriptions are the small, precise sequential steps in an intervention design leading toward problem solution (see examples in Chapter 4).

13. Prescription implementer: Translates prescriptive directives into practice (see Chapter 5).

14. Psychotherapist, dynamic: Approaches treatment of behavior, learning, emotional problems through individual or group therapy methods guided by dynamic principles of personality development and function.

15. Behavior therapist: Approaches treatment of behavior, learning, emotional problems through individual or group methods guided by learning theory and behavior modification principles.

16. Intervention designer: Develops an overall plan of attack on critical problems of an individual, classroom, school, school system, or community to eliminate or nullify conditions precipitating and maintaining the critical problems and introduces conditions and processes designed to eliminate or counteract the negatives to facilitate healthy functioning (see Chapters 4 and 5).

17. Intervention implementer: Applies the guidelines provided by the intervention designer to the target situation (see Chapters 4 and 5).

18. Designer, behavior modification program: Designs a program or plan of intervention (see 16 above) guided by principles of learning and behavior modification (see Chapter 10).

19. Behavior analyst/evaluator: On the basis of controlled class observations and precise recording of behaviors and interval recordings of behavior in a given setting, identifies significant variables eliciting and maintaining problem behaviors. Prepares baseline schedules (see Chapter 10) and designs modification schedules with research (validating) controls to determine the effectiveness of measures taken.

20. Behavior modification consultant: From the premise that deviant behavior is a response to conditions in the physical and social milieus, evaluates presenting problems in these terms (see title 11). Recommends,

supervises, and evaluates intervention programs.

21. Contingency modifier (see Chapter 10): Seeks to modify behaviors through application of contingency schedules (see Premack Principle, Chapter 9).

22. Consultant to school system: Explores critical dimensions of the system in terms of their impacts on the target populations and defines policies and organizational modifications or innovations to facilitate remediations (see Chapters 4 and 5).

23. Community consultant: Explores community mental health needs via epidemiological studies, identifies critical target populations, and determines types of facility and staff needed to deliver appropriate essential services to the community.

24. Research designer/consultant (see Chapters, 4, 5, 6): Provides guidance to systems on research investigations to be conducted by the system staff and/or defines research goals, methods, materials, procedures to explore causes and fitting solutions to presenting problems.

25. Research evaluator (see Chapter 4): Evaluates the reliability and validity of research findings in terms of the fit of the measuring instruments to the variables under investigation, the comparability of the before and after experimental data, and the many controls essential to maintaining purity of variables under study. Determines validity of uses of research results.

26. Research worker: Carries out specific research procedures under direction of research consultant, designer, evaluator, or overall implementer.

27. Curriculum consultant: Explores content, materials, and procedures of current curriculum in terms of dimensions that provoke and maintain presenting problems and offers recommendations for curricular modification to reduce or eliminate precipitating factors. Also recommends curricular innovations where current curriculum fails to meet the needs of special target populations.

28. Learning consultant: Analyzes the specific learning problems of target populations, the milieu and teaching conditions, the materials and teaching procedures that impair, impede, or aggravate learning problems and recommends modifications in milieu, teaching conditions, materials, and procedures to meet the specific learning styles and needs of the target populations.

29. Reading specialist: Expert in all aspects of reading, including learning processes, perceptual dimensions, phonetics, letter and word dimensions, appropriate remediating or compensatory materials, and methods appropriate to remediation of specific individual reading problems.

30. Compensatory program designer (see Chapters 3, 4, 5): Identifies specific gaps in a target population in a given skill or content area and selects or designs teaching and testing materials, procedures, and equipment to fill the gaps and maintain continuing sequential learning or development to expected levels of efficiency.

31. Compensatory program implementer: Follows guidelines set by designer in applying compensatory program to target population.

32. Milieu curricular modifier: Modifies milieu and curricular dimensions operating as obstacles to efficient learning and appropriate behavior in school. Also modifies home and neighborhood milieus (social and physical) that operate to impair learnings and elicit deviant behaviors.

33. Milieu curriculum consultant: Advises on the dimensions of milieu and curriculum that need change to facilitate learnings and appropriate behaviors. Consultant guides modifiers.

34. Group worker, confrontation leader: Seeks to remediate a variety of problems among target populations by group methods on the premise that subjects' behaviors change faster under peer group pressures than

in individually prescribed therapy (dynamic or behavior modification) or under diagnostically prescribed milieu or curricular or teaching/learning modifications.

35. Reality therapist: As the title role implies, seeks to modify deviant behaviors, attitudes, and motivations by rational analysis of situations and reality testing.

36. Conflict resolver/consultant: Studies conflict situations with precision and either applies techniques, methods, practices, and games along with modifications of the organization to facilitate resolution of conflict or trains administrators and staff in these methods, supervising and evaluating their efforts periodically.

37. Mental health interpreter: In essence an educator, informing school personnel, parents, community leaders, agency staffs, and government officials of the critical conditions in these various settings that operate against development and maintenance of mental health in the population and proposes general research based remedies.

38. Family consultant: Confers with families in their homes and in school or at agency conferences, explores and identifies conditions that contribute to critical problems of a child, other family members, or the family *in toto* and recommends intervention procedures to eliminate or modify these provoking circumstances. Works with appropriate agencies toward goals.

39. Paraprofessional trainer/supervisor (see Chapter 11): As the title implies, trains paraprofessional staff in schools and communities to provide certain aspects of professional services under the supervision of professionals.

40. Professional staff trainer/supervisor (see Chapter 11): Again as the title implies, trains lower level professional staff in the given settings to carry out se-

lected professional tasks under supervision of fully qualified professionals.

41. Counseling/guidance (behavioral): Applies counseling and guidance techniques to behavior problem resolution.

42. Counseling/guidance (educational): Applies counseling and guidance techniques to learning problem solutions.

43. Counseling and guidance (psychological): Applies counseling and guidance techniques to resolution of psychological problems.

44. Insight counseling: Through counseling techniques provides insights to subjects into the underlying dynamics of their problems on the premise that insight and understanding of causes facilitates behavior change.

Ordering these many title roles into four levels of complexity from low to high can provide guidelines to graduate level of training. To this end the data in the returned questionnaires were analyzed at four levels of training. It was hoped that the majority of respondents would check the titles discriminately, in terms of levels of complexity of function paralleling levels of graduate training.

ANALYSIS OF DATA

Rapid scanning of the responses revealed that two respondents had checked all title roles and all target populations under levels of training from MA-1 year through the doctoral level. One must assume that these respondents were guided by the challenges that would confront their graduates in the field, once out, rather than by the complexity of the different functions reflected in the title roles. This approach to training blurs the differences in training at the different levels, imposes unrealistic burdens on graduates at the lower levels of training, and misleads the public about who is a qualified professional psychologist.

Three respondents were very discriminating, checking different title roles at different levels of training, without overlap, while three others, also quite discriminating, did overlap a few title roles between levels of training. The overlap in these few cases may reflect an effort to indicate different degrees of proficiency. Two respondents in doctoral clinical programs checked only five or six titles reflecting a strong research orientation, limited service goals, and little if any concern with the changing needs of our population and society.

The data in the school practice returns blurred the distinctions between the four levels of training, that is, between doctoral level and the three master's levels, making separate tabulations meaningless. Accordingly, the data on school practice were tabulated together for all degree levels. It is not surprising that these data were not discriminating, considering the reports on the changing school scene in earlier chapters, which reveal not only blurring of graduate training differences but also blurring of professional lines and even lines between professionals and paraprofessionals. A statement submitted by one of the practicing school respondents provides a telling explanation:

> School psychologists are the General Practitioners of Psychology. They are expected to do everything in the school regardless of the amount of training they have.

Title Roles at Different Training Levels

A discriminating assignment of title roles to training levels must take into account the level of complexity of the functions of each title role so that the levels of complexity parallel levels of graduate training, without overlap. One approach to this assignment would be to review the definitions of each title role and assign each, on the basis of its level of complexity, to an appropriate training level. Had we not obtained data from practice, we might have taken this approach. With data on hand we can arrive at the same results by tabulating the data reported for each degree level, from the MA at 1 year through the MA at 2 years, the MA at 3 years, and the doctoral level, reporting popularly checked title roles at each level, that is, title roles checked by at least 75% of respondents in each category.

Where title roles are repeated at more than one level of training (many of the simpler title roles checked at MA levels were also checked at the doctoral level), they are assigned to the most appropriate level and omitted from the other levels. For example, the title role *IQ tester/scorer/interpreter* was popularly checked at all levels of training in the majority of the reports. Obviously this title role is appropriate to the MA level at 1 year and is so assigned; thus it is omitted from the higher levels of training. Title roles common to doctoral levels in clinical, counseling, and school psychology are so identified, and titles unique to any one of these areas are also identified for each particular area of specialization. This approach is intended to provide a guide to differential levels of training in psychology, to the types and levels of practice for which each program can equip its graduates, and it should reveal those title roles (services) that are at present neglected by graduate training programs. As was indicated earlier, the data on school practice were tabulated for all levels of training combined. These data reveal title roles that psychologists in school practice are called upon to assume as well as those that are not assigned or assumed.

Popular Title Roles

Title Roles Checked by 75% or More Respondents	Popular Target Populations
1. IQ tester/scorer/interpreter 2. Group tester/scorer 3. Educational tester/scorer 4. Test result evaluator/interpreter 5. Psychological examiner/evaluator 6. Psychoeducational evaluator 7. Psychosocial evaluator	Preschoolers Elementary pupils Intermediate pupils Teachers Aids Paraprofessionals Families

2 Year MA level, $N=24$ (5 clinical, 5 counseling, 10 School, 4 educational)

Title Roles checked by 75% or more respondents *	Target Populations
8. Psychodiagnostician 9. Psychological consultant 10. Educational diagnostician 11. Educational consultant 13. Prescription implementer 15. Behavior therapist 17. Intervention implementer 21. Contingency modifier 26. Research worker	All 10 school psychology respondents checked all target populations. Counseling respondents checked college age students and special groups, specifically emotionally disturbed and behavior problems and all adult groups included in questionnaire. Educational respondents checked special groups of children and all adult targets listed. Clinical respondents checked all school children, MR, emotionally disturbed, all adult targets listed in questionnaire.

262

3 Year MA level, $N = 6$ (4 school and 2 counseling)

Title Roles Checked by 5 or 6 Respondents *	Target Populations
20. Behavior modification consultant 22. Consultant to school systems 23. Community consultants 41. Counseling, guidance, behavior 42. Counseling, guidance, educational 43. Counseling guidance, psychological 27. Curriculum consultant ** 28. Learning consultant ** 32. Milieu curricular modifier ** 33. Milieu curricular consultant **	Here again school respondents checked all targets. Counseling respondents checked college students, special child groups, specifically emotional disturbed and behavior problems and all adult targets listed. Title roles 27–33 reflect the unique specialty of school psychology, learning and the educational process.

Doctoral Programs: APA Approved Clinical, $N = 20$

Title Roles Checked by 75% or More Respondents *	Target Populations
12. Prescription writer 14. Psychotherapist, dynamic 16. Intervention designer 18. Behavior modification designer 19. Behavior analyst/evaluator 24. Research designer/consultant 25. Research evaluator 34. Group worker/confrontation leader	All children; special concern with emotionally disturbed and behavior problems and all adult targets.

Doctoral Programs: APA Approved Counseling, $N = 7$

Title Roles Checked by 6 or 7 Respondents *	Target Populations
38. Family consultant 39. Paraprofessional trainer/supervisor 40. Professional trainer/supervisor 44. Insight counseling	College level. Special problem groups: emotionally disturbed; behavior problems; and educationally retarded. Adult targets.

Doctoral School Programs, $N = 17$ (plus 2 educational)

Title Roles Checked by 75% or More Respondents *	Target All Populations

Include title roles checked by 3 Year MA School Psychologists. Only the educational psychology respondents checked reading specialist.

School Practice Respondents, $N = 15$

Title Roles

All title roles were checked by two respondents, across the board. The remaining 13 respondents checked all *except* the following:

24. Research designer/consultant
26. Research worker
29. Reading specialist
30. Compensatory program designer
31. Compensatory program implementer
32. Milieu curricular modifier
33. Milieu curricular consultant
35. Reality therapist
36. Conflict resolver/consultant

SUMMARY OF SURVEY DATA

The tabular data just presented indicate that the majority of graduate school respondents to our questionnaire are cognizant of the many new title roles emerging in our changing school and social scenes and are preparing their students differentially and sequentially at the four stages in the graduate training hierarchy, from the 1 year MA to the doctoral level. These data also appear to blur differences between the different areas of psychology, clinical, counseling, school, and educational. The data also indicate that the differential and sequential title role training in graduate schools is ignored in school settings where the graduates of the different levels are employed. Specificially the data presented above may be summarized as follows.

At the 1 year MA level 9 respondents representing 7 school and 2 counseling graduate programs assigned 7 title roles to the curriculum for this degree level of training. These titles include IQ tester/scorer/interpreter, group tester/scorer, educational tester/scorer/interpreter, test result evaluator/interpreter, psychological examiner/evaluator, psychoeducational evaluator, psychodocial evaluator.

At the 2 year MA level 24 of the 68 respondents, including 15 clinical, 5 counseling, 10 school, and 4 educational psychology training programs, identified 9 titles as popular goals of training for the 2 year MA degree. These popular title roles include psychodiagnostician, psychological consultant, educational diagnostician, educational consultant,

---

* *Note* that all title roles listed above under 1 year MA level were also checked by at least 75% of respondents for this level. Accordingly, they are not repeated here, assuming that these skills are mastered at the 1 year MA level.

** Additional title role checked by school psychology respondents.

prescription implementer, behavior therapist, intervention implementer, contingency modifier, research worker.

Popular title roles at the 3 year MA level identified by 6 respondents from 4 school and 2 counseling graduate programs are behavior modification consultant, consultant to school system, community consultants, guidance / behavior counseling, guidance / educational counseling, guidance / psychological counseling. At this level the 4 respondents from the school psychology programs also identified 4 more title roles: curriculum consultant; learning consultant; milieu curricular modifier; milieu curricular consultant. These title roles identified by school psychology respondents reflect the unique specialty of school psychology, learning and the educational system and processes.

At the doctoral training level the popular title roles identified by 20 clinical respondents, 7 counseling and 17 school graduate program respondents, are prescription writer, dynamic psychotherapist, intervention designer, behavior modification designer, behavior analyst / evaluator, research designer / consultant, research evaluator, group worker / confrontation leader. In addition the 7 counseling respondents identified 4 more title roles, family consultant, paraprofessional trainer / superviser, professional trainer / supervisor, and insight counsel. The 2 educational psychology respondents, included above under school respondents, identified reading specialist as a popular title role at the doctoral level of training.

Finally, the title roles popularly identified by 13 practicing school psychology respondents included all the title roles thus far identified at all levels of training from the 1 year MA level to the doctoral level, without distinction for level of training, *except for the following title roles:* research designer / consultant; research worker; reading specialist; compensatory program designer; compensatory program implementer; milieu curricular modifier; milieu curricular consultant; reality therapist and conflict resolver / consultant. Two school psychology practitioners, on the other hand, identified *every title role* as appropriate to school psychology practice, at all levels of training.

The omission of these nine title roles by practicing school psychologists is surprising in view of the fact that three of these titles—research designer, research worker, and reading specialist—are traditional title roles in psychology and education, skills that school psychologists are expected to master at some graduate training level. The omission of the remaining six title roles is also surprising since these title roles are essential to the designs and implementations of innovative programs introduced into schools and communities over the past decade. Failure on the part of the school psychologists on the job to list these title roles suggests that school administrators, as a group, do not expect psychologists in their schools to participate in ongoing research, in the designing of research, in the designing of remediation or compensatory programs or methods of implementation, in designing milieu/curricular changes, or conflict and crisis interventions. Apparently such roles are generally assigned to other education specialists.

Personal experience and observations in the schools during the past five years supports the preceding interference that school administrators for the most part assign these challenging title roles to educational specialists rather than psychologists in the schools. When psychological staff serving the schools are ill equipped by training and skill to provide these services, it makes good sense not to present them with these challenging roles. However, when psychologists in the schools are doctorally trained and equipped by special training, study, and experience to cope with these tasks, it seems wasteful to bypass them in such critical areas of service to the schools.

A word about the omission of the title role of reality therapist by the practicing school psychologists is in order here. Reality therapy is a title role that may be assumed by psychologists themselves when this intervention method appears to be appropriate to the given problem situation, so omission of this role by our sample of practicing school psychologists suggests that they do not consider this approach useful, or, possibly, that they are not skilled in its application or do not recognize the situations when this type of intervention is appropriate.

Rare Title Roles in Graduate Training Programs

Title roles omitted in the majority returns from graduate training programs include the following: reading specialist, checked only by respondents from educational psychology programs; compensatory program designers and implementers; reality therapist; conflict resolver/consultant; mental health interpreter. Indifference to these title roles suggests that graduate program administrators on the whole are not yet involved, to any serious degree, in the compensatory and experimental educational programs flooding the schools and communities since the early 1960s.

Since the compensatory efforts in education seek to meet critical developmental and learning needs of masses of deprived child populations in the United States, it seems urgent that graduate departments in psychology across the board—clinical, counseling, school, and educational—revamp their curricula to include extensive and intensive study of the learning difficulties among deprived child populations and compensatory approaches to facilitate learning. It appears realistic to expect graduate training programs in psychology, preparing scientifically trained professionals, to strive to contribute scientific knowledges and lend direction and substance to compensatory efforts in the schools to turn the tide which is mounting in spite of all efforts to date.

Popular Target Populations

With regard to the target populations the graduate programs claim to equip their students to serve, the data presented in tabular form indicate that at the 1 year MA level, the 9 graduate school respondents (7 school and 2 counseling) identified 7 targets to be served: preschoolers, elementary and intermediate age level, teachers, aides, other paraprofessionals, and families. At the 2 year MA degree level, the 10 school training respondents checked all target populations listed: all children in the school system, all exceptional children, all school personnel from teacher aides and other paraprofessionals to administrators, the entire school system, the entire community, families, interns, special service staff, and psychological staff. One wonders how well equipped these students can be to cope effectively with such diversified populations. In contrast the counseling program respondents at the 2 year MA level listed only 4 target populations: college students, emotionally and behaviorally disturbed children, and related adult groups. Educational training program respondents appear to limit student training at the 2 year MA level to servicing special groups of children (the exceptional children) and related adult groups, whereas the clinical training respondents listed all school children with special attention to the mentally retarded, emotionally disturbed, and related adult groups.

At the 3 year MA and the doctoral levels of training school respondents listed all targets in the questionnaire; counseling respondents simply added educationally retarded to the targets listed for the 2 year MA; clinical respondents added behaviorally disturbed to the targets listed for the 2 year MA level.

It is somewhat puzzling to note that although most of the graduate training respondents train students at the 2 year MA level and beyond to cope with educationally retarded children and with related adult groups, they do not prepare their students for title roles of reading specialist, compensatory program designers and implementers, conflict and crisis resolver/consultant, or mental health interpreter, all title roles essential to coping effectively with educationally retarded children and related adult groups, particularly in the deprived segments of our population.

The target population data provided by practicing school psychologists indicate that these practitioners cope with all targets listed in the questionnaire in spite of the fact that they do not serve in the title roles uniquely adapted to provide services to many of these target populations. For example, practicing school psychologists do not serve in title roles of research designer/consultant, compensatory program designer/implementer, milieu curricular modifier consultant, or conflict/crisis resolver/consultant, all new title roles adapted to present school and community needs for coping with massive educational retardation among deprived child populations, with parent and community participation in the schools, with the needs of the emerging paraprofessionals, and so on. There seems to be a poor fit between the self-perceived responsibilities of practicing school psychologists and their actual assigned roles and professional skills.

Positive Training Trends Revealed by the Survey

Graduate department administrators and staff responding to the questionnaire generally appear to be expanding their training goals and courses of study, judging from the title roles and targets they checked, to equip their students for the many needs of our new population targets. They appear to be introducing behavior modification theory, principles, and techniques in response to the explosion of research in these areas; they appear to be introducing training and supervision skills to cope with subprofessional staff, the paraprofessionals, the new breed emerging *en masse* from deprived and even from privileged population segments. The graduate programs appear to be training their graduates in consultation skills to cope with the critical problems in education and community mental health, and they appear to have concern with the impacts of milieu structures on learning, development, and functions and the deviations in these processes due to milieu impacts.

IMPLICATIONS

Our data reveal dramatically the changes that mark the field of psychology since midcentury in terms of training, goals, title roles, and targets served. Whereas at midcentury the targets were exceptional children and the services involved testing abilities, aptitudes, and intelligence by graduates at the MA plus 60 credits level while doctoral level graduates were diagnosticians, who used depth testing methods and served as therapists and community consultants, today psychologists serve a multiplicity of targets in a vast variety of methods and at a variety of training levels.

Analyses of our data permit differential assignment of the various title roles to each of the four graduate levels of training. This suggests that the title roles within each category of training have related skills of equivalent complexities. It also suggests that one or more core skills are essential to the title roles within any one training category and the core(s) can be used to define the general rubric of each of the four training levels. Further, if the title roles within each rubric are analyzed for discrete, precisely graded skills, these skills can be assigned differentially to the graded paraprofessional training levels serving professionals.

In the next chapter we attempt to identify the core skill in each category of title role and assign a descriptive title to each general category. Analysis of all title roles for discrete skills is far too space consuming for inclusion in this book, but an approach to the process is presented at the 1 year MA level with description of the paraprofessional hierarchy title roles leading to the general category level. The manner of movement from the 1 year MA to the doctoral level of training is also suggested.

REFERENCES

APA. *Task Force on Standards for Psychological Services and Facilities.* Office of Professional Affairs, No. 3130. Washington, D.C., 1969.

APA. *Directory of Membership.* Washington, D.C., 1970.

APA. *Approved Doctoral Programs in Clinical, Counseling and School Psychology.* Washington, D.C., 1972. (a)

APA. Board of Professional Affairs. *Standards Study No. 3111.* Washington, D.C., 1972. (b)

Bard, B. Report Half of City HS Pupils on Drugs. New York: *New York Post*, Oct. 12–17, 1972.

Bardon, J. I. School Psychology and School Psychologists: An Approach to an Old Problem. *American Psychologist,* 1968, *23,* 189–194.

Bevan, W. Higher Education in the 1970's. A Once and Future Thing. *American Psychologist,* 1971, *26,* 537–545.

Blank, B. D. Who Needs Degrees. *AAUP Bulletin,* Sept. 1972.

Blau, T. H. Exposure to Competence: A Simple Standard for Graduate Training in Professional Psychology. *Professional Psychologist,* 1973, *4,* 133–136.

Center, A. *Committee on Professional Information of the Conference of Psychologist Directors in State, Federal and Territorial Mental Health Programs. 1971.* Salary Data Tables. Richmond: Commonwealth of Virginia, Commissioner's Office, Dec. 1, 1971.

Howe, H., II. *Openness—The New Kick in Education.* Center for the Study of Education. New Haven: Yale University Press, 1972.

Iscoe, I. *Mental Health in the Americas.* Austin: University of Texas, 1972.

Kovacs, A., Blau, T. & Bales, R. A. Ad Hoc Committee on Subdoctoral Training. *Psychotherapy Bulletin,* 1972, *5,* 13–23.

Kurz, R. *Accreditation Procedures and Criteria.* New York: APA Central Office, 1971.

Liddle, G. P. & Reighard, G. W. Directory of Pupil Personnel Services. Who Are They? Where Are They Going? *Psychology in the Schools,* 1966, *3/4.*

Little, K. Is the Responsible Psychologist a Hypothetical Creature? *APA Monitor*, 1972, *3*, 2.

Marland, S. P., Jr. *Education's Time of Questioning*. Center for the Study of Education. New Haven: Yale University Press, 1972.

Matulef, N. J. (ed.) *The Revolution in Professional Training*, 1st ed. National Council on Graduate Education, St Louis: 1970–1971.

Matulef, N. J. To Be or Not To Be. *The Clinical Psychologist, 1972*, 26.

Milgram, N. A. The Subdoctoral Psychologists in the Profession and in APA. *The Clinical Psychologist, 1972*, 26.

Nader, R. Community Mental Health Centers: Calling the Bluff. *Behavior Today, 1972*.

New York State Psychologist. Master's Level Programs Hit by State as Product of Collusive Mediocrity. *New York State Psychologist* 1972, *24*, 1–9.

Nyquist, E. B. The Role of the State in Urban Education. Center for the Study of Education. New Haven: Yale University Press, 1970.

Persons, R. W., Clark, C., Persons, M., Kadish, M. & Patterson, W. Training and Employing Undergraduates as Therapists in a College Counseling Service. *Professional Psychologist, 4*, 1973, p. 170–178.

Pierce, W. H. Behind the Scenes of National Assessment. Center for the Study of Education. New Haven: Yale University Press, 1970.

Proshansky, H. M. For What Are We Training Our Graduate Students? *American Psychologist, 1972*, 27.

Seeman, J. & Seeman, L. Emergent Trends in the Practice of Clinical Psychology. *Professional Psychologist, 1973, 4*, p. 151–157.

Steiner, G. & Roth, L. (eds.) *The Revolution in Professional Training*. National Council on Graduate Education, St. Louis, 1972–1973.

Vardy, M. Role of the Mental Health Professional. *Professional Psychologist, 1972*, 3.

CHAPTER 13

Roles for Psychology Today

ANALYSIS OF CORE SKILL AT DIFFERENTIAL TRAINING LEVELS

As indicated in the preceding chapter, title roles for differential training for delivery of psychological services essential to the needs of today will be formulated through analyses of the core skills critical to each series of popular title roles assigned by university graduate respondents to the four graduate training levels, 1 year MA, 2 year MA, 3 year MA, and doctoral level.

Testing is Core Skill at One Year MA Level

Examination of the title roles assigned to the 1 year MA level reveals a critical core skill throughout these titles,

274

namely, *testing* of abilities, aptitudes, and behaviors. This core skill may be identified by the title *psychometrist*, the traditional designation assigned to MA level graduates in psychology trained to measure mental states and processes. The discrete tasks within these title roles may be roughly ordered in terms of complexity as follows:

1. Test administration (standardized, objective instruments).
2. Test scoring (again standardized, objective processes).
3. Test score interpretations against normal curves of distribution.
4. Trained observations and recordings of behaviors in class, play, home, neighborhood.
5. Test selection for given problem situation.

If we establish high school equivalency attainment or ability as the minimal level of ability essential for success in this paraprofessional ladder, the title roles leading up to rubric psychometrist might be labeled as follows:

Entry Point	*Title Role*
HS equivalency	Psychometric trainee
AA degree in social / human / sciences / services	Junior psychometric technician
BA degree in social / human / sciences / services	Psychometric technician
MA at 1 year	Psychometrist

Incumbents at each level move up to the next level of this ladder upon completion of the prescribed experience, training, and study under tutelage of the psychometrist, who in turn is under direct and close supervision of a fully qualified professional psychologist. In line with present trends, equivalent experience could be offered instead of formal university training, with the candidate demonstrating efficiency in skills, knowledges, and problem solving judgments. Psychometrists could move into the next higher level of operation by fulfilling the additional graduate training appropriate to the specialized core selected in the 2 year MA general classification plus appropriate practicum experience under professional supervision. Training and supervision beyond the 1 year MA level, that is, beyond the level of psychometrist, should be carried out by fully qualified professional psychologists rather than by incumbents at the subdoctoral levels, except where such incumbents demonstrate unique specializations, such as reading specialists, who may not have doctoral degrees.

Several Core Tasks at 2 Year MA Level

Analyses of the title roles assigned to the 2 year MA level reveals several distinct core tasks, for example, psychodiagnostician, educational diagnostician, consultant in psychology and education, behavior therapist, researcher, implementer. Since all these complex core tasks call for sound grounding in basic psychological and social science theories, facts, and skills, it seems reasonable to identify this level of training as psychological, distinguished, however, from full training by the qualifier *assistant psychologist*. Furthermore, since the different core skills within this rubric are highly specialized, it seems wise to further qualify the title roles at this level by each particular specialty. Thus an assistant psychologist might be identified as *assistant psychologist: psychodiagnostician / consultant,* as *assistant psychologist: educational diagnostician / consultant,* or as *assistant psychologist: behavior therapist / contingency modifier.* The title roles of *prescription* and *intervention implementers* and *research worker* fit into all these specialties, so they may be added to any of the specialized titles to define precise training and functions of incumbents in specific positions.

Paraprofessional Steps in 2 Year MA Ladders

To develop parallel paraprofessional ladders to each of these three specialties at the assistant psychologist level, the title roles assigned here can be defined in terms of discrete skills which may then be graded and assigned to differential paraprofessional training tracks. For example, training for the diagnostic specialties might begin in the psychometric hierarchy, move from psychometrist to psychological intern, either in psychological or educational diagnostics and consultation, so designated during the year of graduate training and practicum under full professional supervision and attain or earn the title assistant psychologist upon demonstration of satisfactory proficiency in these high level skills. In the behavior therapy specialty the paraprofessional training might begin with the title contingency technical aid, at precollege level, moving on to the title contingency technician trainee at the AA level, to junior contingency technician at the BA level, contingency technician at the 1 year MA level, and finally to assistant psychologist: behavior therapist/contingency modifier/manager at the 2 year MA level, after demonstrating satisfactory proficiency in those high level skills.

Complex Core Tasks at 3 Year MA Level

At the 3 year MA level of training, the title roles are at a still higher level of complexity and again reflect several complex core skills that call for specialization. The general level of training might be titled associate psychologist, which would be further amplified by the following specialties: behavior modification consultant; school system consultant/currciulum, learning, milieu modifier; community consultant; counseling and guidance specialist.

Paraprofessional Steps in 3 Year MA Ladders

In each of these training ladders, the candidates would specialize in serving the target populations for whom their specialties are most appropriate. Movement toward the title associate psychologist might begin at the assistant psychology level if the candidate wishes to continue his specialty from the assistant psychologist level. In such a case he would assume the title psychological resident for the year of graduate study toward the associate psychology level. During this year he would also do his practicum training under direct supervision of a fully qualified professional psychologist. At the end of the year, with demonstrated efficiency in his specialty, he would earn the title associate psychologist: specialty defined. If the candidate at the assistant psychology level wishes to change his specialty at the associate level he would be required to move back to the psychometry level and traverse the course of study and training called for in the assistant psychology specialty he wishes to enter. Then he would traverse the program as defined above leading to the associate psychology rubric with specialty defined.

Routes to Specialties at Professional
Psychologist Level

At the doctoral level, clinical, counseling, school, and educational, the title roles assigned by university respondents call for high level creative core skills such as designer, evaluator, therapist. At this level the general rubric is *psychologist* augmented by specialties as follows: prescription writer/intervention designer; research designer/evaluator/consultant; psychotherapist dynamic/group worker, confrontation leader/insight counselor; behavior modification designer/evaluator/analyst; family consultant/conflict resolver/mental health consultant/interpreter;

paraprofessional trainer/supervisor and professional trainer /supervisor; compensatory program designer/implementer /evaluator. Entry level for the title psychologist is the doctoral degree with specialization in one or more of the core programs cited above. Movement toward the title *psychologist* would be from the *assistant* or *associate* levels of training, depending on the areas of specialization at these levels of training and their correspondence to the selected cores of specialization at the doctoral level. If the core area of specialization at the associate psychology level is the same as that toward which the candidate wishes to train at the doctoral level, then the associate psychologist would be required to present a dissertation project in this core area of specialization and demonstrate proficiences in each core skill in actual problem situations. With the award of the doctoral degree he becomes eligible for and entitled to the rubric psychologist: specialty defined. On the other hand, if the core area of specialization at the associate level differs from that toward which the candidate strives at the doctoral level, the candidate returns to the assistant level and fulfills the requirements for specialization in the new core area, with practicum during the year of preparation, being identified during this year as a psychological resident, attaining title associate psychologist end of year, then moving on toward the doctorate by submitting a dissertation in his specialty and demonstrating proficiency in each special core skill in actual problem situations.

It is noteworthy that in the training procedures developed here, the specialties of clinical, counseling, school, and educational have disappeared, being replaced by operationally defined core specialties that may be applied to problems of selected target populations as deemed appropriate. The traditional classification of psychology into clinical, counseling, school, and educational have little meaning today, since each implies a specific type of service for a clearly circumscribed population; for example, Clinical = patients; counseling = college students and work age segments of the population; school = children, particularly exceptional; educational = school personnel, particularly teachers.

Diplomate Status

Beyond the title psychologist: specialty defined is the title *diplomate,* which is at present established in traditional fields of psychology, clinical, counseling, school, industrial, by the Admerican Board in Professional Psychology. The approach to training standards and title roles described here makes this diplomate classification meaningless. To bring diplomate status in line with this new classification, awards would be given to psychologists in such specialties as psychologist; prescription writer / intervention designer, psychologist: research designer / evaluator / consultant, psychologist: psychotherapist dynamic / group worker, confrontation leader / insight counselor, and so on.

Award of the diplomate status would call for evidence of five years post doctoral work in the given specialty, evaluated throughout at a high level of performance and efficiency and high level ethical and professional behavior as judged by a group of diplomates. The diplomate would have to display creative function in his specialties in his given work site or, if he is not employed in a site that permits such demonstration, then he is presented with "in basket problems" to demonstrate his expertise. Further study and specialization beyond the diplomate level would be the prerogative of the diplomate himself. However, professionals at this high level would be expected to devise means for continuing education and training for their group members, perhaps through the National Academy of Professional Psychology, Inc. These experts would also be expected to keep ahead of the times and anticipate essential changes and seek to influence the profession to remain fluid so that changes could be effected without need to crack rigidly established tracks and structures.

The procedures defined here would provide a large pool of differentially skilled staff for delivery of services essential to our present populations at reasonable costs and with efficient use of talents, since paraprofessionals trained within the field would be made available to the professionals in large numbers, at end of one year, two years, three years, and so on. These subprofessionals could provide basic services to large numbers of people, under supervision of psychometrists, assistant psychologists, psychological interns, residents, and associate psychologists, who in turn would be under the direct supervision of psychologists who have critical specialized skills essential to coping with current problems of our target populations.

CONCLUDING REMARKS

In short the challenge to psychology by the changing school and social scene can be met by differential training levels, from high school to the doctorate and beyond, with specialization in terms of core skills designed to meet the various needs of the multiple target groups in our population.

Obviously this skeleton of differential training in the hierarchy of psychology from paraprofessional, to precollege, to the professional levels needs to be turned into a dynamic ongoing process by functional analyses of the discrete knowledges and skills comprising all title roles within each major rubric of training. These refined skills must then be assigned sequentially to the appropriate training levels so that appropriately skilled subdoctoral and paraprofessional staff become rapidly available to assist the professionals in each specialty. For example, subdoctoral training in research skills needs to be precisely spelled out so that trainees at the lower levels of the hierarchy are equipped with research skills essential to assist research designers, consultants, and implementers in each specialty of function. Thus, in the field of community consultation/evaluation/implementation, the subprofessionals would need to be skilled in epidemiological methods of collecting appropriate data, under direction of the professionals, since the professionals need these data to make their determinations of needs and interventions.

This task is large and complex and must be assumed by organized psychology, graduate school administrators, and specialized professional staff and professional psychologists with expertise in each specialty to ensure realistic analyses, design, and implementation of the new approaches to such training. Further, these new approaches to the definition of the hierarchy in the profession of psychology need to be communicated deliberately to school, community, and governmental administrators and staffs with the expectation that these allied professionals will contribute to the thinking from their specialized experiences and will develop a refined appreciation of the complexities in the field and a respect for the differential training and functions to the end that they will make realistic optimal use of incumbent psychological staff at all levels of the hierarchy. During this process stereotyped notions about psychologists' functions may well be dissipated. It is expected that in this process mere "seniority" in terms of length of time on a job and the sinecure of tenure per se will be scrapped as criteria of expertise. This enlightened approach to the roles and functions of psychologists in the schools will be successful when hierarchically skilled staff are assigned to deliver to the deprived segments of the population essential services equal to those available to the privileged segments. Finally, it is expected that through this task and a systems analysis approach to differential training and assignment, the roles and functions of members of the psychology hierarchy will remain fluid, so that they may be adaptable to continuing examination and evaluation in terms of meeting current and emerging population needs.

APPENDIX A

APPENDIX A.1. CLASSROOM RECORD: SAMPLE GUIDE TO PRESCRIPTIVE TEACHING, GRADE 1, SECTIONS 3 AND 4

Grade population	VKT (months)			KEI (points)
$N = 160$	P/M	Voc.	Man.	
Grade mean:	73	74	83	4.6
Grade SD:	10.2	15.2	13.6	2.0

	VKT MA–SD (months)			KEI	
Name	P/M	Voc.	Man.	Score	(SD)
JB	96 +3	—	72 −1	2	+2
WM	75 +1	75 +1	80 −1	6	−1
WD	75 +1	69 −1	92 +1	3	+1
CH	75 +1	54 −2 *	108 +2	3	+1
CV	75 +1	48 −2 *	77 −1	7	−2
KJ	72 0	84 +1	72 −1	7	−2;
				5	−10
AW	69 −1	54 −2 *	80 −1	4	+1
MD	63 −1	—	64 −2 *	8	−2 *
HR	63 −1	—	64 −2 *	10	−3 **
JC	63 −1	63 −1	64 −2 *	10	−3 **

* Children with scores that fall below −2 SD.

** Children with scores that fall below −3 SD from the grade mean on each skill.

These data permit the teacher to select the children in need of immediate prescriptive teaching and practice.

APPENDIX A.2. INDIVIDUAL PROGRESS RECORD ON THE VANE KINDERGARTEN TEST AND KEI SCALE

Child's name_____ bd_____age_____

Grade 1 $N=160$ CA	KEI	P/M	Voc.	Man
Mean (months): 82	4.6	73	74	83
SD (months):	2	10	15	13.6

Test	Score SD	Score SD	Score SD	Score SD
Date				
Date				
Date				
Date				

Interpretation

Scores on P/M, Voc., and Man are reported in Mental ages (months). Standard deviations are also in months. The child is ranked against the total grade population mean by comparing his MA to the grade mean in terms of SD's. SD's spread from $+3$ to -3; significant deviations from grade mean fall at or above $+2$ for advanced and -2 for severe lag.

P/M = perceptual motor coordination
VOC = word definitions
MAN = perceptual differentiation and clarity of perceiving human figure details and translating them manually
KEI = emotional adjustment based on Koppitz adjustment scale

APPENDIX A.3. TEACHER GUIDANCE SHEET

Grade: Date:

Name of Child: bd: age:

Vineland Social Maturity Scale (Parent report) Social age:
1. Significant lags in age appropriate autonomy:
2. Significant spurts in age appropriate autonomy:

New York City Child Developmental Scale (Teacher report)
Developmental age:
1. Significant lags in age appropriate autonomy:
2. Significant spurts in age appropriate autonomy:

3DPT: Fein Testing of Limits Dependency and Self Image Scales
TL1 (unstructured setting)
1. Self image attitudes (scale scores)
2. Dependency level attitudes (scale scores)
TL2 (structured setting)
1. Self image attitudes (scale scores)
2. Dependency level attitudes (scale scores)

Suggested Classroom Treatment

Insist on more than average compliance with rules of classroom
    behavior.
Tolerate as much acting out as you can without becoming un-
    comfortable.
Use persistent encouragement and constant feedback to encour-
    age productivity.
Use variable intermittent encouragement (reinforcement) sched-
    ules to firm essential learnings.
Shape behavior by rewarding ever increasing competency in a
    given task.
Emphasize structure. Provide step by step instruction. Use con-
    crete materials. Give as few choices as possible. This child

must be kept aware of exactly what is expected of him at all times.

Give this child as much autonomy and freedom of choice as possible.

Give this child opportunity to learn to make choices by practice with problems calling for decisions hierarchically arranged in complexity, beginning with a simple one out of two choices and increasing units as child masters criteria for choice making.

None of the above apply to this child.

Special Considerations

Use oral gratification to reinforce appropriate responses and behavior emitted.

Use Premack principle of motivation, that is allow child to participate in an activity he likes after he has completed a given task in an activity he does not like to participate in.'

Provide opportunity for withdrawal from the constant noise and hum of the classroom.

Provide contact affection in reassuring amounts.

Provide opportunity for development of sensory-motor skills.

APPENDIX A.4. REPORT TO GRADE PRINCIPAL ON GROUP TEST RESULTS

PSX	Grade 1	$N = 160$	CA mean $= 82$ months	
	Vane KG	Test Means		KEI Means
	P/M	Voc.	Man	Adj. Points
Grade Means (months):	73	74	83	4.6
Grade SD:	10.3	15.2	13.6	2.
1¹ section	66	75	77	5.4
1³⁺⁴	76	63	85	4.4
1⁵	69	87	80	5.3
1⁶	69	69	89	5.
1⁷	77	78	84	3.5
1⁸	88 *	69	88	4.
1⁹	69	85	89	3.5
1¹⁰	68	69	76	4.9

* This class mean falls in +2 SD of the grade mean. It is noteworthy that the teacher of this class was an artist concerned with developing perceptual motor skills in her charges throughout the year. Modeling, shaping, and practice appeared to build perceptual motor skill efficiency in these children.

APPENDIX B

APPENDIX B.1. TWITCHELL-ALLEN 3DPT-FEIN TESTING OF LIMITS DEPENDENCY SCALE

Evaluations of dependency level are based on the manipulations and final resting position of test form 17 in relation to the other two test forms, and/or the manipulations of test forms 12 and 21 in relation to test form 17. The crucial features in the dependency evaluations are the graphic relationships of test form 17 to the other two test forms established by manipulations of forms during and at the end of the task. Dependency level scores are defined operationally and diagrammed below.

It is essential that TL_1 and TL_2 be scored independently of each other. TL_1 represents an ambiguous nonrole structured relationship whereas TL_2 represents a role-structured rela-

289

tionship (with a limited number of perceptual ambiguities.) When subjects present a variety of dependency relationships in one task, each level is scored once. (Repetitions of any dependency level within one task should not be included in the weighting and averaging of the final dependency score, on any scale.)

Score	Dependency Level	Manipulation of Test Form Relationships
1	Independent: Ability to direct the self; no support or limits from authority needed.	Test form 17 is turned or moved so that it faces away from the other two test forms, or the other test forms are so moved that 17 is left facing away from them. Add other scores reflected in performance (see below.)
Ex.		
2	Movement toward independence: Striving for independence while maintaining harmonious relationships with authority.	The distance between test form 17 and the other two test forms is increased but the test forms still face each other. If only one of the other forms is moved apart but still faces 17, score both 2 and 3 (see next). If distance between 17 and others is increased and 17 faces away from the others, score 2 and 1. The essential feature of score 2 is increased distance between 17 and other forms.
Ex.		
3	Accepts status quo: Ability to direct the self within limits set by authority while maintaining harmon-	Test forms are not moved out of the position presented by the examiner. At times the subject picks up and examines the test forms but returns them

Score	Dependency Level	Manipulation of Test Form Relationships
	ious relationships to authority. This level represents average dependency.	to the original position in this case also score 3.

Ex.

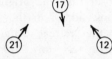

| 4 | Childlike dependency: Resistance to self-direction, bid for increased limits, and closer supervision. | Test form 17 is moved closer to the other test forms, but it does not touch them. Add score (3) if test form 17 is left facing the other test forms. Add score 1 if test form is facing away from the other test forms. The additional scores 3 and/or 1, when present here, are included in the final averaging since they reveal additional dimensions within the framework of a childlike dependency. |

The essential feature of score 4 is the reduction of distance between form 17 and the others, from the original positions, without touching the other test forms.

Ex.

| 5 | Ambivalence, vascillation in dependency: Efforts are made for self-direction but are felt as threatening, sending subject back and forth to "parent | Test form 17 is moved and/ or turned back and forth to and from test forms 12 and/ or 21 without touching them. If test form 17 touches either or both of the other forms in the process, add score 7 or |

291

Score	Dependency Level	Manipulation of Test Form Relationships

or parents" for support

Ex.

8 as the case may be. If test form 17 is moved closer to either or both of the others during vascillation, that is closer than the original positions, add 4 to the score. If on the "retreat to the parent" move test form 17 is not touched but either or both of the other test forms are moved back and forth or to and from test form 17, score 5 is assigned since the implication is the same as above. Add other scores revealed. Note carefully and score the final position of 17 in relation to the other test forms.

6   Confusion in dependency: Efforts made for self-directions or dependency relations leave subject in confusion.

Ex.

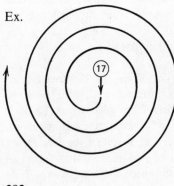

Test form 17 is moved round and round either on the table or held in the hand (score 6). In the final position, if test form 17 is closer to one or both of the other two forms add score 4; if test form 17 is looking away from the forms add score 1; if 17 is left in contact with one or both of the other forms, add score 7 or 8 as indicated. If 17 is in contact and is looking away, while in touch, add 1 to reveal this facet of the relationship but do not include score 1 in the final weighting.

Score	Dependency Level	Manipulation of Test Form Relationships
7	Contact dependency: Infantile dependency on one authority. Subject is fully dependent on one "adult" for direction.	Test form 17 is brought into direct contact with either test form 12 or 21, or either of these forms is brought into direct contact with 17. Here again add 1 if test form 17 is looking away from the other test forms(s), but do not include this score in the weighting.
Ex.		
8	Contact dependency: Infantile dependency on both authority figures (all authorities). Subject cannot direct himself at all.	Test form 17 is brought into direct contact with both 12 and 21 (whether 17 is moved or the others are moved into this position). Again add score 1 if 17 is looking away from the other test forms, but do not include 1 in the weighting. (8 is scored when the three forms are in contact —no matter in what position.)
Ex.		

APPENDIX B.2.   TWITCHELL-ALLEN 3DPT-FEIN TESTING OF LIMITS SELF IMAGE SCALE

Identifications projected onto the test forms in the Testing of Limits tasks appear to reflect the childhood family constellation where test form 17 is seen as the childhood self image, 12 the childhood mother image, and 21 the childhood father image. This inference is supported by clinical experience and verified by statistical evaluations of direct associations to the TL stories and test forms, presented below.

The identifications projected onto test form 17 in TL_1 and

TL$_2$ by the nursing sample were evaluated against a 5 point scale ranging from acceptance of the body image through ambivalence, denial, and finally rejection. Multiple identities projected onto 17 were all scored.

Scale Score Attitude	Definitions	Examples
1. Acceptance of sex and subordinate role.	Responses that acknowledge sex of subject tested. It is expected that the childhood image (structure and subordinate role) will be projected onto test form 17.	Females will project girl, little girl, daughter, young lady, school girl, adolescent girl. Males will project subordinate male roles and structure.
2. Acceptance of sex but not subordinate role.	Responses that acknowledge the sex structure of the subject being tested but assign adult status to test form 17.	Females project pregnant woman, wife, woman carrying child, the other woman, mother, witch, etc. Males project adult male roles.
3. Ambivalence.	Responses that admit human form and life but evade the sex identity of the subject tested.	Females offer boy, man; males offer girl, woman; all references to child, person, people, individual, human creature.
4. Denial.	Responses that reflect evasion of the human quality, assigning sub-	Creature, bird, animal, God, Jesus, Superman, witch, dance step,

Scale			
Score	Attitude	Definitions	Examples
		human or superhuman qualities to this form; also esthetic references, abstractions, symbolism, religious references.	symbol of life, art form, etc.
5.	Rejection.	Responses that reflect destruction, distortion, nonexistence.	Something weird, blot of clay, mangled object, nothing, junk, squashed up thing, a mess, etc.
6.	Confusion.*	Responses reflecting confusion about identity, variety of images projected onto 17 arbitrarily in one story.	Man, child, woman, animal, thief, policeman, etc. projected onto form 17.

* Category 6 was added after this study was completed since this category (confusion) was reflected in the self image responses of the majority of the deprived sample under ambiguous conditions. No. 6 should be scored along with other arbitrary identifications projected onto No. 17.

APPENDIX B.3.   SELF-REFERENCE VALIDATION SCALE

Associations to the Fein-Testing of Limits Self Image Scale

Evidence of the validity of the self-image inferences made from student identifications of test form 17 during the testing of limits tasks was obtained by asking students to give associations to their TL stories. This validation procedure was suggested to the chief investigator by Professor Gordon Allport of Harvard University.

Associations given by the student sample to the TL stories were classifiable in six categories as follows:

Scale Score	Associations	Examples
1.	Wishful family situation.	"Well it is how I wish my marriage will be"; "I wish my house were like that"; "It is like my family only I wish my father were like that"; "I wish my father would build a ranch fence around our house"; "My father yells and sends us out of the room, wish he were like that father I described"; "Well, I sure would like to be married and be looking for a house, wouldn't you?"
2.	Immediate family now.	"It is like our family"; "It is my story"; "It is like my father, he makes me angry sometimes"; "It is like my family but in my family my mother does the disciplining"; "It is my brother, sister, and me"; "I am my father's boy, the boy he never had, so it's me"; "It is my father and me, I am his favorite and my sister is jealous of me"; "It's my father and me and he yelled at me when I was small and I cried and my mother just stood there and did nothing."

Scale Score	Associations	Examples
3.	Friend or relative exclusive of immediate family.	"It reminds me of my girlfriend's family, I feel sorry for her"; "Just one of the student nurses—it is her story"; "It is the story of our neighbor's boy and my mother took care of him"; "It is my cousin's story, I know just how she feels, I hate her mother for not letting her out of the house with boys"; "It's like my f— no uncle, he gets mad too."
4.	Story heard or read, seen on TV, movies, stage, etc. Distant references.	"This reminds me of what I read in the newspaper"; "saw on TV"; "saw in movies"; "heard on radio"; "studied in school about colonial days, primitive days, ancient days, read about India, saw in Germany; read in psychology, sociology," etc.
5.	Denial of associations; vague references.	"Nothing comes to my mind"; "I just made it up"; "It is my imagination at work"; "I just got the story from the forms"; "they look just like that, what else could it be?"
6.	Religious references: these are also stories heard or read but are listed separately because so many students gave such associations.	"This is Christ, the Baby Jesus, the three wise men, the Bible story, Bethlehem, the Virgin Mother and Baby, A nun listening to this sad mother and child," etc.

APPENDIX B.4. STANDARD RECORDING FORM, DEPENDENCY AND SELF IMAGE SCALES (TWITCHELL-ALLEN 3-DPT-FEIN-TESTING OF LIMITS PROCEDURES)

3-DPT-TL₁

Dependency Level =
Self Image Attitudes =

GRT =   VRT =   TT =

Name _____ Age _____ Address _____ School Grade _____

Father _____ Age _____ Occ. _____ Natl. Backgr. _____ Rel. _____

Mother _____ Age _____ Occ. _____ Natl. Backgr. _____ Rel. _____

Siblings _____ Rank _____ Occ. _____ Rel. _____

Directions: These forms have no special names, different people call them different things. You may call them what you wish. Please tell me a story using these pieces in one story.

298

APPENDIX B.5. STANDARD RECORDING FORM, DEPENDENCY AND SELF IMAGE SCALES (TWITCHELL-ALLEN 3-DPT-FEIN-TESTING OF LIMITS PROCEDURES)

3-DPT-TL$_2$

Dependency Level =
Self Image Attitudes =

GRT =   VRT =   TT =

Name	Age	Address	School Grade
Father	Age	Occ.	Natl. Backgr.	Rel.
Mother	Age	Occ.	Natl. Backgr.	Rel.
Siblings		Rank	Occ.	Rel.

Directions: Now I will begin the story:
"This is the mother" (Tch12);
"this is the father" (Tch21);
"and this is the little
girl (or boy)" (Tch17).
Now go on with the story.

APPENDIX C

Fein Identity Questions[*]

Please write a paragraph in answer to each of the following three questions. Take your time and think about these questions before writing your answers. You have 30 minutes to complete this questionnaire.

1. Who am I?

2. How do others see me?

3. How do I want to be seen?

* From Leah Gold Fein, Non-Academic Personality Variables and Success at Nursing School. *International Mental Health Newsletter*. New York: PGCMH, *10,* 1968.

Questionnaire to Directors of Psychology Graduate Departments and Practicing School Psychologists

**Survey of Title Roles for Which
University Programs Prepare
Students for Work in the Schools**

Please check in the appropriate columns of the educational degree ladder the roles for which your students are differentially prepared.

Role	AA	BA	MA (1 yr)	MA (2 yr)	3 yr equi.	Doc-toral
1. IQ tester / scorer / interpreter						
2. Group tester / scorer						
3. Educational tester / scorer						
4. Test results evaluator / interpreter						
5. Psychological examiner / evaluator						
6. Psychoeducational evaluator						
7. Psychosocial evaluator						
8. Psychodiagnostician						
9. Psychological consultant						
10. Educational diagnostician						
11. Educational consultant						
12. Prescription writer						
13. Prescription implementer						
14. Psychotherapist, dynamic						
15. Behavior therapist						
16. Intervention designer						
17. Intervention implementer						
18. Designer behavior, modification programs						
19. Behavior analyst / evaluator						
20. Behavior modification consultant						
21. Contingency modifier						
22. Consultant to school systems						

302

Role	AA	BA	MA (1 yr)	MA (2 yr)	3 yr equi.	Doctoral
23. Community consultant						
24. Research designer / consultant						
25. Research evaluator						
26. Research worker						
27. Curriculum consultant						
28. Learning consultant						
29. Reading specialist						
30. Compensatory program designer						
31. Compensatory program implementer						
32. Milieu / curricular modifier						
33. Milieu / curricular consultant						
35. Group worker / confrontation / leader						
36. Reality therapist						
37. Conflict resolver / consultant						
38. Mental health interpreter						
39. Family consultant						
40. Paraprofessional trainer / supervisor						
41. Professional staff trainer / supervisor						
42. Counseling / guidance (behavioral)						
43. Counseling / guidance (educational)						
44. Counseling / guidance (psychological)						
45. Insight counseling						
46. Other						

**Survey of Title Roles for Which
University Programs Prepare
Students for Work in the Schools**

Target Populations	AA	BA	MA (1 yr)	MA 2 yr)	3 yr equi.	Doc- toral
1. All children in system						
2. Special grades and ages						
a. Preschoolers						
b. Elementary						
c. Intermediate						
d. Secondary						
e. College						
3. Special groups						
a. MR						
b. CP						
c. BD						
d. Emotionally disturbed						
e. Behavior problems						
f. Educationally retarded						
g. Gifted						
h. Other						
4. School personnel						
a. Teachers						
b. Aids						
c. Administrators						
5. Whole school system						
6. Community						
7. Families						
8. Paraprofessionals						
9. Interns						
10. Special service staff						
11. Psychological staff						
12. Other						

Author Index

Subject Index

*Author is consultant and coordinator of the Institute for Relational Management in White Plains, New York which school trains Mental Health Technicians. This program opened September 1973 and is approved by the New York State Board of Education.